ELIZABETHAN VERSE ROMANCES

ROUTLEDGE ENGLISH TEXTS

GENERAL EDITOR: T. S. Dorsch,
Professor of English, University of Durham

ELIZABETHAN VERSE ROMANCES

EDITED BY

M. M. REESE

LONDON

ROUTLEDGE & KEGAN PAUL

NEW YORK: HUMANITIES PRESS

Published 1968
by Routledge & Kegan Paul Ltd
Broadway House, 68–74 Carter Lane
London, EC4V 5EL

Reprinted 1971

Reproduced and Printed in Great Britain by
Redwood Press Limited, Trowbridge & London

ISBN 0 7100 4518 2 (p)
ISBN 0 7100 4517 4 (c)

SERIES EDITOR'S PREFACE

THE ROUTLEDGE ENGLISH TEXTS are designed primarily for the use of sixth-form pupils and undergraduates. Each volume is edited by a scholar who is an authority on the period which it represents and who has also had experience of teaching and examining at the school-leaving or the undergraduate level. The aim is to provide, in the introductions and the notes, both sufficient explanatory material to enable the texts to be read with full understanding, and critical commentary of a kind that will stimulate thought and discussion.

The series will include both single works of some length and collections of shorter works. Where a work is too long to fit within the limits of size necessarily laid down for a textbook series—such a work, for example, as *The Prelude* or *Don Juan*—it will normally be represented by a single extended extract of several consecutive books or cantos rather than by an abridgement of the whole since an abridgement runs the risk of losing the cumulative effects that are important in a work of some scope. In the anthologies a few authors of a particular period will be well represented, in the belief that a reasonably thorough study of a limited field is more profitable than a superficial study of a wide field, and that a more than passing acquaintance is of value in itself.

T. S. DORSCH

CONTENTS

INTRODUCTION

(1) OVID

THE poems collected in this volume were written for pleasure, and it would be foolish not to read them so. They take us into a dreamlike world where every leaf and flower and brook may tell a story, where deities and heroes share the lives of mortal men and women, and rivers, beasts, and trees are sympathetic observers often given to participation and explanatory comment. The tales are sharpened by their recognition of ordinary human appetites, but there is this all-important difference: although the characters may be impelled to extremes of suffering or joy, there is an artistic cunning which keeps their experience at arm's length from reality. If we prick them, they do not bleed.

The creator of these distant perspectives was the Roman poet Ovid, who was born in 43 B.C. and (like Lodge and Marston) was trained to the law but deserted it for literature. In A.D. 8 he was one of the victims of a morality purge instituted by the Emperor Augustus, and he spent the last ten years of his life in plangent exile at Tomi (the modern Constanza), a chilly, desolate town on the Black Sea.

His best-known poems include *Fasti*, a Roman calendar stocked with religious and antiquarian lore, and *Ars Amatoria*, a 'technical' treatise on the arts of love which is still consulted by some; but the works that concern us here are *Metamorphoses*, *Heroides*, and *Amores*. *Metamorphoses*, in fifteen books, is the only major poem in which Ovid uses hexameters instead of his usual elegiac metre. Beginning with the Creation, which transformed Chaos into an ordered universe, it relates the stories of human beings who were changed into some other shape, culminating in the translation of Julius Caesar into a star. These transformations, while they give the stories a connecting link, are often of only incidental importance, and the real value of *Metamorphoses* for later generations was as a wonderful compendium of Greek and Roman legends, told with humour, grace, and point. *Heroides* is a series of letters from heroines to their husbands or lovers, sometimes with male replies, and here Ovid shows some psychological understanding in the presentation of love from the feminine standpoint. Most of his correspondents are reproachful because they have been deserted or betrayed, and the emergent impression is that when a woman falls in love she is on the road to neglect, imprisonment, or death. *Amores* is a collection of love poems in varying moods, some honouring constancy, others not. They feature Corinna, an imaginary or composite figure of the kind the Elizabethans used in their sonnets. Shakespeare only was unusual in not giving his lady a name.

Throughout the Middle Ages Ovid was one of the staples of the academic curriculum in all countries that had come under Roman influence. He was studied as much for the interest of what he wrote as for the linguistic and rhetorical analysis so deeply loved by grammarians, and in England typical adaptations of his tales may be found in Chaucer's *Legend of Good Women* and the *Confessio Amantis* of Chaucer's contemporary Gower. (They both recount the tragedy of Pyramus and Thisbe, which somehow found its way into *Metamorphoses* IV, although its origins were Babylonian.)

Ovid's popularity continued during the Renaissance, when his 'odoriferous flowers of fancy and jerks of invention' delighted profounder scholars than Holofernes (who probably preferred 'the Mantuan' anyway). Caxton printed an English version of *Metamorphoses*, and presently a small flood of translations began in 1560 with *The Fable of Ovid treating of Narcissus, . . . with a moral thereunto, very pleasant to read*, by T. H., who may have been Thomas Howell. It comes from *Metamorphoses* III and cites Narcissus's coldness to Echo and his self-delighting postures as a classic case of pride, of which numerous other examples are provided.

In 1565 Thomas Peend, a London barrister, translated the story of Salmacis and Hermaphroditus from *Metamorphoses* IV. This is the fable in which Ovid explains how hermaphrodites were created, and Peend insists that it is making a grave moral statement. While it is true that Hermaphroditus is a guileless youth who does not know what love is about, Peend glosses the story by presenting him as an innocent who is trapped into sin by Salmacis, a wanton who symbolizes the world's wickedness. In his moralization the poem becomes a demonstration of the viciousness of women and their 'fond and frantic fits'.

In 1567 George Turberville gave the Elizabethans a treasure-house of romantic myth by translating *Heroides*, and in the same year Arthur Golding completed his version of *Metamorphoses*, a work that was certainly known to Shakespeare (cf. VII. 187–206 with the 'elves of hills' passage in *The Tempest*). Golding was a sober and industrious man of puritanical conscience, a member of Archbishop Parker's Society of Antiquaries, and the friend of Burghley and Sir Philip Sidney. He translated many religious, philosophical, and historical works, including Calvin's sermons, Seneca's *De Beneficiis*, and Caesar's *Gallic War*, and he did not approach Ovid with any idea of sensual enjoyment. What he expected of the poem was edification.

Peend had the same exalted notions, and the translator of the *Narcissus* fable also greeted Ovid as 'this poet sure divine', whose tale 'no folly meant'. This was how medieval commentators thought of Ovid, enjoying his narratives but allegorizing his meaning in ways that would have surprised him. In the same eclectic spirit Golding recommends the theme of the poem, this 'dark philosophy of turned shapes', and claims that the metamorphoses denote men's submission to carnal appetites, of which their transformation into beasts is an appropriate symbol. Thus when we read of gods and men changed into animals, stones, or trees, 'it is a mirror for thyself thine own estate to see'. If people give themselves to lust and sin, 'what other kind of shape thereby than filthy can they win?'

But Golding recognized the dangers, and in dedicating the first four books to the Earl of Leicester in 1565, he admits that the poet has contrived some 'excellent devices and fine inventions . . . purporting outwardly most pleasant tales and delectable histories'. It is important to realize, therefore, that these are 'fraughted inwardly with most pithy instructions and wholesome examples'. When the other eleven books appeared two years later, he expanded the dedication to Leicester and added 220 lines of cautious admonition to 'the simple sort of reader'. In these he argues that Ovid's deities should be regarded as personalized symbols of wrongdoing, since 'under feigned names of gods' it was his intention 'the vice and faults of all estates to taunt in covert wise'. Golding even prepared a sort of glossary to explain which human qualities each god was held to personify, and for further illumination he extracted the morals to be gained from each of the fifteen books. Read with the 'skill, heed and judgment' that he so earnestly recommends, the poem is found to be replete with 'counsels wise and sage, . . . reproofs of vice in youth and age'. Indeed, the first book might even be reconciled with a Christian view of the Creation.

There is no special pleading here, or not much. Golding was aware of the multiple significances the poem might contain, and he was entitled to draw from it such instruction as might be sustaining to an upright and religious man. But this was the dying voice of the Middle Ages, and no one would write of Ovid in quite that way again. Golding probably realized that the battle was lost, for in the forty busy years that remained to him he did not again translate any author who might bring him the reproach of being a 'setter out of things that are but light and vain'.

In the vigorous contemporary arguments about the nature and duties of poetry, allegory itself was coming under fire. Sidney mistrusted the conception of poetry as a well where anyone might dip his bucket and withdraw what he had hoped to find. A poem might contain the reality of things, not their semblance; might even mean just what it said. It was generally agreed that there were moral and artistic dangers in crediting a poem with knowledge and insights that possibly were beyond the reach of its creator. In that way many an 'idle text' and 'ragged rhyme' was being valued above its deserts.

Among other things, this was an attack on journalistic

pretentiousness. Ovid was never guilty of that, but sooner or later his work would be stripped of the didactic and allegorical interpretations his medieval readers had laid upon it. This happened, completely and for ever, with the appearance in 1589 of Lodge's *Scylla's Metamorphosis*. It was a youthful and often unsatisfactory experiment by a man who was never a major poet, but it proved to be one of the seminal works of the age. A few years later two men of genius put their hands to this sort of poetry and established a mode, but it is remarkable how many of the ingredients may be found in Lodge.

Through the drench of tears—and no one would deny that Glaucus complains overmuch—the outlines are firm. Here is an erotic story told against a mythological background, but it does not pretend to any 'dark' significance. It has a point, as myths should have, and this only says that girls should relent to lovers who prove their constancy. The prolonged complaint of the scorned Glaucus is a commonplace of Elizabethan poetry, and his release by divine intervention is a frequent occurrence in myth. After that we have the feminine suitor, taken from Ovid and met again in Venus, Echo, Salmacis, Phoebe, and Oenone, all 'poor unskilful maids . . . forc'd to woo'. The tale is localized in England, 'by Isis' flood', and set in the personal framework of the poet's own unhappy love; so that the pagan rout of nymphs and goddesses is brought into homely surroundings, and things that happened in far-off Sicilia acquire the immediacy of a domestic event. This sense of familiarity is heightened by topical and personal allusions and by throwaway aphorisms from the common stock of poetry. Above all, the opulence of the imagery and the abundance of literary and mythological reference keep us at a safe distance from undue philosophizing or genuine feeling. Lodge maintains a comic detachment, and Art, not Nature, is the inspiration of the poem.

The Ovidian poem of the period did not have to include all these elements. Marlowe and Shakespeare, for instance, dispensed with the personal framework and the specifically localized setting—although there is no reason why *Venus and*

Adonis should not have taken place in the woods between Shottery and Stratford where, as like as not, Anne Hathaway met her fate. The charm of this poetry lay in its absence of rules, in its freedom and adaptability. Ovid had created an anthropomorphic world whose phenomena he explained in stories about gods and men. There was nothing definitive about these legends. Greece and Rome had their separate mythologies and traditions, and the gods and heroes may show different qualities in different contexts, here wise and brave, there paltering, lascivious, and equivocal. In trying to categorize their attributes, Golding was showing the inevitable limitations of the allegorical approach. But once the sensuous imagination was allowed free play, emancipated from the need to search for moral significances, these tales had a variety and wealth of association that opened up new opportunities for artistic contrivance.

So it is useless to look for narrative consistency in this poetry. The story was the least important consideration. The writers were content with the basic elements of the myth and displayed their originality in the inventiveness they brought to·it, the interplay of irony and pathos, the decorative richness and rhetorical ingenuity. In this they recaptured the true spirit of Ovid, which generations of his admirers had barely known. They recovered his delight in each activity of the senses, the swift variations of tone and mood, the occasional rhetorical heightening of the plot. Even in the long descriptive passages the sweetness is controlled by the pace and energy of the writing, and if the special flavour of his sophisticated humour is sometimes lacking, we usually find that note of ironic, almost unfeeling detachment that reminds us that the story is just a myth.

What is more, in finding Ovid, the Elizabethan writers also found themselves. These adaptations of a long-dead poet were acclimatized in England and gave their authors a means to self-realization and expression that often failed them in other modes. This is especially true of their sonneteering. In the sonnets, whether through the inherent difficulty of the form or the rigidity of their Petrarchan models, they always seem to be holding something back. The freedom of Ovidian myth was more congenial for personal statement and an address to the world.

Once Lodge had shown the way, there was an abundance of these poems in the next two or three decades. In addition to those printed here, some of the best known are *Oenone and Paris* (1594) by the dramatist Thomas Heywood; *Cephalus and Procris* and *Narcissus* (1595) both by Thomas Edwards; Chapman's *Ovid's Banquet of Sense* (1595), and his completion of *Hero and Leander* (1598); Richard Barnfield's *Cassandra* (1595); John Weever's *Faunus and Melliflora* (1600); *Salmacis and Hermaphroditus* (1602), attributed to the dramatist Beaumont; *Narcissus* (1618) by another playwright, James Shirley, written when he was very young; and another youthful composition, *Pyramus and Thisbe*, written in the 1630s by Abraham Cowley.

(2) SPENSER

Like all popular cultures, Elizabethan poetry was a reconciliation of diverse elements, and these Ovidian tales were rapidly assimilated with older modes like 'pastoral' and the 'complaint'.

There was a lot of romantic nonsense in pastoral, where the endless 'shepherd boys pipe as tho' they would never be old', and Touchstone's thoughts upon Jane Smile offer a healthy corrective. Sidney is said to have had no high opinion of his own *Arcadia*, and it was to a musclebound athlete that Shakespeare gave the famous lines about those fugitive persons who 'fleet the time carelessly, as they did in the golden world'. But as well as giving opportunities for bucolic decoration, pastoral offered a positive ideal of contentment and unwordly self-sufficiency. Before getting involved in more momentous happenings, Paris was a king's son who preferred to live as a shepherd on Mount Ida, and legends of this kind were moralized into an elevation of the simple virtues and a rejection of envy, pride, and ambition. In princely courts 'the worser thrives, the better weeps' (*Complaint of Rosamond*, l. 96) and the betrayed sigh for the life of 'unaffected innocency . . . deck'd with truth' (stanza 79). It required no great transformation, therefore, for Ovid's nymphs to live like shepherdesses and for his gods and heroes to resemble the Florizels who pretended to be shepherds.

The complaint followed pastoral in giving stern warnings against ambition. It derived from medieval presentiments about the arbitrary revolutions of Fortune, which reached for man at the height of his glory and rudely cast him down. This ever-present fear influenced historiography as well as poetry, and in both it took the form of long and plaintive reflections about the insecurity of man's wordly condition.

The intensity of this preoccupation explains the popularity of *A Mirror for Magistrates*, which appeared first in 1559 and was frequently added to in the next thirty years. The *Mirror* is a collection of verse narratives in which, usually, the ghost of a departed statesman appears to the poet and, after describing the causes of his personal tragedy, asks for these to be made public for the guidance of later generations. The tone is lachrymose and self-pitying, and it is heard in various contexts. The sudden fall from prosperity was the earliest and simplest form of tragedy, and behind the melodramatic action (taken in part from Ovid), *Titus Andronicus* is a complaint in dramatic form. Characteristic complaints are uttered by Romeo, by Margaret and Constance, the two wailing queens, and in the 'very tragical mirth' of Pyramus and Thisbe. In romantic poetry it becomes the language of betrayed heroines like Lucrece, or of Ovidian lovers who imitate Petrarch in agonizing over their disdainful ladies.

Both pastoral and the lament were favourite modes of Spenser, and Spenser was the most important non-dramatic poet of his time. He was 'the poets' poet', the consummate professional, and his successors were all in some degree the heirs of his rich endowment. On poetry, and on men's ways of thinking and writing about poetry, his influence was so pervasive that it is difficult to analyse in detail. But *The Shepherd's Calendar* (1579) stimulated pastoral and the pastoral complaint, and *The Faerie Queen* (begun by 1580) affected the development of the Ovidian romance by its use of the long rhyming stanza and by the captivating lushness of its style.

Spenser was the most pictorial of poets. His knights and their ladies give the effect of having been sculpturally posed, and his landscapes seem to have been copied from some vast Renaissance canvas. Readers could enjoy the mythological allusions without concerning themselves with the dark allegorical meanings, and the rich Italianate style, curiously ornamented, was an exciting medium for decorative tales about classical lovers.

Between Spenser and Ovid there was also a philosophical link. The unfinished seventh book of *The Faerie Queen* contains the famous 'Mutability' cantos in which Spenser broods upon a world eroded by time and change. He finds refuge in a Platonic world of everlasting truth and beauty, where things 'are not changed from their first estate' but in the process of change so amplify their being that they 'work their own perfection'.

In a less transcendental way Ovid said much the same thing, showing that, while nothing 'doth in steadfast state remain', nothing either perishes or undergoes substantial alteration. In *Metamorphoses* II Spenser found some of the arguments used by Mutability in its claim to sway the world, and in the final book Ovid outlined the Pythagorean theory of metempsychosis, or transmigration of souls, in which the immortal essence passes to and from men and beasts in a process of purification. 'The soul of our grandam might haply inhabit a bird,' Malvolio said, and even Rosalind thought that she was once an Irish rat. Ovid taught that the gods themselves, while being essentially changeless, were subject to physical metamorphosis. All this was an insurance against Mutability, and it helped serious-minded poets, as well as the other sort, to feel respectable and safe in the company of a pagan like Ovid.

(3) THE HIGHER LOVE

The freedom and sensuousness of Ovid's world were not to
every Elizabethan taste, or not all of the time, and here again
Spenser is important. In the legends of Britomart and Bel-
phoebe (*Faerie Queen* III) he praises 'pure chastity, and virtue
rare', inferring a more exalted condition than the raptures to
which Ovidian lovers, in their unending siege of beauty's
citadel, confidently called their mates.

The general nature of this condition, though unfortunately
not its detail, is described in Drayton's *Endymion and Phoebe*,
ll. 505–22. It involved the Neo-Platonic idea of the soul,
'exempt from vile and gross corruption', working through the
senses to raise the mind to a knowledge of ideal love and truth
and beauty. This conception was also stated by Chapman in
Ovid's Banquet of Sense (1595), where he wrestles with the
Neo-Platonic paradox that to feast the senses is a means to free
the soul.

The narrative shows Ovid in a garden, duly banqueting his
senses on Corinna bathing in a fountain. These are enraptured
one by one, and as soon as each pleasure is granted, it turns into
the immaterial. When at the climax Corinna is to be touched,
she becomes a mistress who rises above the flesh to feed the
mind. This preliminary wooing through the senses is a neces-
sary stage, since the soul cannot apprehend experience by
direct means; it can only be stirred through the mind, and the
mind has first to be excited through the senses. Flesh, which is
the servant of the divine soul, is itself glorified by this communi-
cation, and perfect love is only attainable through sensuous
excitement. Chapman says that Nature does not give us
sensual gifts without intending that they shall be used (557–8),
and before the mind can be moved, the body 'must her content-
ment find'. The conclusion is that

We therefore must procure the sense delighted,
That so the soul may use her faculty. (562–3)

However much he may insist that the true communication
is not 'of lips or bodies, but of bodies' virtues', and is to be

valued for its approximation to 'natural divinity', we must be aware of some speciousness here, of an attempt to make the best of both worlds. It is indeed comforting to know that the attainment of virtue is a consistently pleasurable activity. But Chapman was a serious man, not knowingly given to absurdity, and he was not a hypocrite. It may be strange to use an erotic poem as a means to strive after heavenly knowledge, but the grandeur of the marriage service itself is in a way an attempt to give dignity and purpose to common appetites. This graver sort of poetry provided a necessary balance to the frank sensuality of Ovidian myth, and most contemporary poets felt the need for both kinds of expression. We cannot properly understand Elizabethan romantic poetry without recognising this. Chapman's Ovid was not alone among mankind in seeking some deeper emotion to raise 'the poorness of his flesh's faculty' (954).

(4) BEAUTY'S LOSS

Apart from *Rosamond*, the poems in this selection are myths, and myths have two functions. The lesser one, although it often gives shape to the narrative, is to explain why certain things in the world are as they are: how Adonis in dying created the anemone, or Pyramus the mulberry; how roses turned from white to red because they blushed to see Hermaphroditus naked; why there is light and darkness, winter and summer; how Echo became a disembodied voice; why love is cruel, or scholars are always poor. This is the characteristic stuff of myth the world over, whether in *Genesis* or the *Just So Stories*.

Myth's second function is to permit the author, under cover of the fable, to say certain things of his own. What the poets in this book want to say, through all the varieties of poetic style and narrative method, is that they are preoccupied with Time and Beauty.

Life was briefer then, its hazards more sudden and irrevocable, and men knew that their own lease, like summer's, had all too short a date. The quest for Beauty was the symbol of their fear, and they expressed it through the familiar image of the flower that is doomed to fade. *Carpe diem,* and put no trust in tomorrow: at one level it was just a plea for reckless sensuality, since we shall all be damnably mouldy a hundred years hence. But the usual method is to entreat the lover to surrender, with the reminder that if she (or he) is reluctant, youth and beauty perish as surely as the rose. Against Time's scythe Beauty's only defence is generation. This is the most powerful strain in Elizabethan sonnets and romantic verse, and it continues far into the following century with Herrick, Lovelace, Marvell, and Waller's invocation to the 'lovely rose'. The settings are erotic and personal, but only incidentally so. Marvell's address to his coy mistress is his way of saying that he hates the idea of growing old.

Even the moralizing translator of the *Narcissus* fable in 1560 concluded that the boy's metamorphosis into a flower signified

> That youth and beauty come, and soon be past,
> Even as the flower that withereth full fast.

It was his punishment for refusing the nymph who loved him. So these poems contain many examples of the *suasio*, the rhetorical set-piece which states the arguments against coyness and chastity. The most brilliant—although addressed to a girl who had not much need of it—is Leander's (I. 199–294), with its insistence that 'one is no number' and women are only 'untun'd golden strings' until joined in harmony with men. 'The richest corn dies if it be not reap'd' (I. 327). But the persuasions of Venus (*passim*) are more profound and sensitive. Whereas Leander, like Rosamond's wrinkled bawd, finds it necessary to demolish the arguments for chastity and honour, it never occurs to Venus that chastity may be a relevant consideration. She entreats for pleasure, and this quite brazenly, but at a deeper level her persuasion is for Beauty's sake, which 'within itself should not be wasted' (130), and rightly should desire increase, just as 'torches are made to light, and jewels to wear' (163). The lover's refusal is a defiance of Nature's own imperatives. With 'Beauty dead, black Chaos comes again'

SUASIO

(1020), and her final complaint over the dead Adonis (1075 ff.) is
a lament over the 'waste' of Beauty.

Even Phoebe, whose intents are pure, tempts Endymion by
listing love's delights. With Scylla, Salmacis, Oenone, and
several others, the feminine wooer is a common feature of
Ovidian verse. Perhaps the men were hoping to transfer to their
natural persecutors their own dread certainties about Time's
winged chariot. More probably it was a shared masculine joke,
the fun of seeing the ladies take their turn as victims of disdain.

'My dear Lady Disdain' is Benedick's first insult to Beatrice,
and male lovers had good reason for this attitude. 'Disdain' is
the solicitor's rude word for the whole range of feminine feel-
ings from chastity as a religious ideal to honour, pride, married
loyalty, flirtatiousness, and physical revulsion. Sir Guyon, the
knight of Temperance, overcame Acrasia in her bower of bliss
(*Faerie Queene* II. xii), and there were maidens well able to
protect themselves against the combined assaults of Night,
Opportunity, and Lust. Drayton drew one in his *Legend of
Matilda* (1594), and in the same year (in which Lucrece, too,
did her best, and certainly tried harder than Rosamond) ap-
peared *Willobie his Avisa*, an anonymous poem about an
innkeeper's wife who shielded her virtue for reasons which
reflected the emergence of a Puritan bourgeoisie.

But Ovidian poetry was written for courtiers, gallants, and
the law-students of the Inns, and here the apologists of virtue
needed to be more sophisticated than Avisa. The most eloquent
piece of counter-persuasion comes from Adonis (415–20,
523–8), and one feels that he gets rather the better of Venus
dialectically. He turns the analogy from Nature against its
expositors by reminding her that 'the mellow plum doth fall'
while the green is sour to taste. 'Who plucks the bud before one
leaf put forth?' More formally, Rosamond too praises 'chastity's
attires',

> Th' unstain'd veil which innocence adorns,
> Th' ungather'd rose, defended with the thorns. (216–17)

But ultimately these arguments are powerless against the
sovereign rights of Beauty. Adonis does not defeat Venus, any

more than she defeats him, because we never know what might have happened if he had returned safely from his hunting expedition. The action between them is drawn until it is resolved by the appearance of a *diabolus ex machina*, the boar, who is the incarnation of evil in the world because he robs it of Beauty and leaves it desolate. Leander scornfully says that it is only 'hare-brain'd and illiterate hinds' who have hard hearts and minds obdurate to love (II. 217–18); and Rosamond, while she has some severe things to say about girls who let the side down, comes in the end to understand the grief of Venus. She moves from self-pity to resentment at the untimely extinction of Beauty, buried within walls fashioned by 'the credulous devout'. Her plea is to be remembered for the youth and loveliness she once possessed; remembered and also vindicated, because for Beauty's sake it is not wrong to employ the 'sweet silent rhetoric of persuading eyes' (128). One of the legends on the ornamental casket teaches her that Beauty's only sin is 'cruelty, which yields unto no prayer' (406).

The worship of Beauty passed into extravagant absurdity in the *Narcissus* of Thomas Edwards (1595), in which Narcissus appears as a ghost lamenting his own physical perfection because it has been the cause of his destruction. But as a much-loved symbol of life's transience, Beauty continued to be the inspiration of Ovidian romance. Even the austerely philosophical Chapman found that the love which it provokes is wiser than all the 'judgments graven in Stoic gravity' (486). It is 'the feast of souls, the glory of the light . . . The sum and court of all proportion' (462, 466).

(5) *SCYLLA'S METAMORPHOSIS*

The importance of Lodge's work, which much outweighs its poetic merits, has already been discussed. He declares his satirical intention in his sub-title, which says that Scylla's transformation is 'interlaced with the unfortunate love of Glaucus, . . . containing the detestable tyranny of Disdain, and the comical triumph of Constancy, very fit for young Courtiers to peruse and coy Dames to remember'. Lodge is not so much entranced by Beauty as disgusted with its exploitation by flirtatious women. The tone is comic-rueful, and the conclusion, which threatens a punishment as dreadful as Scylla's to ladies who scorn their faithful lovers, is hardly the assertion of a deep conviction.

In fact there is no deep feeling anywhere. The poem is a courtly persuasion to love, and Glaucus's grief is poured out in the form of a conventional complaint. Its assuagement by divine intervention is an artificial device that forbids emotional participation, and in any case it would be difficult to respond very warmly to a poem so copiously washed by tears. We are unlikely to pity either Glaucus or the scorned and translated Scylla, although we are invited to do both.

The tears also weaken the comic point, and here Lodge is soft-centred in a way that, say, Marlowe or Marston would never be. They would not spoil the joke by allowing the narrator and the onlookers to feel sorry for Scylla in the humiliation she has brought upon herself by rejecting a faithful lover.

But Lodge does not try to turn his story into an allegory. For what it is worth, he tells it for its own sake, lingering happily over the erotic and pictorial images it allows him to develop. Feeling is dissolved in a beautiful world of gods and nymphs and enchanted landscapes, and the rivers and trees are gladly drawn into the story. This is the anthropomorphic Nature of which Ovid wrote, and its naturalization in England is Lodge's most memorable achievement. For the sake of those who later drew upon his inspiration we may forget that his pioneering poem is too static and rhetorical to be more than mildly enjoyable.

Lodge

(6) *THE COMPLAINT OF ROSAMOND*

This differs from other poems in the book in deriving itself from the *Mirror*, whose complaint pattern it largely imitates.

The ghost of Rosamond bewails her fall and offers it as an *exemplum* for the unborn generations, 'to teach to others what I learn'd too late' (67). The method is homiletic, and except in the short passage about the casket, Daniel shuns decoration and mythological allusion. Even this casket, depicting the 'heady riots' of the sportive gods, enforces the moral significance of Rosamond's fall, and this is the purpose of the imagery throughout.

But the complaint was quite a common feature in other types of Elizabethan romantic verse, and the poem has several Ovidian features. It studies the male-female relationship with the sort of psychological realism that Ovid attempts in *Heroides*; the narrative is punctuated with sententious comment; there is the personal reference in the appeal to Delia and the poet to rescue the heroine from oblivion and shame; and ultimately we are left in no doubt that Beauty is the sovereign grace.

Our frailty's doom is written in the flowers,
Which flourish now, and fade ere many hours. (251–2)

The *Mirror* stories are seldom consistent in their attitude. In describing their fall, the ghostly narrators, whether warriors, statesmen, or dishonoured ladies, like to linger on the days of their pride. They cannot resist making the point that, although since fallen, they once were great; and their relish in recalling this brings into question the sincerity of the shame and repentance they now profess. There is a half-conscious inclination to lay the blame on Fate rather than their own guilty actions.

We find this in Rosamond. For one thing, she is ambivalent in her attitude to her lover and their passion. She blames his lust, and denounces the intrigues and ambition of the designing folk who tore her from her pastoral innocence and exposed her to such temptations; but there are times, too, when she glories in the association and thinks of its forbidden fruits as their own sweet reward. She is highly indignant with Eleanor for depriving her of them, and her grief for Henry in his bereavement is tender and true.

The emotional situation is confusing, because these sentiments are not consistent with her frequent references to her

shame and to the lessons she intends to teach. In this salva-
tionist mood she dwells upon the sad 'downfall of my slipp'ry
state', when 'disgrace dark'd honour, sin did cloud my brow'
(76), and she 'lost the flower which honour keeps' (95). She
cannot really have it both ways, and she resolves the difficulty by
deciding that her end was foredoomed. We cannot avoid our
destiny even when we know it; things must happen as Fate
has decreed them, even if there is an element of personal
responsibility in it (418-20). 'For will in us is over-rul'd by
Fate' (*Hero and Leander* I. 168).

Like Edwards's Narcissus, Rosamond rues her own beauty as
the cause of her misfortune, but she differs from him because
she would not have had it otherwise. Her final message to
Delia (and what really is the poem if not a *suasio* to Delia?) is
that love and beauty are woman's highest gifts and her true
endowment. She herself was lovely once, and this, and not her
wretched fall, is what she wants the world to remember.

The impact of Daniel's poem (evident in other respects in
Shakespeare's *Rape of Lucrece*) appeared immediately in two
re-workings of the story—already becoming a folk-myth—of
the courtesan Jane Shore: Anthony Chute's *Beauty Dishon-
oured* and the ancient Churchyard's revision of his earlier poem.
Now both tread lightly on the old idea of moral recrimination,
and the emphasis is on the new theme of Beauty brought to a
tragic end; and Churchyard specifically refers to Daniel's
noble rendering of this. In the same year, 1593, Drayton cheer-
fully accepts the moral obliquity of *Piers Gaveston* and his
companions and asks for them to be applauded as Beauty's
acolytes and persons of high romance. Thus already the in-
fluence of Ovid has worked upon *Mirror* poetry and converted
it into an erotic celebration: a metamorphosis indeed.

(7) HERO AND LEANDER

If we say that *Hero and Leander* is perfect of its kind, this is a
constricting judgment that ignores all the things it might be

but is not. It is commonly acknowledged to be the most Ovidian of all the Ovidian imitations, diamond-hard and glittering, witty, sensuous, and wonderfully integrated; artistically the best thing that Marlowe ever did.

It achieves its self-sufficient effect by ignoring the moral implications of the material. It is the tale of two young people who espy each other, stand amazed, and, after a courtly minuet of wooing, consummate their love. Neptune, trying to seduce the boy as he swims towards more conventional pleasures, burlesques the human passion; there is a long digression which explains why the Parcae feel crotchety about Cupid; and the narrative, written in a surge of hard, end-stopped couplets, is unified by the poet's knowing aphoristic comments. Only Cupid's 'languishment' (I. 378) and the single line suggesting that personal decision is overwhelmed by Fate (I. 168) hint at the tragic sequel which Marlowe never told. It is a poem without reverberations. It stands full in the sunlight and casts no shadow.

The mocking asides control the romanticism, the speed of the narrative leaves the honey-sweetness as just a fragrance hanging in the air. There is no tenderness, just a cynical detachment from the lovers as emanations of the comic spirit, helplessly magnetised into sensual gratification. But the mockery is warmed by Marlowe's relish for the spectacle, and the opulence of his imagination creates for it a golden mythical world where everything in Nature is pledged to the service of love.

(8) *VENUS AND ADONIS*

It must have been written almost simultaneously with *Hero and Leander*, and readers have been wondering ever since which is the better poem. Marlowe's is more consistent in tone. It perfectly harmonizes content and form, and for all his knowing detachment—itself part of the joke—the poet is intimately identified with the mood of his characters. But if we then conclude that *Hero and Leander* is 'a better work of art', this may be no more than aesthetic shadow-boxing in the deserted arena of the 'Art versus Nature' controversy. If, as Jonson complained, Shakespeare lacked Art, his unique prodigality made up for it. *Venus and Adonis* has insights beyond Marlowe's knowledge.

Myth was congenial to Shakespeare because, like the drama of his time, it demanded the double vision that sees the characters not wholly as human beings nor wholly as embodiments of certain fixed attitudes. In both the author may stand apart from his creations and employ them for multiple purposes. In drama Ben Jonson was rare in trying to achieve a rigid psychological consistency; and while myths were supposed to have a 'point' (explaining, for instance, why the year falls into seasons), they had grown out of the medieval trick of moralizing. A precisian like Golding thought he could infer a single meaning from Ovid's fables. But when from the story of Venus and Adonis he concludes that Adonis's death proves that 'manhood strives Against forewarning, though men see the peril of their lives', he only shows that he did not appreciate the nature of myth and did not understand this particular fable at all.

Shakespeare allows Venus to make a potent persuasion to love, but he was incapable of viewing the subject with Marlowe's single-minded absorption. He knew too much about the pathos of those who are led 'prisoner in a red-rose chain' (110), and too much also about love's blindfold foraging and the sweating indignities that cause the lover's face to reek and smoke (555). Strengthless doves carry off to heaven the goddess who makes no footprints on the sand and cannot bruise the primroses with her weight. But passion finds her in some unseemly postures, pulling Adonis off his horse, tucking him under her arm, heaving up his hat, confessing that were she a boar, her kisses would have torn his cheeks. The instinctive behaviour of the two horses turns her avowals to fustian, and the erotic exchanges are often described with deliberate hyperbole (451–6, 482) or ironic comment (607–10). Coleridge claimed too much when he said that Shakespeare 'here represented the animal impulse, so as to preclude all sympathy with

it', but Venus's wooing invites the same sort of laughter as
Titania's courtship of Bottom.

When, on the other hand, Adonis denounces lust and exalts
a love that is mutual and passionless (769–804), we are not
allowed to forget that this is an immature young man overpos-
sessed by outdoor sports. He witholds Beauty's fee and denies
increase; his rejection of Venus, who is the goddess of fecund-
ity, is unnatural; and it may only be his inexperience that
drives her passion to such extremes that he misinterprets it as
lust.

So we do not have to look for moral conclusions in the poem.
Shakespeare is aloof from his characters, entering into their
emotional predicaments but working, as Coleridge said,
'exactly as if of another planet, as describing the movements of
two butterflies'. At the end (1135–64) he announces the point,
that 'sorrow on love hereafter shall attend'. Venus resolves to
'immure herself and not be seen', and mortals will never again
have unalloyed enjoyment of her gifts.

In the superfluity of his genius Shakespeare gives us other
things beside, notably those images from Nature (the snail, the
gentle lark, the hunted hare) which arouse more immediate
feelings than anything the characters say or do. Imagery as
direct as this, rising so much above the ordinary requirements
of decorative embellishment, is at odds with the essential
artificiality of myth, and the sourer critics may be right when
they account it an artistic flaw. But Coleridge would not agree,
and in a notable passage in *Biographia Literaria* (Chapter XV)
he says how he found in the poem an imaginative consistency
which 'reduces multitude into unity of effect', and also an
intuitive power that works by an unbroken chain of images to
provide a 'visual substitute' for the language used by actors on
the stage. Shakespeare, he thinks, is aloof from the feelings of
which he is the painter and the analyst, but the imagery is
unified by a predominant passion in which 'the creative power
and the intellectual energy wrestle in a war embrace'. The
versification shows a 'delight in richness and sweetness of
sound', and this sense of musical delight is also a gift of the

imagination which may be cultivated but never learned. *Poeta nascitur non fit.*

(9) *ENDYMION AND PHOEBE*

The poems by Shakespeare and Marlowe were an instant and lasting success, and no man was truly a gallant unless he kept copies under his pillow and was free with his quotations. To Marlowe's potency Shakespeare paid his tribute in *As You Like It*, and there are many witnesses to his own. In 1598 Francis Meres reported that 'the sweet witty soul of Ovid lives in mellifluous and honey-tongued Shakespeare', and at about the same time Gabriel Harvey said—not without regret—that 'the younger sort takes much delight in Shakespeare's *Venus and Adonis*'. A character in one of the *Parnassus* plays (*c.* 1600) was still asking 'Who loves not Adon's love?'

Lesser poets rushed in with their imitations, and probably Marston's squib was already being circulated when Drayton seems to have decided that it was time to call a halt. A minor poet but acute literary observer, John Davies of Hereford, applauded the 'fine wit' of *Venus and Adonis*, but thought it would have been finer 'if not attir'd in such bawdy gear'. This view was not uncommon, and Drayton (conveniently forgetting *Piers Gaveston*) undertook to show that an erotic romance did not have to be lewd.

His poem is a noble and eloquent declaration of the love of which Adonis possibly had a vision, the celestial stirring that transcends earthly passion and is purged of destructive sensuality. Drayton interprets mythological eroticism in Platonic terms, and the love of a goddess for a mortal is a symbol of the divine inspiration which raises chosen men above the common clay. No boar lurks for Endymion.

But the theme was beyond the poet's imaginative reach. Phoebe's promises are glowing and passionate, and Drayton is at his best when most influenced by the originals he wants to rebuke. The fluctuations in mood are disturbing, and although

the poem ends with a demonstration of curious knowledge, it is
bookish stuff, generalised and non-intellectual when compared
with the sinewy arguments of Venus or Leander. Drayton was
determined to avoid a sensuous climax, but he had nothing to
put in its place. He was ill-advised also to borrow Marlowe's
metre, because the fluid but rather monotonous movement of
his couplets marks as great a contrast in style as in conception
and mood.

It is an enjoyable poem all the same. Pastoral is freshened and
elevated by a touch of the heroic, and however fatigued we may
be by the parade of astronomic and philosophical quaintness,
there is an unfading pleasure in the luxuriant setting and the
wealth of delicate, fantastic ornament.

(10) *THE METAMORPHOSIS OF PYGMALION'S IMAGE*

Marston too reacted against the licentiousness of Ovidian
romance, but in a very different spirit from Drayton. In what
was probably a teenage composition he isolated the theme of
erotic desire so as to titillate the 'gaping ears that swallow up
my lines'.

The result is a sick poem, Ovid with the bloom off. Vanished
are the colour, warmth, and gaiety of myth. Love has declined
from sportiveness to calculating carnality, and there are no
nymphs or smiling rivers to sweeten it, no refining comment,
only the poet's sour asides to his own unresponsive mistress.
The old game of courtship is degraded by the assumption that
women will always relent when the lover's advances are bold
enough, and they are advised not to take seriously the vows of
men 'who do not unto more than kissing move you' (120). The
question of 'disdain' does not arise, since by a cruelly satirical
stroke the heroine of the poem is in no position to dictate her
own responses; while Adonis's vision of an untainted love, the
love, 'that comforteth like sunshine after rain', is dismissed
as the foolery of such youths as 'seriously protest That love
respects not actual luxury' (110–11). As for the reader, he

is exposed to a kind of strip-tease, encouraged to expect lasci-vious revelations that do not occur, and then ridiculed for having allowed himself to expect them.

Later Marston said that his aim had always been satirical: romantic poetry was debasing itself, and he would make it worse. By 1598, when the poem was printed, he had probably convinced himself that this was indeed his attitude, because by then his mind was more robust and he had settled into his chosen posture as a satirist with a prescription to rebuke 'th' immodest looseness of our age'. This he did to such purpose that a character in a contemporary comedy begged that 'an old knight might have his wench in a chimney corner without any satires or epigrams'. Marston had a pedagogic obsession about all this, and he wrote of it in the strident, monotonous tones of Thersites.

But this apart, there is a dark splendour in his rancorous defiance of the world and his confidence in the therapeutic properties of his poetry. Here he is a Timon scorning all man-kind's vanities, indifferent to praise or blame because 'my soul . . . knows his sacred parentage'. 'He that thinks worse of my rhymes than myself, I scorn him, for he cannot; he that thinks better, is a fool.' His *Scourge of Villainy* (1598) is dedi-cated 'To Detraction', the spirit of envious calumny, which he despised as much as its own contemptible objects. 'I am myself, so is my poesy.'

His *Pygmalion* has more merit than is sometimes allowed. The mocking contempt of the reader is a bar to complete enjoyment, but the poem has Marlowe's speed and clarity as well as his cynicism. The style is swift and unencumbered, and Marston here avoids the harsh obscurity of language that makes much of his work so difficult. We may not much like the poem but we have to admire its artistic control.

SAMUEL DANIEL

The Complaint of Rosamond

(1592)

1

'OUT from the horror of infernal deeps
My poor afflicted ghost comes here to plain it,
Attended with my shame that never sleeps,
The spot wherewith my kind and youth did stain it.
My body found a grave where to contain it:
    A sheet could hide my face, but not my sin,
    For fame finds never tomb t'enclose it in.

2

'And which is worse, my soul is now denied
Her transport to the sweet Elysian rest,
The joyful bliss for ghosts repurified,   10
The ever-springing gardens of the blest:
Charon denies me waftage with the rest,
    And says my soul can never pass the river
    Till lovers' sighs on earth shall it deliver.

3

'So shall I never pass; for how should I
Procure this sacrifice amongst the living?
Time hath long since worn out the memory
Both of my life and life's unjust depriving;
Sorrow for me is dead, for aye reviving.
    Rosamond hath little left her but her name,   20
    And that disgrac'd, for time hath wrong'd the same.

C

4

'No Muse suggests the pity of my case;
Each pen doth overpass my just complaint,
Whilst others are preferr'd, though far more base;
Shore's wife is grac'd, and passes for a saint;
Her legend justifies her foul attaint;
   Her well-told tale did such compassion find
   That she is pass'd, and I am left behind.

5

'Which seen with grief, my miserable ghost
(Whilom invested in so fair a veil   30
Which, whilst it liv'd, was honour'd of the most,
And being dead, gives matter to bewail)
Comes to solicit thee, whilst others fail,
   To take this task, and in thy woeful song
   To form my case and register my wrong.

6

'Although I know thy just lamenting Muse,
Toil'd in th' affliction of thine own distress,
In others' cares hath little time to use,
And therefore mayst esteem of mine the less;
Yet as thy hopes attend happy redress,   40
   The joys depending on a woman's grace,
   So move thy mind a woeful woman's case.

7

'Delia may hap to deign to read our story,
And offer up her sighs among the rest,
Whose merit would suffice for both our glory,
Whereby thou might'st be grac'd and I be blest;
That indulgence would profit me the best,
   Such power she hath, by whom thy youth is led,
   To joy the living and to bless the dead.

8

'So I, by beauty made the woefull'st wight,   50
By beauty might have comfort after death:
That dying fairest, by the fairest might
Find life above on earth, and rest beneath.
She that can bless us with one happy breath
   Give comfort to thy Muse to do her best,
    That thereby thou mayst joy and I might rest.'

9

Thus said: forthwith mov'd with a tender care
And pity (which myself could never find),
What she desir'd my Muse deign'd to declare,
And therefore will'd her boldly tell her mind.   60
And I, more willing, took this charge assign'd,
   Because her griefs were worthy to be known,
    And telling hers, might hap forget mine own.

10

'Then write (quoth she) the ruin of my youth,
Report the downfall of my slipp'ry state:
Of all my life recall the simple truth,
To teach to others what I learn'd too late;
Exemplify my frailty, tell how Fate
   Keeps in eternal dark our fortunes hidden,
    And ere they come, to know them is forbidden.   70

11

'For whilst the sunshine of my fortune lasted,
I joy'd the happiest warmth, the sweetest heat,
That ever yet imperious beauty tasted;
I had what glory ever flesh could get.
But this fair morning had a shameful set:
   Disgrace dark'd honour, sin did cloud my brow,
    As note the sequel, and I'll tell thee how.

12

'The blood I stain'd was good and of the best;
My birth had honour, and my beauty fame:
Nature and Fortune join'd to make me blest,   80
Had I had grace t' have known to use the same.
My education show'd from whence I came,
    And all concurr'd to make me happy first,
    That so great hope might make me more accurst.

13

'Happy liv'd I whilst parents' eye did guide
The indiscretion of my feeble ways,
And country home kept me from being ey'd,
Where best unknown I spent my sweetest days:
Till that my friends mine honour sought to raise
    To higher place, which greater credit yields,   90
    Deeming such beauty was unfit for fields.

14

'From country then to court I was preferr'd,
From calm to storms, from shore into the deeps:
There where I perish'd, where my youth first err'd,
There where I lost the flower which honour keeps,
There where the worser thrives, the better weeps;
    Ah me, poor wench, on this unhappy shelf
    I grounded me, and cast away myself.

15

'There whereas frail and tender beauty stands
With all assaulting powers environed,   100
Having but prayers and weak feeble hands
To hold their honour's fort unvanquished;
There where to stand, and be unconquered,
    Is to b' above the nature of our kind,
    That cannot long for pity be unkind.

16

'For thither com'd, when years had arm'd my youth
With rarest proof of beauty ever seen;
When my reviving eye had learnt the truth,
That it had power to make the winter green,
And flower affections whereas none had been;   110
    Soon could I teach my brow to tyrannize,
    And make the world do homage to mine eyes.

17

'For age I saw (though years with cold conceit
Congeal'd their thoughts against a warm desire)
Yet sigh their want, and look at such a bait;
I saw how youth was wax before the fire;
I saw by stealth, I fram'd my look a liar,
    Yet well perceiv'd how Fortune made me then
    The envy of my sex, and wonder unto men.

18

'Look how a comet at the first appearing   120
Draws all men's eyes with wonder to behold it;
Or as the saddest tale at sudden hearing
Makes silent list'ning unto him that told it:
So did my speech when rubies did unfold it;
    So did the blazing of my blush appear,
    T'' amaze the world, that holds such sights so dear.

19

'Ah, Beauty! siren, fair enchanting good,
Sweet silent rhetoric of persuading eyes;
Dumb eloquence, whose power doth move the blood
More than the words or wisdom of the wise;   130
Still harmony, whose diapason lies
    Within a brow, the key which passions move
    To ravish sense and play a world in love.

20

'What might I then not do, whose power was such?
What cannot women do, that know their power?
What women knows it not (I fear too much),
How bliss or bale lies in their laugh or lour,
Whilst they enjoy their happy blooming flower,
 Whilst Nature decks them in their best attires
 Of youth and beauty, which the world admires? 140

21

'Such one was I. My beauty was mine own,
No borrowed blush which bankrupt beauties seek:
That new-found shame, a sin to us unknown,
Th' adulterate beauty of a falsed cheek:
Vild stain to honour, and to women eke,
 Seeing that time our fading must detect,
 Thus with defect to cover our defect.

22

'Impiety of times, chastity's abater;
Falsehood wherein thyself thyself deniest;
Treason to counterfeit the seal of Nature, 150
The stamp of heaven, impressed by the Highest;
Disgrace unto the world, to whom thou liest;
 Idol unto thyself, shame to the wise
 And all that honour these idolatries.

23

'Far was that sin from us whose age was pure,
When simple beauty was accounted best;
The time when women had no other lure
But modesty, pure cheeks, a virtuous breast:
This was the pomp wherewith my youth was blest;
 These were the weapons which mine honour won 160
 In all the conflicts which mine eyes begun.

24

'Which were not small: I wrought on no mean object.
A crown was at my feet, sceptres obey'd me:
Whom Fortune made my king, Love made my subject;
Who did command the land most humbly pray'd me:
Henry the Second, that so highly weigh'd me,
　　Found well, by proof, the privilege of beauty,
　　That it had power to countermand all duty.

25

'For after all his victories in France,
And all the triumphs of his honour won,   170
Unmatch'd by sword, was vanquish'd by a glance;
And hotter wars within his breast begun,
Wars whom whole legions of desires drew on:
　　Against all which my chastity contends,
　　With force of honour, which my shame defends.

26

'No armour might be found that could defend
Transpiercing rays of crystal-pointed eyes;
No stratagem, no reason, could amend,
No, not his age; yet old men should be wise,
But shows deceive, outward appearance lies: 180
　　Let none, for seeming so, think saints of others,
　　For all are men, and all have suck'd their mothers.

27

'Who would have thought a monarch would have ever
Obey'd his handmaid of so mean estate?
Vulture ambition feeding on his liver,
Age having worn his pleasures out of date;
But hap comes never, or it comes too late:
　　For such a dainty which his youth found not
　　Unto his feeble age did chance allot.

28

'Ah, Fortune, never absolutely good,   190
For that some cross still counterchecks our luck:
As here behold, th' incompatible blood
Of age and youth was that whereon we stuck:
Whose loathing we from Nature's breasts do suck,
     As opposite to what our blood requires;
     For equal age doth equal like desires.

29

'But mighty men, in highest honour sitting,
Nought but applause and pleasure can behold:
Sooth'd in their liking, careless what is fitting,
May not be suffer'd once to think they're old: 200
Not trusting what they see, but what is told.
     Miserable fortune, to forget so far
     The state of flesh, and what our frailties are.

30

'Yet must I needs excuse so great defect;
For drinking of the Lethe of mine eyes,
He's forc'd forget himself, and all respect
Of majesty whereon his state relies,
And now of loves and pleasures must devise:
     For thus reviv'd again, he serves and su'th
     And seeks all means to undermine my youth: 210

31

'Which never by assault he could recover;
So well encamp'd in strength of chaste desires,
My clean-arm'd thoughts repell'd an unchaste lover.
The crown that could command what it requires
Is lesser priz'd than chastity's attires,
     Th' unstain'd veil which innocence adorns,
     Th' ungather'd rose, defended with the thorns.

32

'And safe mine honour stood, till that, in truth,
One of my sex, of place and nature bad,
Was set in ambush to entrap my youth: 220
One in the habit of like frailty clad,
One who the liv'ry of like weakness had;
    A seeming matron, yet a sinful monster,
    As by her words the chaster sort may conster.

33

'She set upon me with the smoothest speech
That court and age could cunningly devise:
Th' one, authentic, made her fit to teach,
Th' other made her fit to subtilize:
Both were enough to circumvent the wise:
    A document that well might teach the sage   230
    That there's no truth in youth, nor hope in age.

34

'"Daughter (said she), behold thy happy chance,
That hath the lot cast down into thy lap
Whereby thou mayst thy honour great advance,
Whilst thou, unhappy, wilt not see thy hap:
Such fond respect thy youth doth so enwrap,
    T' oppose thyself against thine own good fortune
    That points thee out and seems thee to importune.

35

'"Dost thou not see how that thy king—thy love—
Lightens forth glory on thy dark estate,   240
And showers down gold and treasure from above,
Whilst thou dost shut thy lap against thy Fate?
Fie, fondling, fie! thou wilt repent too late
    The error of thy youth, that canst not see
    What is the fortune that doth follow thee.

36

' "Thou must not think thy flower can always flourish,
And that thy beauty will be still admir'd;
But that those rays which all these flames do nourish,
Cancell'd with time, will have their date expir'd,
And men will scorn what is so desir'd.   250
    Our frailty's doom is written in the flowers,
    Which flourish now, and fade ere many hours.

37

' "Read in my face the ruins of my youth,
The wrack of years upon my aged brow.
I have been fair (I must confess the truth)
And stood upon as nice respects as thou.
I lost my time, and I repent it now;
    But were I to begin my youth again,
    I would redeem the time I spent in vain.

38

' "But thou hast years, and privilege to use them: 260
Thy privilege doth bear beauty's great seal.
Besides, the Law of Nature doth excuse them
To whom thy youth may have a just appeal.
Esteem not fame more than thou dost thy weal:
    Fame, whereof the world seems to make such choice,
    Is but an echo and an idle voice.

39

' "Then why should this respect of honour bound us
In th' imaginary lists of reputation?
Titles which cold severity hath found us,
Breath of the vulgar, foe to recreation,   270
Melancholy's opinion, custom's relation,
    Pleasure's plague, beauty's scourge, hell to the fair,
    To leave the sweet for castles in the air.

40

' "Pleasure is felt, opinion but conceiv'd,
Honour a thing without us, not our own;
Whereof we see how many are bereav'd
Which should have reap'd the glory they had sown:
And many have it (yet unworthy) known.
 So breathes his blast this many-headed beast,
 Whereof the wisest have esteemed least.   280

41

' "The subtle city-women, better learn'd,
Esteem them chaste enough that best seem so:
Who, though they sport, it shall not be discern'd:
Their face bewrays not what their bodies do.
'Tis wary walking that dost safeliest go,
 With show of virtue, as the cunning knows:
 Babes are beguil'd with sweets, and men with shows.

42

' "Then use thy talent: youth shall be thy warrant.
And let not honour from thy sports detract:
Thou must not fondly think thyself transparent,   290
That those who see thy face can judge thy fact.
Let her have shame that cannot closely act,
 And seem thee chaste, which is the chiefest art:
 For what we seem, each sees; none knows our heart.

43

' "The mighty, who can with such sins dispense,
Instead of shame do honours great bestow.
A worthy author doth redeem th' offence,
And makes the scarlet sin as white as snow.
The majesty that doth descend so low
 Is not defil'd, but pure remains therein;   300
 And being sacred, sanctifies the sin.

44

' "What, dost thou stand on this, that he is old?
Thy beauty hath the more to work upon.
Thy pleasure's want shall be supplied with gold.
Cold age doth dote the most when heat of youth is gone:
Enticing words prevail with such a one;
   Alluring shows most deep impression strikes,
   For age is prone to credit what it likes."

45

'Here interrupt, she leaves me in a doubt,
When, lo, began a combat in my blood: 310
Seeing my youth environ'd round about,
The ground uncertain where my reasons stood,
Small my defence to make my party good
   Against such powers which were so surely laid
   To overthrow a poor unskilful maid.

46

'Treason was in my bones, myself conspiring,
To sell myself to lust, my soul to sin;
Pure blushing shame was even in retiring,
Leaving the sacred hold it gloried in.
Honour lay prostrate for my flesh to win,   320
   When cleaner thoughts my weakness gan upbray
   Against myself, and shame did force me say:

47

' "Ah, Rosamond, what doth thy flesh prepare?
Destruction to thy days, death to thy fame!
Wilt thou betray that honour held with care,
T' entomb with black reproach a spotted name,
Leaving thy blush the colours of thy shame?
   Opening thy feet to sin, thy soul to lust,
   Graceless to lay thy glory in the dust?

48

' "Nay, first let th' earth gape wide to swallow thee,   330
And shut thee up in bosom with her dead,
Ere serpent tempt thee taste forbidden tree
Or feel the warmth of an unlawful bed;
Suff'ring thyself by lust to be misled,
   So to disgrace thyself and grieve thine heirs,
   That Clifford's race should scorn thee one of theirs.

49

' "Never wish longer to enjoy the air
Than that thou breath'st the air of chastity,
Longer than thou preferr'st thy soul as fair
As is thy face, free from impurity: 340
Thy face that makes th' admir'd in every eye,
   Where Nature's care such rarities enrol:
   Which us'd amiss may serve to damn thy soul.

50

' "But what? He is my king, and may constrain me;
Whether I yield or not, I live defam'd.
The world will think authority did gain me;
I shall be judg'd his love, and so be sham'd:
We see the fair condemn'd that never gam'd.
   And if I yield, 'tis honourable shame;
   If not, I live disgrac'd, yet thought the same.   350

51

' "What way is left thee then, unhappy maid,
Whereby thy spotless foot may wander out
This dreadful danger, which thou seest is laid,
Wherein thy shame doth compass thee about?
Thy simple years cannot resolve this doubt,
   Thy youth can never guide thy foot so even
   But in despite some scandal will be given."

52

'Thus stood I balanc'd equally precise,
Till my frail flesh did weigh me down to sin,
Till world and pleasure made me partialize,   360
And glittering pomp my vanity did win:
When to excuse my faults my lusts begin,
And impious thoughts alleg'd this wanton clause,
That though I sinn'd, my sin had honest cause.

53

'So well the golden balls cast down before me
Could entertain my course, hinder my way:
Whereat my wretchless youth, stooping to store me,
Lost me the goal, the glory and the day.
Pleasure had set my well-school'd thoughts to play,
    And bade me use the virtue of mine eyes,   370
    For sweetly it fits the fair to wantonize.

54

'Thus wrought to sin, soon was I train'd from court
T' a solitary grange, there to attend
The time the king should thither make resort,
Where he love's long-desired work should end.
Thither he daily messages doth send,
    With costly jewels, orators of love,
    Which (ah, too well men know) do women move.

55

'The day before the night of my defeature
He greets me with a casket richly wrought,   380
So rare that Art did seem to strive with Nature
T' express the cunning workman's curious thought:
The mystery whereof I prying sought,
    And found engraven on the lid above
    Amymone, how she with Neptune strove:

56

'Amymone, old Danaus' fairest daughter,
As she was fetching water all alone
At Lerna, whereas Neptune came and caught her:
From whom she striv'd and struggled to be gone,
Beating the air with cries and piteous moan.   390
   But all in vain, with him she's forc'd to go:
   'Tis shame that men should use poor maidens so.

57

'There might I see described how she lay
At those proud feet, not satisfied with prayer:
Wailing her heavy hap, cursing the day,
In act so piteous to express despair;
And by how much more griev'd, so much more fair:
   Her tears upon her cheeks, poor careful girl,
   Did seem against the sun crystal and pearl:

58

'Whose pure clear streams, which, lo, so fair appears,   400
Wrought hotter flames. O, miracle of love
That kindles fire in water, heat in tears,
And makes neglected beauty mightier prove,
Teaching afflicted eyes affects to move;
   To show that nothing ill-becomes the fair
   But cruelty, which yields unto no prayer.

59

'This having view'd, and therewith something mov'd,
Figur'd I find within the other squares
Transformed Io, Jove's dearly lov'd,
In her affliction how she strangely fares: 410
Strangely distress'd (O, beauty, born to cares),
   Turn'd to a heifer, kept with jealous eyes,
   Always in danger of her hateful spies.

60

'These precedents presented to my view,
Wherein the presage of my fall was shown,
Might have forewarn'd me well what would ensue,
And others' harms have made me shun mine own.
But Fate is not prevented, though foreknown:
   For that must hap, decreed by heavenly powers,
   Who work our fall, yet make the fault still ours.   420

61

'Witness the world, wherein is nothing rifer
Than miseries unkenn'd before they come.
Who can the characters of chance decipher,
Written in clouds of our concealed doom?
Which though perhaps have been reveal'd to some,
   Yet that so doubtful (as success did prove them)
   That men must know they have the Heavens above them.

62

'I saw the sin wherein my foot was ent'ring;
I saw how that dishonour did attend it;
I saw the shame whereon my flesh was vent'ring,   430
Yet had I not the power for to defend it.
So weak is sense when error hath condemn'd it:
   We see what's good, and thereto we consent,
   But yet we choose the worst, and soon repent.

63

'And now I come to tell the worst of illness,
Now draws the date of mine affliction near.
Now when the dark had wrapp'd up all in stillness,
And dreadful black had dispossess'd the clear,
Com'd was the night, mother of sleep and fear,
   Who with her sable mantle friendly covers   440
   The sweet-stol'n sport of joyful-meeting lovers.

64

'When, lo, I joy'd my lover, not my love,
And felt the hand of lust most undesir'd;
Enforc'd th' unproved bitter-sweet to prove,
Which yields no natural pleasure when 'tis hir'd.
Love's not constrain'd, nor yet of due requir'd:
    Judge they who are unfortunately wed
    What 'tis to come unto a loathed bed.

65

'But soon his age receiv'd his short contenting,
And sleep seal'd up his languishing desires.   450
When he turns to his rest, I to repenting;
Into myself my waking thought retires.
My nakedness had prov'd my senses liars:
    Now open'd were mine eyes to look therein;
    For first we taste the fruit, then see our sin.

66

'Now did I find myself unparadis'd
From those pure fields of my so clean beginning;
Now I perceiv'd how ill I was advis'd,
My flesh gan loathe the new-felt touch of sinning.
Shame leaves us by degrees, not at first winning: 460
    For Nature checks a new offence with loathing,
    But use of sin doth make it seem as nothing.

67

'And use of sin did work in me a boldness,
And love in him incorporates such a zeal
That jealousy increas'd with age's coldness,
Fearing to lose the joy of all his weal;
Or doubting time his stealth might else reveal,
    He's driven to devise some subtle way
    How he might safeliest keep so rich a prey.

D

68

'A stately palace he forthwith did build,   470
Whose intricate innumerable ways
With such confused errors so beguil'd
Th' unguided ent'rers, with uncertain strays
And doubtful turnings, kept them in delays;
   With bootless labour leading them about,
   Able to find no way, nor in nor out.

69

'Within the closed bosom of which frame,
That serv'd a centre to that goodly round,
Were lodgings, with a garden to the same,
With sweetest flowers that e'er adorn'd the ground, 480
And all the pleasures that delight hath found
   T' entertain the sense of wanton eyes:
   Fuel of love, from whence lust's flames arise.

70

'Here I, enclos'd from all the world asunder,
The Minotaur of shame, kept for disgrace,
The monster of Fortune and the world's wonder,
Liv'd cloister'd in so desolate a case.
None but the king might come into the place,
   With certain maids that did attend my need,
   And he himself came guided by a thread.   490

71

'O, jealousy, daughter of envy and love,
Most wayward issue of a gentle sire,
Foster'd with fears, thy father's joys t' improve,
Mirth-marring monster, born a subtle liar;
Hateful unto thyself, flying thine own desire,
   Feeding upon suspect that doth renew thee,
   Happy were lovers if they never knew thee.

72

'Thou hast a thousand gates thou enterest by,
Condemning trembling passions to our heart;
Hundred-ey'd Argus, ever-waking spy, 500
Pale hag, infernal Fury, pleasure's smart,
Envious observer, prying in every part,
    Suspicious, fearful, gazing still about thee,
    O, would to God love could be without thee.

73

'Thou didst deprive (through self-suggesting fear)
Him of content, and me of liberty—
The only good that women hold so dear—
And turn'st my freedom to captivity,
First made a prisoner, ere an enemy:
    Enjoin'd the ransom of my body's shame, 510
    Which though I paid, could not redeem the same.

74

'What greater torment ever could have been
Than to enforce the fair to live retir'd?
For what is beauty if it be not seen?
Or what is't to be seen if not admir'd,
And though admir'd, unless in love desir'd?
    Never were cheeks of roses, locks of amber,
    Ordain'd to live imprison'd in a chamber.

75

'Nature created beauty for the view,
Like as the fire for heat, the sun for light: 520
The fair do hold this privilege as due
By ancient charter, to live most in sight,
And she that is debarr'd it hath not right.
    In vain our friends from this do us dehort,
    For beauty will be where is most resort.

76

'Witness the fairest streets that Thames doth visit,
The wondrous concourse of the glitt'ring fair:
For what rare woman deck'd with beauty is it
That thither covets not to make repair?
The solitary country may not stay her: 530
   Here is the centre of all beauties best,
   Excepting Delia, left t' adorn the west.

77

'Here doth the curious with judicial eyes
Contemplate beauty gloriously attir'd:
And herein all our chiefest glory lies,
To live where we are prais'd and most desir'd.
O, how we joy to see ourselves admir'd,
   Whilst niggardly our favours we discover:
   We love to be belov'd, yet scorn the lover.

78

'Yet would to God my foot had never mov'd   540
From country safety, from the fields of rest,
To know the danger to be highly lov'd
And live in pomp to brave among the best.
Happy for me, better had I been blest,
   If I unluckily had never stray'd,
   But liv'd at home a happy country-maid:

79

'Whose unaffected innocency thinks
No guileful fraud, as doth the courtly liver.
She's deck'd with truth: the river where she drinks
Doth serve her for her glass, her counsel-giver;   550
She loves sincerely, and is loved ever;
   Her days are peace, and so she ends her breath:
   True life, that knows not what's to die till death.

80

'So should I never have been regist'red
In the black book of the unfortunate,
Nor had my name enroll'd with maids misled
Which bought their pleasures at so high a rate;
Nor had I taught, through my unhappy fate,
     This lesson, which myself learnt with expense,
     How most it hurts that most delights the sense.   560

81

'Shame follows sin, disgrace is duly given,
Impiety will out, never so closely done:
No walls can hide us from the eye of Heaven,
For shame must end what wickedness begun.
Forth breaks reproach when least we think thereon,
     And this is ever proper unto courts,
     That nothing can be done but fame reports.

82

'Fame doth explore what lies most secret hidden,
Ent'ring the closet of the palace-dweller,
Abroad revealing what is most forbidden;   570
Of truth and falsehood both an equal teller,
There's not a guard can serve for to expel her;
     The sword of justice cannot cut her wings
     Nor stop her mouth from utt'ring secret things.

83

'And this our stealth she could not long conceal
From her whom such a forfeit most concern'd:
The wronged queen, who could so closely deal,
That she the whole of all our practice learn'd,
And watch'd a time when least it was discern'd,
     In absence of the king, to wreak her wrong   580
     With such revenge as she desired long.

84

'The labyrinth she enter'd by that thread
That serv'd a conduct to my absent lord,
Left there by chance, reserv'd for such a deed,
Where she surpris'd me whom she so abhorr'd;
Enrag'd with madness, scarce she speaks a word,
    But flies with eager fury to my face,
    Off'ring me most unwomanly disgrace.

85

'Look how a tigress that hath lost her whelp
Runs fiercely ranging through the woods astray,   590
And seeing herself depriv'd of hope or help,
Furiously assaults what's in her way,
To satisfy her wrath, not for a prey:
    So fell she on me in outrageous wise
    As could disdain and jealousy devise.

86

'And after all her vile reproaches us'd,
She forc'd me take the poison she had brought,
To end the life that had her so abus'd,
And free her fears, and ease her jealous thought.
No cruelty her wrath could leave unwrought,   600
    No spiteful act that to revenge is common;
    No beast being fiercer than a jealous woman.

87

' "Here take (saith she), thou impudent unclean,
Base graceless strumpet, take this next your heart;
Your lovesick heart, that overcharg'd hath been
With pleasure's surfeit, must be purg'd with art.
This potion hath a power that will convart
    To naught those humours that oppress'd you so,
    And, girl, I'll see you take it ere I go.

88

' "What, stand you now amaz'd, retire you back?   610
Tremble you, minion? Come, dispatch with speed;
There is no help, your champion now you lack,
And all these tears you shed will nothing steed;
Those dainty fingers needs must do the deed.
   Take it, or I will drench you else by force;
   And trifle not, lest that I use you worse."

89

'Having this bloody doom from hellish breath,
My woeful eyes on every side I cast:
Rigour about me, in my hand my death,
Presenting me the horror of my last: 620
All hope of pity and of comfort past;
   No means, no power; no forces to contend;
   My trembling hands must give myself my end.

90

'Those hands that beauty's ministers had bin,
They must give death that me adorn'd of late;
That mouth that newly gave consent to sin
Must now receive destruction in thereat;
That body which my lust did violate
   Must sacrifice itself t' appease the wrong:
   So short is pleasure, glory lasts not long.   630

91

'And she no sooner saw I had it taken
But forth she rushes, proud with victory,
And leaves m' alone, of all the world forsaken,
Except of death, which she had left with me.
Death and myself alone together be,
   To whom she did her full revenge refer:
   Oh, poor weak conquest both for him and her.

92

'Then straight my conscience summons up my sin
T' appear before me in a hideous face.
Now doth the terror of my soul begin,   640
When ev'ry corner of that hateful place
Dictates mine error and reveals disgrace,
    Whilst I remain oppress'd in every part,
    Death in my body, horrors at my heart.

93

'Down on my bed my loathsome self I cast,
The bed that likewise gives in evidence
Against my soul and tells I was unchaste,
Tells I was wanton, tells I follow'd sense;
And therefore cast by guilt of mine offence.
    Must here the right of Heaven needs satisfy,   650
    And where I wanton lay must wretched die.

94

'Here I began to wail my hard mishap,
My sudden, strange, unlook'd-for misery,
Accusing them that did my youth entrap,
To give me such a fall of infamy.
"And poor distressed Rosamond (said I),
    Is this thy glory got, to die forlorn
    In deserts where no ear can hear thee mourn?

95

' "Nor any eye of pity to behold
The woeful end of thy sad tragedy;   660
But that thy wrongs unseen, thy tale untold,
Must here in secret silence buried lie;
And with thee thine excuse together die,
    Thy sin reveal'd, but thy repentance hid,
    Thy shame alive, but dead what thy death did.

96

' "Yet breathe out to these walls the breath of moan,
Tell th' air thy plaints, since men thou canst not tell;
And though thou perish desolate alone,
Tell yet thyself what thyself knows too well:
Utter thy grief wherewith thy soul doth dwell,   670
   And let thy heart pity thy heart's remorse,
   And by thyself the mourner and the corse.

97

' "Condole thee here, clad all in black despair,
With silence only, and a dying bed,
Thou that of late, so flourishing, so fair,
Didst glorious live, admir'd and honoured;
And now from friends, from succour, hither led,
   Art made a spoil to lust, to wrath, to death,
   And in disgrace, forc'd here to yield thy breath.

98

' "Did Nature for this good ingeniate,   680
To show in thee the glory of her best,
Framing thine eye the star of thy ill fate,
Making thy face the foe to spoil the rest?
O, beauty, thou an enemy profess'd
   To chastity and us that love thee most,
   Without thee, how w' are loath'd, and with thee lost!

99

' "You, you that proud with liberty and beauty
(And well you may be proud that you be so)
Glitter in court, lov'd and observ'd of duty,
Would God I might to you but ere I go   690
Speak what I feel, to warn you by my woe,
   To keep your feet in cleanly paths of shame,
   That no enticing may divert the same.

100

' "See'ng how against your tender weakness still
The strength of wit and gold and all is bent;
And all th' assaults that ever might or skill
Can give against a chaste and clean intent:
Ah, let not greatness work you to consent:
   The spot is foul, though by a monarch made:
   Kings cannot privilege what God forbade.   700

101

' "Lock up therefore the treasure of your love
Under the surest keys of fear and shame,
And let no powers have power chaste thoughts to move
To make a lawless entry on your fame.
Open to those the comfort of your flame
   Whose equal love shall march with equal pace
   In those pure ways that lead to no disgrace.

102

' "For see how many discontented beds
Our own aspiring, or our parents' pride,
Have caus'd whilst that ambition vainly weds   710
Wealth and not love, honour and nought beside:
Whilst married but no titles, we abide
   As wedded widows, wanting what we have,
   When shadows cannot give us what we crave.

103

' "Or whilst we spend the freshest of our time,
The sweet of youth, in plotting in the air.
Alas, how oft we fall, hoping to climb,
Or wither as unprofitably fair;
Whilst those decays which are without repair
   Make us neglected, scorned and reprov'd: 720
   And, oh, what are we if we be not lov'd?

104

' "Fasten therefore upon occasions fit,
Lest this, or that, or like disgrace as mine
Do overtake your youth, or ruin it,
And cloud with infamy your beauty's shine:
Seeing how many seek to undermine
   The treasury that's unpossess'd of any;
   And hard 'tis kept that is desir'd of many.

105

' "And fly, O fly, these bed-brokers unclean,
The monsters of our sex, that make a prey   730
Of their own kind, by an unkindly mean;
And even, like vipers, eating out a way
Through th' womb of their own shame, accursed they
   Live by the death of fame, the gain of sin,
   The filth of lust uncleanness wallows in.

106

' "As if 'twere not enough that we—poor we!—
Have weakness, beauty, gold and men our foes,
But we must have some of ourselves to be
Traitors unto ourselves, to join with those
Such as our feeble forces do disclose,   740
   And still betray our cause, our shame, our youth,
   To lust, to folly and to men's untruth.

107

' "Hateful confounders both of blood and laws,
Vild orators of shame that plead delight;
Ungracious agents in a wicked cause,
Factors for darkness, messengers of night,
Serpents of guile, devils that do invite
   The wanton taste of that forbidden tree
   Whose fruit, once pluck'd, will show how foul we be.

108

‘ "You in the habit of a grave aspect,   750
In credit by the trust of years, can show
The cunning ways of lust, and can direct
The fair and wily wantons how to go;
Having your loathsome selves your youth spent so,
   And in uncleanness ever have been fed
   By the revenue of a wanton bed.

109

‘ "By you have been the innocent betray’d,
The blushing fearful bolden’d unto sin,
The wife made subtil, subtil made the maid,
The husband scorn’d, dishonoured the kin,   760
Parents disgrac’d, children infamous bin,
   Confus’d our race, and falsified our blood,
   Whilst fathers’ sons possess wrong fathers’ good."

110

‘This and much more I would have utter’d then,
A testament to be recorded still,
Sign’d with my blood, subscrib’d with conscience’ pen,
To warn the fair and beautiful from ill:
Though I could wish, by the example of my will,
   I had not left this note unto the fair,
   But died intestate, to have had no heir.   770

111

‘By now the poison, spread through all my veins,
Gan dispossess my living senses quite;
And nought-respecting death, the last of pains,
Plac’d his pale colours (th’ ensign of his might)
Upon his new-got spoil before his right;
   Thence chas’d my soul, setting my day ere noon,
   When I least thought my joys could end so soon.

112

'And as convey'd t' untimely funerals,
My scarce-cold corse not suffer'd longer stay,
Behold, the king, by chance returning, falls   780
T' encounter with the same upon the way,
As he repair'd to see his dearest joy:
   Not thinking such a meeting could have been,
   To see his love, and seeing bin unseen.

113

'Judge, those whom chance deprives of sweetest treasure,
What 'tis to lose a thing we hold so dear,
The best delight, wherein our soul takes pleasure,
The sweet of life, that penetrates so near;
What passions feels that heart enforc'd to bear
   The deep impression of so strange a sight   790
   That overwhelms us, or confounds us quite!

114

'Amaz'd he stands: nor voice nor body stirs,
Words had no passage, tears no issue found,
For sorrow shut up words, wrath kept in tears;
Confus'd affects each other do confound;
Oppress'd with grief, his passions had no bound:
   Striving to tell his woes, words would not come,
   For light cares speak, when mighty griefs are dumb.

115

'At length extremity breaks out a way,
Through which th' imprison'd voice, with tears attended, 800
Wails out a sound that sorrows do bewray;
With arms a-cross and eyes to heaven bended,
Vapouring out sighs that to the skies ascended,
   Sighs (the poor ease calamity affords)
   Which serve for speech when sorrow wanteth words.

116

' "O, Heavens (quoth he), why do mine eyes behold
The hateful rays of this unhappy sun?
Why have I light to see my sins controll'd,
With blood of mine own shame thus vildly done?
How can my sight endure to look thereon?   810
　　Why doth not black eternal darkness hide
　　That from mine eyes my heart cannot abide?

117

' "What saw my life wherein my soul might joy?
What had my days, whom troubles still afflicted,
But only this to counterpoise annoy?
This joy, this hope, which death hath interdicted,
This sweet, whose loss hath all distress inflicted,
　　This, that did season all my flower of life,
　　Vex'd still at home with broils, abroad in strife;

118

' "Vex'd still at home with broils, abroad in strife,   820
Dissension in my blood, jars in my bed;
Distrust at board, suspecting still my life,
Spending the night in horror, days in dread:
Such life hath tyrants, and this life I led.
　　These miseries go mask'd in glittering shows,
　　Which wise men see, the vulgar little knows."

119

'Then as these passions do him overwhelm,
He draws him near my body to behold it;
And as the vine married unto the elm
With strict embraces, so doth he enfold it;   830
And as he in his careful arms doth hold it,
　　Viewing the face that even death commends,
　　On senseless lips millions of kisses spends.

120

' "Pitiful mouth (saith he) that living gavest
The sweetest comfort that my soul could wish,
Oh, be it lawful now that dead thou havest
This sorrowing farewell of a dying kiss;
And you, fair eyes, containers of my bliss,
 Motives of love, born to be matched never,
  Entomb'd in your sweet circles, sleep for ever. 840

121

' "Ah, how methinks I see death, dallying, seeks
To entertain itself in love's sweet place;
Decay'd roses of discolour'd cheeks
Do yet retain dear notes of former grace;
And ugly death sits fair within her face,
 Sweet remnants resting of vermilion red
  That death itself doubts whether she be dead.

122

' "Wonder of beauty, oh, receive these plaints,
These obsequies, the last that I shall make thee:
For, lo, my soul that now already faints 850
(That lov'd thee living, dead will not forsake thee)
Hastens her speedy course to overtake thee.
 I'll meet my death, and free myself thereby,
  For, ah! what can he do that cannot die?

123

' "Yet ere I die, thus much my soul doth vow
Revenge shall sweeten death with ease of mind:
And I will cause posterity shall know
How fair thou wert above all womankind;
And after-ages monuments shall find
 Showing thy beauty's title, not thy name, 860
  Rose of the world, that sweeten'd so the same."

124

'This said, though more desirous yet to say,
(For sorrow is unwilling to give over)
He doth repress what grief would else bewray,
Lest he too much his passion should discover;
And yet respect scarce bridles such a lover,
　　So far transported that he knows not whither,
　　For love and majesty dwell ill together.

125

'Then were my funerals not long deferr'd,
But done with all the rites pomp could devise,　　870
At Godstow, where my body was interr'd,
And richly tomb'd in honourable wise:
Where yet as now scarce any note descries
　　Unto these times the memory of me,
　　Marble and brass so little lasting be.

126

'For those walls, which the credulous devout
And apt-believing ignorant did found,
With willing zeal that never call'd in doubt
That Time their works should ever so confound,
Lie like confused heaps as underground;　　880
　　And what their ignorance esteem'd so holy
　　The wiser ages account as folly.

127

'And were it not thy favourable lines
Re-edified the wrack of my decays,
And that thy accents willingly assigns
Some farther date, and give me longer days,
Few in this age had known my beauty's praise.
　　But thus renew'd, my fame redeems some time
　　Till other ages shall neglect thy rhyme.

128

'Then when confusion in her course shall bring   890
Sad desolation on the times to come,
When mirthless Thames shall have no swan to sing,
All music silent, and the Muses dumb;
And yet even then it must be known to some
   That once they flourish'd, though not cherish'd so,
   And Thames had swans as well as ever Po.

129

'But here an end, I may no longer stay;
I must return t' attend at Stygian flood.
Yet ere I go, this one word more I pray:
Tell Delia now her sigh may do me good,   900
And will her note the frailty of our blood;
   And if I pass unto those happy banks,
   Then she must have her praise, thy pen her thanks.'

130

So vanish'd she, and left me to return
To prosecute the tenor of my woes,
Eternal matter for my Muse to mourn.
But yet the world hath heard too much of those:
My youth such errors must no more disclose.
   I'll hide the rest, and grieve for what hath been;
   Who made me known must make me live unseen.   910

THOMAS LODGE

Scylla's Metamorphosis:
Interlaced with the unfortunate love of Glaucus
(1589)

1

Walking alone (all only full of grief)
Within a thicket near to Isis' flood,
Weeping my wants, and wailing scant relief,
Wringing mine arms (as one with sorrow wood);
    The piteous streams, relenting at my moan,
    Withdrew their tides, and stayed to hear me groan.

2

From forth the channel, with a sorrowing cry
The sea-god Glaucus (with his hallow'd ears
Wet in the tears of his sad mother's dye)
With piteous looks before my face appears;   10
    For whom the nymphs a mossy coat did frame,
    Embroider'd with his Scylla's heavenly name.

3

And as I sat under a willow tree,
The lovely honour of fair Thetis' bower
Repos'd his head upon my faintful knee:
And when my tears had ceas'd their stormy shower
    He dried my cheeks, and then bespake him so,
    As when he wail'd I straight forgot my woe:

4

'Unfortunate, why wand'reth thy content
From forth his scope as wearied of itself?   20
Thy books have school'd thee from this fond repent,
And thou canst talk by proof of wavering pelf:
   Unto the world such is inconstancy,
   As sap to tree, as apple to the eye.

5

'Mark, how the morn in roseate colour shines,
And straight with clouds the sunny tract is clad;
Then see how pomp through wax and wane declines,
From high to low, from better to the bad:
   Take moist from sea, take colour from his kind,
   Before the world devoid of change thou find.   30

6

'With secret eye look on the earth awhile,
Regard the changes Nature forceth there;
Behold the heavens, whose course all sense beguile;
Respect thyself, and thou shalt find it clear
   That infantlike thou art become a youth,
   And youth forespent, a wretched age ensu'th.

7

'In searching then the schoolmen's cunning notes,
Of heaven, of earth, of flowers, of springing trees,
Of herbs, of metal, and of Thetis' floats,
Of laws and nurture kept among the bees: 40
   Conclude and know times change by course of fate;
   Then mourn no more, but moan my hapless state.'

8

Here gan he pause and shake his heavy head,
And fold his arms, and then unfold them straight;

Fain would he speak, but tongue was charm'd by dread,
Whilst I that saw what woes did him await,
  Comparing his mishaps and moan with mine,
  Gan smile for joy and dry his drooping eyne.

9

But (lo) a wonder; from the channel's glide
A sweet melodious noise of music rose   50
That made the stream to dance a pleasant tide,
The weeds and sallows near the bank that grows
  Gan sing, as when the calmest winds accord
  To greet with balmy breath the fleeting ford.

10

Upon the silver bosom of the stream
First gan fair Themis shake her amber locks,
Whom all the nymphs that wait on Neptune's realm
Attended from the hollow of the rocks.
  In brief, while these rare paragons assemble,
  The wat'ry world to touch their teats do tremble.   60

11

Footing it featly on the grassy ground,
These damsels, circling with their brightsome fairs
The lovesick god and I, about us wound
Like stars that Ariadne's crown repairs:
  Who once hath seen or pride of morn or day,
  Would deem all pomp within their cheeks did play.

12

Nais, fair nymph with Bacchus' ivory touch,
Gan tune a passion with such sweet reports.
And every word, note, sigh, and pause was such,
And every cadence fed with such consorts,   70

As were the Delian harper bent to hear,
Her stately strains might tempt his curious ear.

13

Of love (God wot) the lovely nymph complain'd:
But so of love as forced Love to love her;
And even in love such furious love remain'd,
As searching out his powerful shaft to prove her,
  He found his quiver emptied of the best,
  And felt the arrow sticking in his breast.

14

Under a poplar Themis did repose her,
And from a briar a sweetful branch did pluck: 80
When midst the briar ere she could scarce suppose her
A nightingale gan sing: but woe the luck;
  The branch so near her breast, while she did quick her
  To turn her head, on sudden gan to prick her.

15

Whilst smiling Clore, midst her envious blushes,
Gan blame her fear and prettily said thus:
'Worse pricks than these are found among these bushes,
 And yet such pricks are scarcely fear'd of us.'
  'Nay soft (said Chelis), pricks do make birds sing,
  But pricks in ladies' bosoms often sting.'   90

16

Thus jest they on the nightingale's report,
And on the prickle of the eglantine,
On Nais' song, and all the whole consort
In public this sweet sentence did assign:
  That while some smile, some sigh through change of time;
  Some smart, some sport, amidst their youthly prime.

17

Such wreaths as bound the Theban's ivory brow,
Such gay-trick'd garlands plait these jolly dames;
The flowers themselves, when as the nymphs gan vow,
Gan vail their crests in honour of their names: 100
    And smil'd their sweet and woo'd with so much glee,
    As if they said, 'Sweet nymph, come gather me.'

18

But pensive Glaucus, passionate with painings,
Amidst their revel thus began his ruth:
'Nymphs, fly these groves late blasted with my plainings,
For cruel Scylla nill regard my truth:
    And leave us two consorted in our groanings,
    To register with tears our bitter moanings.

19

'The floods do fail their course to see our cross,
The fields forsake their green to hear our grief,   110
The rocks will weep whole springs to mark our loss,
The hills relent to store our scant relief,
    The air repines, the pensive birds are heavy,
    The trees to see us pain'd no more are leafy.

20

'Ay me, the shepherds let their flocks want feeding,
And flocks to see their paly face are sorry;
The nymphs to spy the flocks and shepherds needing,
Prepare their tears to hear our tragic story:
    Whil'st we, surpris'd with grief, cannot disclose them,
    With sighing wish the world for to suppose them.   120

21

'He that hath seen the sweet Arcadian boy
Wiping the purple from his forced wound,

His pretty tears betokening his annoy,
His sighs, his cries, his falling on the ground,
  The echoes ringing from the rocks his fall,
  The trees with tears reporting of his thrall:

22

'And Venus starting at her love-mate's cry,
Forcing her birds to haste her chariot on;
And full of grief at last with piteous eye
Seeing where all pale with death he lay alone,   130
  Whose beauty quail'd, as wont the lilies droop
  When wasteful winter winds do make them stoop:

23

'Her dainty hand address'd to daw her dear,
Her roseal lip allied to his pale cheek,
Her sighs, and then her looks and heavy cheer,
Her bitter threats, and then her passions meek;
  How on his senseless corpse she lay a-crying,
  As if the boy were then but new a-dying.

24

'He that hath view'd Angelica the fair
Bestraught with fancy near the Caspian springs,   140
Renting the tresses of her golden hair;
How on her harp with piteous notes she sings
  Of Roland's ruth, of Medor's false depart,
  Sighing each rest from centre of her heart;

25

'How now she writes upon a beechen bough
Her Medor's name, and bedlam-like again
Calls all the heaven to witness of his vow,
And straight again begins a mournful strain,

And how in thought of her true faith forsooken
He fled her bowers, and how his league was broken. 150

26

'Ay me, who marks her harp hang up again
Upon the willows water'd with her tears,
And how she rues to read her Roland's pain,
When but the shadow of his name appears,
    Would make more plainings from his eyes to flee
    Than tears distil from amber-weeping tree.

27

'He that hath known the passionate mishaps
That near Olympus fair Lucina felt
When as her Latmian love her fancy traps,
How with suspect her inward soul doth melt;   160
    Or mark'd the morn her Cephalus complaining;
    May then recount the course of all our paining.

28

'But tender nymphs, to you belongs no teen;
Then favour me in flying from this bower
Whereas but care and thought of crosses been;
Leave me, that lose myself through fancy's power;
    Through fancy's power, which had I leave to lose it,
    No fancy then should see me for to choose it.

29

'When you are fled, the heaven shall lour for sorrow,
The day o'ercast shall be betime with sable,   170
The air from sea such streaming showers shall borrow
As earth to bear the brunt shall not be able,
    And ships shall safely sail whereas beforn
    The ploughman watch'd the reaping of his corn.

30

'Go you in peace to Neptune's wat'ry sound;
No more may Glaucus play him with so pretty,
But shun resort where solace nill be found,
And plain my Scylla's pride and want of pity:
  Alas sweet nymphs, my godhead's all in vain,
  For why this breast includes immortal pain.   180

31

'Scylla hath eyes, but too sweet eyes hath Scylla;
Scylla hath hands, fair hands, but coy in touching;
Scylla in wit surpasseth grave Sibylla;
Scylla hath words, but words well stor'd with grutching;
  Scylla a saint in look, no saint in scorning:
  Look saint-like, Scylla, lest I die with mourning.

32

'Alas, why talk I? Sea-god, cease to mourn her,
'For in her nay my joys are ever ceasing:
Cease life or love, then shall I never blame her;
But neither love nor life may find decreasing.   190
  A mortal wound is my immortal being,
  Which passeth thought, or eyes' advised seeing.'

33

Herewith his falt'ring tongue, by sighs oppress'd,
Forsook his office, and his blood resorted
To feed the heart that wholly was distress'd,
Whilst pale (like Pallas' flower) my knee supported
  His feeble head and arm, so full of anguish,
  That they which saw his sorrows gan to languish.

34

Themis, the coyest of this beauteous train,
On hilly tops the wond'rous moly found,   200

Which dipp'd in balmy dew she gan to strain,
And brought her present to recure his wound:
  Clore she gathered Amaranthus' flower,
  And Nais Ajax' blossom in that stour.

35

Some chafe his temples with their lovely hands,
Some sprinkle water on his pale wan cheeks,
Some weep, some wake, some curse affection's bands,
To see so young, so fair, become so weak:
  But not their piteous herbs or springs have working
  To ease that heart where wanton love is lurking.   210

36

Natheless, though loth to show his holy kindness,
On every one he spent a look for favour,
And pray'd their pardon, vouching Cupid's blindness,
(Oh, fancies fond that naught but sorrows savour);
  To see a lovely god leave sea nymphs so,
  Who cannot doom upon his deadly woe?

37

Themis, that knew that waters long restrain'd
Break forth with greater billows than the brooks
That sweetly float through meads with flowers distain'd,
With cheerful lays did raise his heavy looks,   220
  And bade him speak and tell what him aggriev'd:
  For griefs disclos'd (said she) are soon reliev'd.

38

And as she wish'd, so all the rest did woo him;
By whose incessant suits at last invited,
He thus discover'd that which did undo him,
And orderly his hideous harms recited,

When first with finger's wag he gan to still them,
And thus with dreary terms of love did fill them.

39

'Ah nymphs,' (quoth he), 'had I by reason learnt
That secret art which birds have gain'd by sense,   230
By due foresight misfortune to prevent;
Or could my wit control mine eyes' offence:
  You then should smile, and I should tell such stories
  As woods and waves should triumph in our glories.

40

'But Nereus' daughters, sea-borne saints, attend:
Lake-breeding geese, when from the eastern clime
They list unto the western waters wend
To choose their place of rest by course of time,
  Approaching Taurus' haughty-topped hill
  They charm their cackle by this wondrous skill.   240

41

'The climbing mountain, neighbouring air well-nigh,
Hath harbour'd in his rocks and desert haunts
Whole eeries of eagles, prest to fly,
That gazing on the sun their birthright vaunts;
  Which birds of Jove with deadly feud pursue
  The wandering geese, when so they press in view.

42

'These fearful flitting troops, by Nature taught,
Passing these dangerous places of pursuit,
When all the desert vales they through have sought,
With pebbles stop their beaks to make them mute,   250
  And by this means their dangerous deaths prevent
  And gain their wished waters of frequent.

43

'But I, fond God, I god complain thy folly;
Let birds by sense exceed my reason far:
Whilom than I who was more strong and jolly,
Who more contemn'd affection's wanton war?
   Who less than I lov'd lustful Cupid's arrows,
   Who now with curse and plague poor Glaucus harrows?

44

'How have I leapt to hear the Tritons play
A harsh retreat unto the swelling floods?   260
How have I kept the dolphins at a bay,
When as I meant to charm their wanton moods?
   How have the angry winds grown calm for love,
   When as these fingers did my harp strings move?

45

'Was any nymph, you nymphs, was ever any
That tangled not her fingers in my tress?
Some well I wot, and of that some full many,
Wish'd or my fair or their desire were less:
   Even Ariadne, gazing from the sky,
   Became enamour'd of poor Glaucus' eye.   270

46

'Amidst this pride of youth and beauty's treasure
It was my chance, you floods can tell my chancing,
Fleeting along Sicilian bounds for pleasure,
To spy a nymph of such a radiant glancing,
   As when I look'd, a beam of subtil firing
   From eye to heart incens'd a deep desiring.

47

'Ah, had the veil of reason clad mine eye,
This foe of freedom had not burnt my heart:

But birds are blest, and most accurs'd am I
Who must report her glories to my smart: 280
   The nymph I saw and lov'd her, all too cruel,
   Scylla, fair Scylla, my fond fancy's jewel.

48

'Her hair not truss'd but scatter'd on her brow,
Surpassing Hybla's honey for the view,
Or soften'd golden wires; I know not how
Love with a radiant beauty did pursue
   My too judicial eyes, in darting fire
   That kindled straight in me my fond desire.

49

'Within these snares first was my heart entrapp'd,
Till through those golden shrouds mine eyes did see   290
An ivory-shadow'd front, wherein was wrapp'd
Those pretty bowers where graces couched be:
   Next which her cheeks appear'd like crimson silk,
   Or ruddy rose bespread on whitest milk.

50

'Twixt which the nose in lovely tenor bends,
(Too traitorous pretty for a lover's view):
Next which her lips like violets commends
By true proportion that which doth ensue;
   Which when they smile present unto the eyes
   The ocean's pride and ivory paradise.   300

51

'Her polish'd neck of milk-white snows doth shine,
As when the moon in winter night beholds them:
Her breast of alabaster clear and fine,
Whereon two rising apples fair unfolds them,

Like Cynthia's face when in her full she shineth,
And blushing to her love-mate's bower declineth.

52

'From whence in length her arms do sweetly spread
Like two rare branchy saples in the spring,
Yielding five lovely sprigs from every head,
Proportion'd alike in everything;   310
  Which featly sprout in length like spring-born friends,
  Whose pretty tops with five sweet roses ends.

53

'But why, alas, should I that marble hide
That doth adorn the one and other flank,
From whence a mount of quicken'd snow doth glide;
Or else the vale that bounds this milk-white bank,
  Where Venus and her sisters hide the fount
  Whose lovely nectar doth all sweets surmount.

54

'Confounded with descriptions, I must leave them;
Lovers must think, and poets must report them: 320
For silly wits may never well conceive them,
Unless a special grace from heaven consort them.
  Aye's me, these fairs attending Scylla won me:
  But now (sweet nymphs) attend what hath undone me.

55

'The lovely breast where all this beauty rested
Shrouded within a world of deep disdain:
For where I thought my fancy should be feasted
With kind affect, alas (unto my pain)
  When first I wooed, the wanton straight was flying,
  And gave repulse before we talk'd of trying.   330

56

'How oft have I (too often have I done so)
In silent night when every eye was sleeping,
Drawn near her cave, in hope her love were won so,
Forcing the neighbouring waters through my weeping
    To wake the winds, who did afflict her dwelling
    Whilst I with tears my passion was a-telling.

57

'When midst the Caspian seas the wanton play'd
I drew whole wreaths of coral from the rocks
And in her lap my heavenly presents laid:
But she unkind rewarded me with mocks;   340
    Such are the fruits that spring from ladies' coying,
    Who smile at tears and are entrapp'd with toying.

58

'Tongue might grow weary to report my wooings,
And heart might burst to think of her denial:
May none be blam'd but heaven for all these doings,
That yield no helps in midst of all my trial.
    Heart, tongue, thought, pen nill serve me to repent me;
    Disdain herself should strive for to lament me:

59

'Wretched Love, let me die, end my love by my death;
Dead, alas I live. Fly, my life! fade, my love!   350
Out, alas, love abides, still I 'joy vital breath:
Death is love, love is death: woe is me that do prove.
    Pain and woe, care and grief every day about me hovers:
    Then but death what can quell all the plagues of hapless lovers?

60

'Ay me, my moanings are like water drops
That need an age to pierce her marble heart;

I sow'd true zeal, yet fruitless were my crops:
I plighted faith, yet falsehood wrought my smart:
  I prais'd her looks, her looks despised Glaucus;
  Was ever amorous sea-god scorned thus?   360

61

'A hundred swelling tides my mother spent
Upon these locks, and all her nymphs were prest
To pleat them fair when to her bower I went:
He that hath seen the wand'ring Phoebus' crest
  Touch'd with the crystal of Eurotas' spring,
  The pride of these my bushy locks might sing.

62

'But short discourse beseems my bad success.
Each office of a lover I perform'd:
So fervently my passions did her press,
So sweet my lays, my speech so well reform'd,   370
  That (cruel) when she saw naught would beguile me,
  With angry looks the nymph did thus exile me:

63

' "Pack hence, thou fondling, to the western seas,
Within some calmy river shroud thy head:
For never shall my fair thy love appease,
Since fancy from this bosom late is fled:
  And if thou love me, show it in departing:
  For why thy presence doth procure my smarting."

64

'This said, with angry looks away she hasted
As fast as fly the floods before the winds: 380
When I (poor soul), with wretched sorrows wasted,
Exclaim'd on love, which wit and reason blinds:

THOMAS LODGE 73

And banish'd from her bower, with woeful posting
I bent myself to seek a foreign coasting.

65

'At last in wand'ring through the greater seas
It was my chance to pass the noted straits:
And wearied sore in seeking after ease,
Amidst the creeks, and wat'ry cool receipts,
  I spied from far, by help of sunny beams,
  A fruitful isle begirt with ocean streams.   390

66

'Westward I fleeted, and with heedful eye
Beheld the chalky cliffs that tempt the air,
Till at the last it was my chance to spy
A pleasant entrance to the floods' repair;
  Through which I press'd, and wond'ring there beheld
  On either side a sweet and fruitful field.

67

'Isis (the lady of that lovely stream)
Made holiday in view of my resort;
And all the nymphs of that her wat'ry realm
Gan trip for joy, to make me mickle sport: 400
  But I (poor soul) with no such joys contented,
  Forsook their bowers, and secretly lamented.

68

'All solitary roam I hereabout,
Now on the shore, now in the stream I weep;
Fire burns within, and ghastly fear without,
No rest, no ease, no hope of any sleep:
  Poor banish'd god, here have I still remain'd,
  Since time my Scylla hath my suits disdain'd.

69

'And here consort I now with hapless men,
  Yielding them comfort, thought my wound be cureless.   410
Songs of remorse I warble now and then,
  Wherein I curse fond Love and Fortune dureless;
    Wanhope my weal, my trust but bad adventure,
    Circumference is care, my heart the centre.'

70

Whilst thus he spake, fierce Ate charm'd his tongue,
His senses fail'd, his arms were folded straight,
And now he sighs, and then his heart is stung;
Again he speaks 'gainst fancy's fond deceit,
    And tears his tresses with his fingers fair,
    And rents his robes, half-mad with deep despair.   420

71

The piteous nymphs that view'd his heavy plight,
And heard the sequel of his bad success,
Did loose the springs of their remorseful sight,
And wept so sore to see his scant redress
    That of their tears there grew a pretty brook,
    Whose crystals clear the clouds of pensive look.

72

Alas, woe's me, how oft have I bewept
So fair, so young, so lovely, and so kind;
And whilst the god upon my bosom slept,
Beheld the scars of his afflicted mind,   430
    Imprinted in his ivory brow by care
    That fruitless fancy left unto his share.

73

My wand'ring lines, bewitch not so my senses:
But, gentle Muse, direct their course aright;

Delays in tragic tales procure offences:
Yield me such feeling words that whilst I write
  My working lines may fill mine eyes with languish,
  And they to note my moans may melt with anguish.

74

The woeful Glaucus, thus with woes attainted,
The pensive nymphs aggriev'd to see his plight,   440
The floods and fields with his laments acquainted,
Myself amaz'd to see this heavy sight;
  On sudden, Thetis with her train approach'd,
  And gravely thus her amorous son reproach'd:

75

'My son (said she), immortal have I made thee;
Amidst my wat'ry realms who may compare
Or match thy might? Why then should care invade thee,
That art so young, so lovely, fresh and fair?
  Alas, fond god, it merits great reproving
  In states of worth to dote on foolish loving.   450

76

'Come, wend with me, and midst thy father's bower
Let us disport and frolic for a while
In spite of love: although he pout and lour,
Good exercise will idle lusts beguile:
  Let wanton Scylla coy her where she will,
  Live thou, my son, by reason's level still.'

77

Thus said the goddess: and although her words
Gave signs of counsel, pomp and majesty,
Yet natheless her piteous eye affords
Some pretty witness to the standers-by   460

That in her thoughts (for all her outward show)
She mourn'd to see her son amated so.

78

But (welladay) her words have little force;
That hapless lover, worn with working woe,
Upon the ground lay pale as any corse,
And were not tears which from his eyes did flow,
    And sighs that witness he enjoy'd his breath,
    They might have thought him citizen of Death.

79

Which spectacle of care made Thetis bow,
And call on Glaucus, and command her son   470
To yield her right, and her advice allow.
But (woe) the man whom fancy had undone
    Nill mark her rules: nor words nor weeping tears
    Can fasten counsel in the lover's ears.

80

The Queen of Sea, with all her nymphs, assur'd
That no persuasion might relieve his care,
Kneeling adown, their falt'ring tongues enur'd
To tempt fair Venus by their vowed prayer:
    The course whereof, as I could bear in mind,
    With sorrowing sobs they utter'd in this kind: 480

81

'Born of the sea, thou Paphian Queen of Love,
Mistress of sweet conspiring harmony:
Lady of Cyprus, for whose sweet behove
The shepherds praise the youth of Thessaly:
    Daughter of Jove and sister to the Sun,
    Assist poor Glaucus, late by love undone.

82

'So mayst thou bain thee in th' Arcadian brooks,
And play with Vulcan's rival when thou list,
And calm his jealous anger by thy looks,
And knit thy temples with a roseate twist,   490
  If thou thyself and thine almighty son
  Assist poor Glaucus, late by love undone.

83

'May earth still praise thee for her kind increase,
And beasts adore thee for their fruitful wombs,
And fowls with notes thy praises never cease,
And bees admire thee for their honeycombs:
  So thou thyself and thine almighty son
  Assist poor Glaucus, late by love undone.'

84

No sooner from her reverent lips were past
Those latter lines but, mounting in the east,   500
Fair Venus in her ivory coach did haste,
And toward those pensive dames her course address'd;
  Her doves so plied their waving wings with flight
  That straight the sacred goddess came in sight.

85

Upon her head she bare that gorgeous crown
Wherein the poor Amyntas is a star;
Her lovely locks her bosom hung adown
(Those nets that first ensnar'd the God of War):
  Delicious lovely shine her pretty eyes,
  And on her cheeks carnation clouds arise;   510

86

The stately robe she ware upon her back
Was lily-white, wherein with coloured silk

Her nymphs had blaz'd the young Adonis' wrack,
And Leda's rape by swan as white as milk,
  And on her lap her lovely son was plac'd,
  Whose beauty all his mother's pomp defac'd.

87

A wreath of roses hemm'd his temples in,
His tress was curl'd and clear as beaten gold;
Haught were his looks, and lovely was his skin,
Each part as pure as heaven's eternal mould,   520
  And on his eyes a milk-white wreath was spread,
  Which 'longst his back with pretty plaits did shed.

88

Two dainty wings of parti-coloured plumes
Adorn his shoulders, dallying with the wind;
His left hand wields a torch that ever fumes:
And in his right, his bow that fancies bind,
  And on his back his quiver hangs, well stor'd
  With sundry shafts that sundry hearts have gor'd.

89

The deities arriv'd in place desir'd,
Fair Venus her to Thetis first bespake: 530
'Princess of Sea' (quoth she), 'as you requir'd,
From Sestos with my son my course I take:
  Frolic, fair goddess, nymphs, forsake your plaining,
  My son hath power and favour yet remaining.'

90

With that the reverend powers each other kiss'd,
And Cupid smil'd upon the nymphs for pleasure:
So naught but Glaucus' solace there was miss'd:
Which to effect the nymphs withouten measure

Entreat the god, who at the last drew nigh
The place where Glaucus full of care did lie;   540

91

And from his bow a furious dart he sent
Into that wound which he had made before:
That like Achilles' sword became the taint
To cure the wound that it had carv'd before:
   And suddenly the sea-god started up,
   Reviv'd, reliev'd, and free from fancy's cup.

92

No more of love, no more of hate he spoke,
No more he forc'd the sighs from out his breast:
His sudden joy his pleasing smiles provoke,
And all aloft he shakes his bushy crest,   550
   Greeting the gods and goddesses beside,
   And every nymph upon that happy tide.

93

Cupid and he together, hand in hand,
Approach the place of this renowned train:
'Ladies' (said he), 'releas'd from amorous band,
Receive my prisoner to your grace again.'
   Glaucus gave thanks, when Thetis, glad with bliss,
   Embrac'd his neck and his kind cheeks did kiss.

94

To see the nymphs in flocks about him play,
How Nais kempt his head, and wash'd his brows: 560
How Thetis check'd him with his welladay,
How Clore told him of his amorous vows,
   How Venus prais'd him for his faithful love,
   Within my heart a sudden joy did move.

95

Whilst in this glee this holy troop delight,
Along the stream afar fair Scylla floated,
And coyly vaunts her crest in open sight:
Whose beauties all the tides with wonder noted,
   'Fore whom Palemon and the Tritons danc'd
     Whilst she her limbs upon the tide advanc'd: 570

96

Whose swift approach made all the godheads wonder:
Glaucus gan smile to see his lovely foe,
Rage almost rent poor Thetis' heart asunder:
Was never happy troop confused so
   As were these deities and dainty dames,
     When they beheld the cause of Glaucus' blames.

97

Venus commends the carriage of her eye,
Nais upbraids the dimple in her chin,
Cupid desires to touch the wanton's thigh,
Clore she swears that every eye doth sin   580
   That likes a nymph that so contemneth love
     As no attempts her lawless heart may move.

98

Thetis, impatient of her wrong sustain'd,
With envious tears her roseate cheeks afflicted,
And thus of Scylla's former pride complain'd;
'Cupid' (said she) 'see her that hath inflicted
   The deadly wound that harm'd my lovely son,
     From whom the offspring of my care begun.

99

'Oh, if there dwell within my breast, my boy,
  Or grace, or pity, or remorse (said she),   590

Now bend thy bow, abate yon wanton's joy,
And let these nymphs thy rightful justice see.'
   The god, soon won, gan shoot, and cleft her heart
   With such a shaft as caus'd her endless smart.

100

The tender nymph, attainted unawares,
Fares like the Libyan lioness that flies
The hunter's lance that wounds her in his snares;
Now gins she love, and straight on Glaucus cries;
   Whilst on the shore the goddesses rejoice,
   And all the nymphs afflict the air with noise.   600

101

To shore she flits, and swift as Afric wind
Her footing glides upon the yielding grass,
And wounded by affect, recure to find
She suddenly with sighs approach'd the place
   Where Glaucus sat, and weary with her harms
   Gan clasp the sea-god in her amorous arms.

102

'Glaucus, my love' (quoth she), 'look on thy lover,
Smile, gentle Glaucus, on the nymph that likes thee.'
But stark as stone sat he, and list not prove her:
Ah, silly nymph, the selfsame god that strikes thee   610
   With fancy's dart, and hath thy freedom slain,
   Wounds Glaucus with the arrow of disdain.

103

Oh, kiss no more, kind nymph, he likes no kindness,
Love sleeps in him, to flame within thy breast;
Clear'd are his eyes, where thine are clad with blindness;
Freed be his thoughts, where thine must taste unrest:

Yet nill she leave, for never love will leave her,
But fruitless hopes and fatal haps deceive her.

104

Lord, how her lips do dwell upon his cheeks;
And how she looks for babies in his eyes: 620
And how she sighs, and swears she loves and leeks,
And how she vows, and he her vows envies:
   Trust me, the envious nymphs, in looking on,
   Were forc'd with tears for to assist her moan.

105

How oft with blushes would she plead for grace,
How oft with whisperings would she tempt his ears:
How oft with crystal did she wet his face:
How oft she wip'd them with her amber hairs:
   So oft, methought, I oft in heart desir'd
   To see the end whereto Disdain aspir'd.   630

106

Palemon with the Tritons roar for grief,
To see the mistress of their joys amated:
But Glaucus scorns the nymph, that waits relief:
And more she loves, the more the sea-god hated;
   Such change, such chance, such suits, such storms, believe
    me,
   Poor silly wretch, did heartily aggrieve me.

107

As when the fatal bird of augury,
Seeing a stormy dismal cloud arise
Within the south, foretells with piteous cry
The weeping tempest that on sudden hies: 640
   So she, poor soul, in view of his disdain
   Began to descant on her future pain.

108

And fixing eye upon the fatal ground,
Whole hosts of floods drew dew from out her eyes;
And when through inward grief the lass did sound,
The soften'd grass like billows did arise
    To woo her breasts, and wed her limbs so dainty,
    Whom wretched love had made so weak and fainty.

109

Aye's me, methinks I see here Thetis' fingers
Renting her locks as she were woe-begone her;   650
And now her lips upon his lipping, lingers:
Oh, ling'ring pain, where love nill list to moan her:
    Rue me that writes, for why her ruth deserves it:
    Hope needs must fail, where sorrow scarce preserves it.

110

To make long tale were tedious to the woeful,
Woeful that read what woeful she approved:
In brief her heart with deep despair was full,
As since she might not win her sweet beloved,
    With hideous cries like wind born back, she fled
    Unto the sea, and toward Sicilia sped.   660

111

Sweet Zephyrus upon that fatal hour
In hapless tide midst wat'ry world was walking;
Whose milder sighs, alas, had little power
To whisper peace amongst the godheads talking:
    Who all in one conclude for to pursue
    The hapless nymph, to see what would ensue.

112

Venus herself and her fair son gan hie
Within their ivory coach, drawn forth by doves,

After this hapless nymph, their power to try:
The nymphs, in hope to see their vowed loves,   670
   Gan cut the wat'ry bosom of the tide,
   As in Caÿster Phoebus' birds do glide.

113

Thetis in pomp upon a Triton's back
Did post her straight, attended by her train;
But Glaucus, free from love by lovers' wrack,
Seeing me pensive where I did remain,
   Upon a dolphin hors'd me as he was;
   Thus on the ocean hand in hand we pass.

114

Our talk midway was nought but still of wonder,
Of change, of chance, of sorrow, and her ending;   680
I wept for want: he said, 'Time brings men under,
And secret want can find but small befriending.'
   And as he said, in that before I tried it,
   I blam'd my wit forewarn'd, yet never spied it.

115

What need I talk the order of my way
(Discourse was steersman while my bark did sail,
My ship conceit, and fancy was my bay:
If these fail me, then faint, my muse, and fail)
   Hast brought us where the hapless nymph sojourn'd,
   Beating the weeping waves that for her mourn'd?   690

116

He that hath seen the northern blasts despoil
The pomp of prime, and with a whistling breath
Blast and disperse the beauties of the soil,
May think upon her pains more worse than death.

Alas, poor lass, the echoes in the rocks
Of Sicily her piteous plaining mocks.

117

Echo herself, when Scylla cried out, 'O love,'
With piteous voice from out her hollow den
Return'd these words, these words of sorrow, '*No love.*'
'No love (quoth she), then fie on traitorous men,   700
   Then fie on hope:' *Then fie on hope* (quoth Echo).
   To every word the nymph did answer so.

118

For every sigh, the rocks return a sigh;
For every tear, the fountains yield a drop;
Till we at last the place approached nigh,
And heard the nymph that fed on sorrow's sop
   Make woods, and waves, and rocks, and hills admire
   The wondrous force of her untam'd desire.

119

'Glaucus (quoth she) is fair:' whilst Echo sings
Glaucus is fair: 'But yet he hateth Scylla',   710
The wretch reports: and then her arms she wrings
Whilst Echo tells her this, *He hateth Scylla*,
   'No hope (quoth she): *No hope* (quoth Echo) then.
   Then *fie on men*: when she said, 'Fie on men.'

120

Fury and Rage, Wanhope, Despair, and Woe,
From Ditis' den by Ate sent, drew nigh:
Fury was red, with rage his eyes did glow,
Whole flakes of fire from forth his mouth did fly,
   His hands and arms ibath'd in blood of those
   Whom fortune, sin, or fate made country's foes.   720

121

Rage, wan and pale, upon a tiger sat,
Gnawing upon the bones of mangled men;
Naught can he view, but he repin'd thereat:
His locks were snakes bred forth in Stygian den;
    Next whom, Despair, that deep-disdained elf,
    Delightless liv'd, still stabbing of herself.

122

Woe, all in black, within her hands did bear
The fatal torches of a funeral;
Her cheeks were wet, dispersed was her hair,
Her voice was shrill (yet loathsome therewithal):   730
    Wanhope (poor soul) on broken anchor sits,
    Wringing his arms as robbed of his wits.

123

These five at once the sorrowing nymph assail,
And captive lead her bound into the rocks,
Where howling still she strives for to prevail;
With no avail yet strives she: for her locks
    Are chang'd with wonder into hideous sands,
    And hard as flint become her snow-white hands.

124

The waters howl with fatal tunes about her,
The air doth scout when as she turns within them,   740
The winds and waves with puffs and billows scout her;
Waves storm, air scouts, both wind and waves begin them
    To make the place this mournful nymph doth weep in
    A hapless haunt whereas no nymph may keep in.

125

The seaman, wand'ring by that famous isle,
Shuns all with fear, dispairing Scylla's bower;

Nymphs, sea-gods, sirens, when they list to smile
Forsake the haunt of Scylla in that stour:
  Ah, nymphs, thought I, if every coy one felt
  The like mishaps, their flinty hearts would melt.   750

126

Thetis rejoic'd to see her foe depress'd,
Glaucus was glad, since Scylla was enthrall'd;
The nymphs gan smile, to boast their Glaucus' rest:
Venus and Cupid, in their thrones install'd,
  At Thetis' beck to Neptune's bower repair,
  Whereas they feast amidst his palace fair.

127

Of pure immortal nectar is their drink,
And sweet ambrosia dainty do repast them,
The Tritons sing, Palemon smiles to think
Upon the chance, and all the nymphs do haste them 760
  To trick up mossy garlands where they woon,
  For lovely Venus and her conquering son.

128

From forth the fountains of his mother's store,
Glaucus let fly a dainty crystal bain
That wash'd the nymphs, with labour tir'd before:
Cupid he trips among this lovely train;
  Alonely I apart did write this story
  With many a sigh and heart full sad and sorry.

129

Glaucus, when all the goddesses took rest,
Mounted upon a dolphin full of glee: 770
Convey'd me friendly from this honour'd feast,
And by the way, such sonnets sang to me,

That all the dolphins neighbouring of his glide
Danc'd with delight, his reverend course beside.

130

At last he left me where at first he found me,
Willing me let the world and ladies know
Of Scylla's pride; and then by oath he bound me
To write no more of that whence shame doth grow:
   Or tie my pen to penny-knaves' delight,
   But live with fame and so for fame to write.   780

Envoy

Ladies, he left me, trust me I missay not,
But so he left me as he will'd me tell you,
That nymphs must yield, when faithful lovers stray not,
Lest through contempt almighty love compel you
   With Scylla in the rocks to make your biding,
   A cursed plague, for women's proud back-sliding.

CHRISTOPHER MARLOWE
(1598)

Hero and Leander

First Sestiad

On Hellespont, guilty of true love's blood,
In view, and opposite, two cities stood,
Sea borderers, disjoin'd by Neptune's might;
The one Abydos, the other Sestos hight.
At Sestos, Hero dwelt; Hero the fair,
Whom young Apollo courted for her hair,
And offer'd as a dower his burning throne,
Where she should sit for men to gaze upon.
The outside of her garments were of lawn,
The lining purple silk, with gilt stars drawn;   10
Her wide sleeves green, and border'd with a grove,
Where Venus in her naked glory strove
To please the careless and disdainful eyes
Of proud Adonis, that before her lies;
Her kirtle blue, whereon was many a stain,
Made with the blood of wretched lovers slain.
Upon her head she ware a myrtle wreath,
From whence her veil reach'd to the ground beneath.
Her veil was artificial flowers and leaves,
Whose workmanship both man and beast deceives.   20
Many would praise the sweet smell as she pass'd,
When 'twas the odour which her breath forth cast;
And there for honey bees have sought in vain,
And, beat from thence, have lighted there again.
About her neck hung chains of pebble-stone,
Which, lighten'd by her neck, like diamonds shone.

She ware no gloves, for neither sun nor wind
Would burn or parch her hands, but to her mind,
Or warm or cool them, for they took delight
To play upon those hands, they were so white,   30
Buskins of shells all silver'd used she,
And branch'd with blushing coral to the knee,
Where sparrows perch'd, of hollow pearl and gold,
Such as the world would wonder to behold:
Those with sweet water oft her handmaid fills,
Which, as she went, would chirrup through the hills.
Some say, for her the fairest Cupid pin'd,
And, looking in her face, was strooken blind.
But this is true, so like was one the other,
As he imagin'd Hero was his mother;   40
And oftentimes into her bosom flew,
About her naked neck his bare arms threw,
And laid his childish head upon her breast,
And with still panting rock'd, there took his rest.
So lovely fair was Hero, Venus' nun,
As Nature wept, thinking she was undone,
Because she took more from her than she left,
And of such wondrous beauty her bereft;
Therefore, in sign her treasure suffer'd wrack,
Since Hero's time hath half the world been black.   50
Amorous Leander, beautiful and young,
(Whose tragedy divine Musaeus sung)
Dwelt at Abydos; since him dwelt there none
For whom succeeding times make greater moan.
His dangling tresses that were never shorn,
Had they been cut and unto Colchos borne,
Would have allur'd the venturous youth of Greece
To hazard more than for the golden fleece.
Fair Cynthia wish'd his arms might be her sphere;
Grief makes her pale, because she moves not there.   60
His body was as straight as Circe's wand;
Jove might have sipp'd out nectar from his hand.
Even as delicious meat is to the taste,

So was his neck in touching, and surpass'd *feminine*
The white of Pelops' shoulder. I could tell ye
How smooth his breast was, and how white his belly,
And whose immortal fingers did imprint
That heavenly path, with many a curious dint,
That runs along his back; but my rude pen
Can hardly blazon forth the loves of men, 70
Much less of powerful gods; let it suffice
That my slack muse sings of Leander's eyes,
Those orient cheeks and lips, exceeding his
That leapt into the water for a kiss
Of his own shadow, and despising many,
Died ere he could enjoy the love of any.
Had wild Hippolytus Leander seen,
Enamour'd of his beauty had he been;
His presence made the rudest peasant melt,
That in the vast uplandish country dwelt; 80
The barbarous Thracian soldier, mov'd with nought,
Was mov'd with him, and for his favour sought.
Some swore he was a maid in man's attire,
For in his looks were all that men desire,
A pleasant smiling cheek, a speaking eye,
A brow for love to banquet royally;
And such as knew he was a man, would say,
'Leander, thou art made for amorous play;
Why art thou not in love, and lov'd of all?
Though thou be fair, yet be not thine own thrall.' 90
    The men of wealthy Sestos, every year,
For his sake whom their goddess held so dear,
Rose-cheek'd Adonis, kept a solemn feast.
Thither resorted many a wandering guest
To meet their loves; such as had none at all,
Came lovers home from this great festival.
For every street, like to a firmament,
Glister'd with breathing stars, who, where they went,
Frighted the melancholy earth, which deem'd
Eternal heaven to burn, for so it seem'd 100

As if another Phaeton had got
The guidance of the sun's rich chariot.
But, far above the loveliest, Hero shin'd,
And stole away th' enchanted gazer's mind;
For like sea-nymphs' inveigling harmony,
So was her beauty to the standers-by.
Nor that night-wand'ring pale and wat'ry star
(When yawning dragons draw her thirling car
From Latmus' mount up to the gloomy sky,
Where, crown'd with blazing light and majesty,   110
She proudly sits) more over-rules the flood
Than she the hearts of those that near her stood.
Even as, when gaudy nymphs pursue the chase,
Wretched Ixion's shaggy-footed race,
Incens'd with savage heat, gallop amain
From steep pine-bearing mountains to the plain;
So ran the people forth to gaze upon her,
And all that view'd her were enamour'd on her.
And as in fury of a dreadful flight,
Their fellows being slain or put to flight,   120
Poor soldiers stand with fear of death dead strooken,
So at her presence all, surpris'd and tooken,
Await the sentence of her scornful eyes;
He whom she favours lives, the other dies.
There might you see one sigh, another rage,
And some, their violent passions to assuage,
Compile sharp satires; but alas! too late,
For faithful love will never turn to hate.
And many, seeing great princes were denied,
Pin'd as they went, and thinking on her, died.   130
On this feast day, oh, cursed day and hour!
Went Hero thorough Sestos, from her tower
To Venus' temple, where unhappily,
As after chanc'd, they did each other spy.
So fair a church as this had Venus none;
The walls were of discolour'd jasper stone,
Wherein was Proteus carv'd, and o'erhead

A lively vine of green sea-agate spread,
Where by one hand light-headed Bacchus hung,
And with the other wine from grapes out-wrung.   140
Of crystal shining fair the pavement was;
The town of Sestos call'd it Venus' glass.
There might you see the gods in sundry shapes,
Committing heady riots, incest, rapes:
For know that underneath this radiant floor
Was Danae's statue in a brazen tower;
Jove slyly stealing from his sister's bed
To dally with Idalian Ganymede,
And for his love Europa bellowing loud,
And tumbling with the rainbow in a cloud;   150
Blood-quaffing Mars heaving the iron net
Which limping Vulcan and his Cyclops set;
Love kindling fire to burn such towns as Troy;
Silvanus weeping for the lovely boy
That now is turn'd into a cypress tree,
Under whose shade the wood-gods love to be.
And in the midst a silver altar stood;
There Hero sacrificing turtles' blood,
Vail'd to the ground, veiling her eyelids close,
And modestly they open'd as she rose: 160
Thence flew love's arrow with the golden head,
And thus Leander was enamoured.
Stone-still he stood, and evermore he gaz'd,
Till with the fire that from his countenance blaz'd
Relenting Hero's gentle heart was strook;
Such force and virtue hath an amorous look.

   It lies not in our power to love or hate,
For will in us is over-rul'd by Fate.   ] Fate
When two are stripp'd, long ere the course begin
We wish that one should lose, the other win;   170
And one especially do we affect
Of two gold ingots, like in each respect.
The reason no man knows; let it suffice,
What we behold is censur'd by our eyes.

Where both deliberate, the love is slight;
Who ever lov'd, that lov'd not at first sight?
 He kneel'd, but unto her devoutly pray'd;
Chaste Hero to herself thus softly said:
'Were I the saint he worships, I would hear him;'
And as she spake these words, came somewhat 180
 near him.
He started up; she blush'd as one asham'd;
Wherewith Leander much more was inflam'd.
He touch'd her hand; in touching it she trembl'd;
Love deeply grounded hardly is dissembl'd.
These lovers parled by the touch of hands;
True love is mute, and oft amazed stands.
Thus while dumb signs their yielding hearts entangl'd,
The air with sparks of living fire was spangl'd,
And Night, deep drench'd in misty Acheron,
Heav'd up her head, and half the world upon 190
Breath'd darkness forth (dark night is Cupid's day).
And now begins Leander to display
Love's holy fire with words, with sighs and tears,
Which like sweet music enter'd Hero's ears;
And yet at every word she turn'd aside,
And always cut him off as he replied.
At last, like to a bold sharp sophister,
With cheerful hope thus he accosted her:
 'Fair creature, let me speak without offence;
I would my rude words had the influence 200
To lead thy thoughts as thy fair looks do mine;
Then shouldst thou be his prisoner who is thine.
Be not unkind and fair; misshapen stuff
Are of behaviour boisterous and rough.
O! shun me not, but hear me ere you go;
God knows I cannot force love, as you do.
My words shall be as spotless as my youth,
Full of simplicity and naked truth.
This sacrifice, whose sweet perfume descending
From Venus' altar to your footsteps bending, 210

Doth testify that you exceed her far
To whom you offer, and whose nun you are.
Why should you worship her? her you surpass
As much as sparkling diamonds flaring glass.
A diamond set in lead his worth retains;
A heavenly nymph, belov'd of human swains,
Receives no blemish, but oft-times more grace;
Which makes me hope, although I am but base,
Base in respect of thee, divine and pure,
Dutiful service may thy love procure;   220
And I in duty will excel all other,
As thou in beauty dost exceed Love's mother.
Nor heaven, nor thou, were made to gaze upon;
As heaven preserves all things, so save thou one.
A stately-builded ship, well rigg'd and tall,
The ocean maketh more majestical:
Why vowest thou then to live in Sestos here,
Who on Love's seas more glorious would appear?
Like untun'd golden strings all women are,
Which, long time lie untouch'd, will harshly jar.   230
Vessels of brass, oft handl'd, brightly shine;
What difference betwixt the richest mine
And basest mould, but use? for both, not us'd,
Are of like worth. Then treasure is abus'd,
When misers keep it; being put to loan,
In time it will return us two for one.
Rich robes themselves and others do adorn;
Neither themselves nor others, if not worn.
Who builds a palace, and rams up the gate,
Shall see it ruinous and desolate.   240
Ah, simple Hero, learn thyself to cherish;
Lone women, like to empty houses, perish.
Less sins the poor rich man that starves himself
In heaping up a mass of drossy pelf,
Than such as you; his golden earth remains,
Which after his decease some other gains;
But this fair gem, sweet in the loss alone,

When you fleet hence, can be bequeath'd to none.
Or if it could, down from th' enamell'd sky
All heaven would come to claim this legacy,   250
And with intestine broils the world destroy,
And quite confound Nature's sweet harmony.
Well therefore by the gods decreed it is
We human creatures should enjoy that bliss.
One is no number; maids are nothing, then,
Without the sweet society of men.
Wilt thou live single still? One shalt thou be
Though never-singling Hymen couple thee.
Wild savages, that drink of running springs,
Think water far excels all earthly things,   260
But they that daily taste neat wine despise it.
Virginity, albeit some highly prize it,
Compar'd with marriage, had you tried them both,
Differs as much as wine and water doth.
Base bullion for the stamp's sake we allow;
Even so for men's impression do we you,
By which alone, our reverend fathers say,
Women receive perfection every way.
This idol which you term virginity
Is neither essence subject to the eye,   270
No, nor to any exterior sense;
Nor hath it any place of residence,
Nor is 't of earth or mould celestial,
Or capable of any form at all.
Of that which hath no being do not boast;
Things that are not at all are never lost.
Men foolishly do call it virtuous;
What virtue is it, that is born with us?
Much less can honour be ascrib'd thereto;
Honour is purchas'd by the deeds we do.   280
Believe me, Hero, honour is not won
Until some honourable deed be done.
Seek you for chastity, immortal fame,
And know that some have wrong'd Diana's name?

Whose name is it, if she be false or not,
So she be fair, but some vile tongues will blot?
But you are fair, ay me! so wondrous fair,
So young, so gentle, and so debonair,
As Greece will think, if thus you live alone,
Some one or other keeps you as his own,   290
Then, Hero, hate me not, nor from me fly,
To follow swiftly-blasting infamy.
Perhaps thy sacred priesthood makes thee loth;
Tell me, to whom madest thou that heedless oath?'
    'To Venus,' answer'd she, and as she spake,
Forth from those two tralucent cisterns brake
A stream of liquid pearl, which down her face
Make milk-white paths, whereon the gods might trace
To Jove's high court. He thus replied: 'The rites
In which Love's beauteous empress most delights   300
Are banquets, Doric music, midnight revel,
Plays, masques, and all that stern age counteth evil.
Thee as a holy idiot doth she scorn,
For thou, in vowing chastity, hast sworn
To rob her name and honour, and thereby
Commit'st a sin far worse than perjury,
Even sacrilege against her deity,
Through regular and formal purity.
To expiate which sin, kiss and shake hands;
Such sacrifice as this Venus demands.'   310
    Thereat she smil'd, and did deny him so
As, put thereby, yet might he hope for mo.
Which makes him quickly reinforce his speech,
And her in humble manner thus beseech:
'Though neither gods nor men may thee deserve,
Yet for her sake whom you have vow'd to serve,
Abandon fruitless cold virginity,
The gentle queen of love's sole enemy.
Then shall you most resemble Venus' nun,
When Venus' sweet rites are perform'd and done.   320
Flint-breasted Pallas joys in single life,

But Pallas and your mistress are at strife.
Love, Hero, then, and be not tyrannous,
But heal the heart that thou hast wounded thus;
Nor stain thy youthful years with avarice;
Fair fools delight to be accounted nice.
The richest corn dies, if it be not reap'd;
Beauty alone is lost, too warily kept.'
These arguments he us'd, and many more,
Wherewith she yielded, that was won before.   330
Hero's looks yielded, but her words made war;
Women are won when they begin to jar.
Thus having swallow'd Cupid's golden hook,
The more she striv'd, the deeper was she strook;
Yet, evilly feigning anger, strove she still,
And would be thought to grant against her will.
So having paus'd a while, at last she said:
'Who taught thee rhetoric to deceive a maid?
Ay me! such words as these should I abhor,
And yet I like them for the orator.'   340
    With that Leander stoop'd to have embrac'd her,
But from his spreading arms away she cast her,
And thus bespake him: 'Gentle youth, forbear
To touch the sacred garments which I wear.
Upon a rock, and underneath a hill,
Far from the town, where all is whist and still,
Save that the sea, playing on yellow sand,
Sends forth a rattling murmur to the land,
Whose sound allures the golden Morpheus
In silence of the night to visit us,   350
My turret stands; and there, God knows, I play
With Venus' swans and sparrows all the day.
A dwarfish beldame bears me company,
That hops about the chamber where I lie,
And spends the night, that might be better spent,
In vain discourse and apish merriment.
Come thither.' As she spake this, her tongue tripp'd.
For unawares 'Come thither' from her slipp'd;

And suddenly her former colour chang'd,
And here and there her eyes through anger rang'd.   360
And like a planet moving several ways
At one self instant, she, poor soul, assays,
Loving, not to love at all, and every part
Strove to resist the motions of her heart:
And hands so pure, so innocent, nay such
As might have made heaven stoop to have a touch,
Did she uphold to Venus, and again
Vow'd spotless chastity, but all in vain.
Cupid beats down her prayers with his wings;
Her vows above the empty air he flings;   370
All deep enrag'd, his sinewy bow he bent,
And shot a shaft that burning from him went;
Wherewith she strooken look'd so dolefully
As made Love sigh to see his tyranny.
And as she wept, her tears to pearl he turn'd,
And wound them on his arm, and for her mourn'd.
Then towards the palace of the Destinies,
Laden with languishment and grief, he flies,
And to those stern nymphs humbly made request,
Both might enjoy each other, and be blest.   380
But with a ghastly dreadful countenance,
Threatening a thousand deaths at every glance,
They answer'd Love, nor would vouchsafe so much
As one poor word, their hate to him was such.
Hearken awhile, and I will tell you why:
Heaven's winged herald, Jove-born Mercury,
The self-same day that he asleep had laid
Enchanted Argus, spied a country maid,
Whose careless hair, instead of pearl t' adorn it,
Glister'd with dew, as one that seem'd to scorn it: 390
Her breath as fragrant as the morning rose,
Her mind pure, and her tongue untaught to gloze;
Yet proud she was, for lofty pride that dwells
In tower'd courts is oft in shepherds' cells,
And too too well the fair vermilion knew,

And silver tincture of her cheeks, that drew
The love of every swain. On her this god
Enamour'd was, and with his snaky rod
Did charm her nimble feet, and made her stay,
The while upon a hillock down he lay,   400
And sweetly on his pipe began to play,
And with smooth speech her fancy to assay;
Till in his twining arms he lock'd her fast,
And then he woo'd with kisses, and at last,
As shepherds do, her on the ground he laid,
And tumbling in the grass, he often stray'd
Beyond the bounds of shame, in being bold
To eye those parts which no eye should behold;
And like an insolent commanding lover,
Boasting his parentage, would needs discover   410
The way to new Elysium: but she,
Whose only dower was her chastity,
Having striven in vain, was now about to cry,
And crave the help of shepherds that were nigh.
Herewith he stay'd his fury, and began
To give her leave to rise; away she ran;
After went Mercury, who us'd such cunning
As she, to hear his tale, left off her running.
Maids are not won by brutish force and might,
But speeches full of pleasure and delight;   420
And knowing Hermes courted her, was glad
That she such loveliness and beauty had
As could provoke his liking, yet was mute,
And neither would deny not grant his suit.
Still vow'd he love; she, wanting no excuse
To feed him with delays, as women use,
Or thirsting after immortality—
All women are ambitious naturally—
Impos'd upon her lover such a task
As he ought not perform, nor yet she ask.   430
A draught of flowing nectar she requested,
Wherewith the king of gods and men is feasted.

He, ready to accomplish what she will'd,
Stole some from Hebe (Hebe Jove's cup fill'd)
And gave it to his simple rustic love;
Which being known (as what is hid from Jove?)
He inly storm'd, and wax'd more furious
Than for the fire filch'd by Prometheus,
And thrusts him down from heaven: he wandering here,
In mournful terms, with sad and heavy cheer,   440
Complain'd to Cupid. Cupid, for his sake,
To be reveng'd on Jove did undertake;
And those on whom heaven, earth, and hell relies,
I mean the adamantine Destinies,
He wounds with love, and forc'd them equally
To dote upon deceitful Mercury.
They offer'd him the deadly fatal knife
That shears the slender threads of human life;
At his fair, feather'd feet the engines laid
Which th' earth from ugly Chaos' den upway'd.   450
These he regarded not, but did entreat
That Jove, usurper of his father's seat,
Might presently be banish'd into hell,
And aged Saturn in Olympus dwell.
They granted what he crav'd, and once again
Saturn and Ops began their golden reign.
Murder, rape, war, lust, and treachery
Were with Jove clos'd in Stygian empery.
But long this blessed time continu'd not;
As soon as he his wished purpose got,   460
He, reckless of his promise, did despise
The love of th' everlasting Destinies.
They seeing it, both Love and him abhorr'd,
And Jupiter unto his place restor'd.
And but that Learning, in despite of Fate,
Will mount aloft, and enter heaven gate,
And to the seat of Jove itself advance,
Hermes had slept in hell with Ignorance;
Yet as a punishment they added this,

That he and poverty should always kiss.   470
And to this day is every scholar poor;
Gross gold from them runs headlong to the boor.
Likewise, the angry sisters, thus deluded,
To venge themselves on Hermes have concluded
That Midas' brood shall sit in Honour's chair,
To which the Muses' sons are only heir;
And fruitful wits that in aspiring are
Shall, discontent, run into regions far;
And few great lords in virtuous deeds shall joy,
But be surpris'd with every garish toy;   480
And still enrich the lofty servile clown,
Who with encroaching guile keeps Learning down.
Then muse not Cupid's suit no better sped,
Seeing in their loves the Fates were injured.

Second Sestiad

By this, sad Hero, with love unacquainted,
Viewing Leander's face, fell down and fainted.
He kiss'd her and breath'd life into her lips,
Wherewith as one displeas'd away she trips.
Yet as she went, full often look'd behind,
And many poor excuses did she find
To linger by the way, and once she stay'd
And would have turn'd again, but was afraid,
In offering parley, to be counted light.
So on she goes, and in her idle flight,   10
Her painted fan of curled plumes let fall,
Thinking to train Leander therewithal.
He, being a novice, knew not what she meant,
But stay'd, and after her a letter sent,
Which joyful Hero answer'd in such sort
As he had hope to scale the beauteous fort
Wherein the liberal graces lock'd their wealth,
And therefore to her tower he got by stealth.
Wide open stood the door, he need not climb;

And she herself before the 'pointed time   20
Had spread the board, with roses strew'd the room,
And oft look'd out, and mus'd he did not come.
At last he came; O! who can tell the greeting
These greedy lovers had at their first meeting.
He ask'd, she gave, and nothing was denied;
Both to each other quickly were affied.
Look how their hands, so were their hearts united,
And what he did she willingly requited.
Sweet are the kisses, the embracements sweet,
When like desires and affections meet;   30
For from the earth to heaven is Cupid rais'd,
Where fancy is in equal balance peis'd.
Yet she this rashness suddenly repented,
And turn'd aside, and to herself lamented,
As if her name and honour had been wrong'd
By being possess'd of him for whom she long'd;
Ay, and she wish'd, albeit not from her heart,
That he would leave her turret and depart.
The mirthful god of amorous pleasure smil'd
To see how he this captive nymph beguil'd;   40
For hitherto he did but fan the fire,
And kept it down that it might mount the higher.
Now wax'd she jealous lest his love abated,
Fearing her own thoughts made her to be hated.
Therefore unto him hastily she goes,
And like light Salmacis, her body throws
Upon his bosom, where with yielding eyes
She offers up herself a sacrifice,
To slake his anger if he were displeas'd.
O! what god would not therewith be appeas'd?   50
Like Aesop's cock, this jewel he enjoy'd,
And as a brother with his sister toy'd,
Supposing nothing else was to be done,
Now he her favour and good will had won.
But know you not that creatures wanting sense
By nature have a mutual appetence,

And wanting organs to advance a step,
Mov'd by love's force, unto each other leap?
Much more in subjects having intellect
Some hidden influence breeds like effect.   60
Albeit Leander, rude in love and raw,
Long dallying with Hero, nothing saw
That might delight him more, yet he suspected
Some amorous rites or other were neglected.
Therefore unto his body hers he clung;
She, fearing on the rushes to be flung,
Striv'd with redoubl'd strength; the more she striv'd,
The more a gentle pleasing heat reviv'd,
Which taught him all that elder lovers know;
And now the same 'gan so to scorch and glow,   70
As in plain terms, yet cunningly, he crav'd it;
Love always makes those eloquent that have it.
She, with a kind of granting, put him by it,
And ever as he thought himself most nigh it,
Like to the tree of Tantalus she fled,
And, seeming lavish, sav'd her maidenhead.
Ne'er king more sought to keep his diadem,
Than Hero this inestimable gem.
Above our life we love a steadfast friend,
Yet when a token of great worth we send,   80
We often kiss it, often look thereon,
And stay the messenger that would be gone;
No marvel then though Hero would not yield
So soon to part from that she dearly held.
Jewels being lost are found again, this never;
'Tis lost but once, and once lost, lost for ever.
  Now had the Morn espi'd her lover's steeds,
Whereat she starts, puts on her purple weeds,
And, red for anger that he stay'd so long,
All headlong throws herself the clouds among.   90
And now Leander, fearing to be miss'd,
Embrac'd her suddenly, took leave, and kiss'd.
Long was he taking leave, and loth to go,

And kiss'd again, as lovers use to do.
Sad Hero wrung him by the hand and wept,
Saying, 'Let your vows and promises be kept.'
Then, standing at the door, she turn'd about,
As loth to see Leander going out.
And now the sun that through th' horizon peeps,
As pitying these lovers, downward creeps,   100
So that in silence of the cloudy night,
Though it was morning, did he take his flight.
But what the secret trusty night conceal'd,
Leander's amorous habit soon reveal'd;
With Cupid's myrtle was his bonnet crown'd,
About his arms the purple riband wound,
Wherewith she wreath'd her largely spreading hair;
Nor could the youth abstain, but he must wear
The sacred ring wherewith she was endow'd
When first religious chastity she vow'd;   110
Which made his love through Sestos to be known,
And thence unto Abydos sooner blown
Than he could sail; for incorporeal Fame,
Whose weight consists in nothing but her name,
Is swifter than the wind, whose tardy plumes
Are reeking water and dull earthly fumes.
Home when he came, he seem'd not to be there,
But like exil'd air thrust from his sphere,
Set in a foreign place; and straight from thence,
Alcides-like, by mighty violence   120
He would have chas'd away the swelling main,
That him from her unjustly did detain.
Like as the sun in a diameter
Fires and inflames objects removed far,
And heateth kindly, shining laterally,
So beauty sweetly quickens when 'tis nigh,
But being separated and remov'd,
Burns where it cherish'd, murders where it lov'd.
Therefore even as an index to a book,
So to his mind was young Leander's look.   130

O! none but gods have power their love to hide;
Affection by the countenance is descried.
The light of hidden fire itself discovers,
And love that is conceal'd betrays poor lovers.
His secret flame apparently was seen;
Leander's father knew where he had been,
And for the same mildly rebuk'd his son,
Thinking to quench the sparkles new begun.
But love, resisted once, grows passionate,
And nothing more than counsel lovers hate;   140
For as a hot proud horse highly disdains
To have his head controll'd, but breaks the reins,
Spits forth the ringled bit, and with his hooves
Checks the submissive ground, so he that loves,
The more he is restrain'd, the worse he fares.
What is it now but mad Leander dares?
'O Hero, Hero!' thus he cried full oft,
And then he got him to a rock aloft,
Where having spi'd her tower, long star'd he on 't,
And pray'd the narrow toiling Hellespont   150
To part in twain, that he might come and go;
But still the rising billows answer'd 'No.'
With that he stripp'd him to the ivory skin,
And crying, 'Love, I come,' leap'd lively in.
Whereat that sapphire-visag'd god grew proud,
And made his capering Triton sound aloud,
Imagining that Ganymede, displeas'd,
Had left the heavens; therefore on him he seiz'd.
Leander striv'd; the waves about him wound,
And pull'd him to the bottom, where the ground   160
Was strew'd with pearl, and in low coral groves
Sweet singing mermaids sported with their loves
On heaps of heavy gold, and took great pleasure
To spurn in careless sort the shipwreck treasure:
For here the stately azure palace stood
Where kingly Neptune and his train abode.
The lusty god embrac'd him, call'd him love,

And swore he never should return to Jove.
But when he knew it was not Ganymede,
For under water he was almost dead,   170
He heav'd him up, and looking on his face,
Beat down the bold waves with his triple mace,
Which mounted up, intending to have kiss'd him,
And fell in drops like tears, because they miss'd him.
Leander, being up, began to swim,
And looking back, saw Neptune follow him;
Whereat aghast, the poor soul 'gan to cry:
'O! let me visit Hero ere I die!'
The god put Helle's bracelet on his arm,
And swore the sea should never do him harm.   180
He clapp'd his plump cheeks, with his tresses play'd,
And smiling wantonly, his love bewray'd.
He watch'd his arms, and as they open'd wide,
At every stroke betwixt them would he slide,
And steal a kiss, and then run out and dance,
And as he turn'd, cast many a lustful glance,
And throw him gaudy toys to please his eye,
And dive into the water, and there pry
Upon his breast, his thighs, and every limb,
And up again, and close behind him swim,   190
And talk of love. Leander made reply:
'You are deceiv'd, I am no woman, I.'
Thereat smil'd Neptune, and then told a tale,
How that a shepherd, sitting in a vale,
Play'd with a boy so lovely fair and kind
As for his love both earth and heaven pin'd;
That of the cooling river durst not drink
Lest water-nymphs should pull him from the brink;
And when he sported in the fragrant lawns,
Goat-footed satyrs and up-staring fauns   200
Would steal him thence. Ere half this tale was done,
'Ay me!' Leander cried, 'th' enamour'd sun,
That now should shine on Thetis' glassy bower,
Descends upon my radiant Hero's tower.

O! that these tardy arms of mine were wings!'
And as he spake, upon the waves he springs.
Neptune was angry that he gave no ear,
And in his heart revenging malice bare
He flung at him his mace; but as it went
He call'd it in, for love made him repent.   210
The mace returning back his own hand hit,
As meaning to be veng'd for darting it.
When this fresh-bleeding wound Leander view'd,
His colour went and came, as if he rued
The grief which Neptune felt. In gentle breasts
Relenting thoughts, remorse, and pity rests;
And who have hard hearts and obdurate minds
But vicious, hare-brain'd and illiterate hinds?
The god, seeing him with pity to be mov'd,
Thereon concluded that he was belov'd.   220
(Love is too full of faith, too credulous,
With folly and false hope deluding us.)
Wherefore, Leander's fancy to surprise,
To the rich ocean for gifts he flies.
'Tis wisdom to give much; a gift prevails
When deep persuading oratory fails.
By this, Leander being near the land
Cast down his weary feet, and felt the sand.
Breathless albeit he were, he rested not
Till to the solitary tower he got,   230
And knock'd and call'd, at which celestial noise
The longing heart of Hero much more joys
Than nymphs or shepherds when the timbrel rings,
Or crooked dolphin when the sailor sings.
She stay'd not for her robes, but straight arose,
And drunk with gladness, to the door she goes;
Where seeing a naked man, she screech'd for fear,
(Such sights as this to tender maids are rare)
And ran into the dark herself to hide.
Rich jewels in the dark are soonest spied.   240
Unto her was he led, or rather drawn,

By those white limbs which sparkl'd through the lawn.
The nearer that he came, the more she fled,
And seeking refuge, slipp'd into her bed.
Whereon Leander sitting, thus began,
Through numbing cold all feeble, faint, and wan:
'If not for love, yet, love, for pity sake,
Me in thy bed and maiden bosom take;
At least vouchsafe these arms some little room,
Who, hoping to embrace thee, cheerly swum;   250
This head was beat with many a churlish billow,
And therefore let it rest upon thy pillow.'
Herewith affrighted, Hero shrunk away,
And in her lukewarm place Leander lay,
Whose lively heat, like fire from heaven fet,
Would animate gross clay, and higher set
The drooping thoughts of base-declining souls,
Than dreary Mars carousing nectar bowls.
His hands he cast upon her like a snare:
She, overcome with shame and sallow fear,   260
Like chaste Diana, when Actaeon spied her,
Being suddenly betray'd, div'd down to hide her;
And as her silver body downward went,
With both her hands she made the bed a tent,
And in her own mind thought herself secure,
O'ercast with dim and darksome coverture.
And now she lets him whisper in her ear,
Flatter, entreat, promise, protest, and swear;
Yet ever as he greedily assay'd
To touch those dainties, she the Harpy play'd,   270
And every limb did, as a soldier stout,
Defend the fort and keep the foeman out.
For though the rising ivory mount he scal'd,
Which is with azure-circling lines empal'd,
Much like a globe (a globe may I term this,
By which love sails to regions full of bliss),
Yet there with Sisyphus he toil'd in vain,
Till gentle parley did the truce obtain.

Wherein Leander on her quivering breast
Breathless spoke something, and sigh'd out the rest;   280
Which so prevail'd as he with small ado
Enclos'd her in his arms and kiss'd her too.
And every kiss to her was as a charm,
And to Leander as a fresh alarm,
So that the truce was broke, and she, alas!
Poor silly maiden, at his mercy was.
Love is not full of pity, as men say,
But deaf and cruel where he means to prey.
Even as a bird, which in our hands we wring,
Forth plungeth and oft flutters with her wing,   290
She trembling strove; this strife of hers, like that
Which made the world, another world begat
Of unknown joy. Treason was in her thought,
And cunningly to yield herself she sought.
Seeming not won, yet won she was at length;
In such wars women use but half their strength.
Leander now, like Theban Hercules
Enter'd the orchard of th' Hesperides,
Whose fruit none rightly can describe but he
That pulls or shakes it from the golden tree.   300
And now she wish'd this night were never done,
And sigh'd to think upon th' approaching sun;
For much it griev'd her that the bright daylight
Should know the pleasure of this blessed night,
And them like Mars and Erycina display,
Both in each other's arms chained as they lay.
Again she knew not how to frame her look,
Or speak to him who in a moment took
That which so long so charily she kept;
And fain by stealth away she would have crept,   310
And to some corner secretly have gone,
Leaving Leander in the bed alone.
But as her naked feet were whipping out,
He on the sudden cling'd her so about
That mermaid-like unto the floor she slid,

One half appear'd, the other half was hid.
Thus near the bed she blushing stood upright,
And from her countenance behold ye might
A kind of twilight break, which through the hair,
As from an orient cloud, glims here and there;   320
And round about the chamber this false morn
Brought forth the day before the day was born.
So Hero's ruddy cheek Hero betray'd,
And her all naked to his sight display'd;
Whence his admiring eyes more pleasure took
Than Dis on heaps of gold fixing his look.
By this, Apollo's golden harp began
To sound forth music to the ocean;
Which watchful Hesperus no sooner heard
But he the day's bright-bearing car prepar'd,   330
And ran before, as harbinger of light,
And with his flaring beams mock'd ugly Night
Till she, o'ercome with anguish, shame and rage,
Dang down to hell her loathsome carriage.

Desunt nonnulla

WILLIAM SHAKESPEARE

Venus and Adonis

(1593)

1

Even as the sun with purple-colour'd face
Had ta'en his last leave of the weeping morn,
Rose-cheek'd Adonis hied him to the chase,
Hunting he lov'd, but love he laugh'd to scorn:
   Sick-thoughted Venus makes amain unto him,
   And like a bold-fac'd suitor 'gins to woo him.

2

'Thrice fairer than myself, (thus she began)
The field's chief flower, sweet above compare,
Stain to all nymphs, more lovely than a man,
More white, and red, than doves or roses are: 10
   Nature that made thee with herself at strife
   Saith that the world hath ending with thy life.

3

'Vouchsafe, thou wonder, to alight thy steed,
And rein his proud head to the saddle bow;
If thou wilt deign this favour, for thy meed
A thousand honey secrets shalt thou know:
   Here come and sit, where never serpent hisses,
   And being set, I'll smother thee with kisses.

4

'And yet not cloy thy lips with loath'd satiety,
But rather famish them amid their plenty,   20
Making them red, and pale, with fresh variety:
Ten kisses short as one, one long as twenty:
    A summer's day will seem an hour but short,
    Being wasted in such time-beguiling sport.'

5

With this she seizeth on his sweating palm,
The precedent of pith and livelihood,
And, trembling in her passion, calls it balm,
Earth's sovereign salve to do a goddess good.
    Being so enrag'd, desire doth lend her force
    Courageously to pluck him from his horse. —   30

6

Over one arm the lusty courser's rein,
Under her other was the tender boy,
Who blush'd and pouted in a dull disdain,
With leaden appetite, unapt to toy;
    She red and hot as coals of glowing fire,
    He red for shame, but frosty in desire.

7

The studded bridle in a ragged bough
Nimbly she fastens, (oh, how quick is love!)
The steed is stalled up, and even now
To tie the rider she begins to prove: 40
    Backward she push'd him, as she would be thrust,
    And govern'd him in strength though not in lust.

8

So soon was she along as he was down,
Each leaning on their elbows and their hips:

Now doth she stroke his cheek, now doth he frown,
And 'gins to chide, but soon she stops his lips,
    And kissing speaks, with lustful language broken,
    'If thou wilt chide, thy lips shall never open.'

9

He burns with bashful shame, she with her tears
Doth quench the maiden burning of his cheeks;   50
Then with her windy sighs and golden hairs
To fan and blow them dry again she seeks.
    He saith, she is immodest, blames her miss;
    What follows more she murders with a kiss.

10

Even as an empty eagle, sharp by fast,
Tires with her beak on feathers, flesh, and bone,
Shaking her wings, devouring all in haste,
Till either gorge be stuff'd, or prey be gone:
    Even so she kiss'd his brow, his cheek, his chin,
    And where she ends, she doth anew begin.   60

11

Forc'd to content, but never to obey,
Panting he lies, and breatheth in her face.
She feedeth on the steam as on a prey,
And calls it heavenly moisture, air of grace,
    Wishing her cheeks were gardens full of flowers,
    So they were dew'd with such distilling showers.

12

Look how a bird lies tangled in a net,
So fasten'd in her arms Adonis lies;
Pure shame and aw'd resistance made him fret,
Which bred more beauty in his angry eyes: 70

Rain added to a river that is rank
Perforce will force it overflow the bank.

13

Still she entreats, and prettily entreats,
For to a pretty ear she tunes her tale.
Still is he sullen, still he lours and frets,
'Twixt crimson shame and anger ashy pale;
   Being red she loves him best, and being white,
   Her best is better'd with a more delight.

14

Look how he can, she cannot choose but love,
And by her fair immortal hand she swears   80
From his soft bosom never to remove,
Till he take truce with her contending tears,
   Which long have rain'd, making her cheeks all wet,
   And one sweet kiss shall pay this countless debt.

15

Upon this promise did he raise his chin,
Like a divedapper peering through a wave,
Who, being look'd on, ducks as quickly in:
So offers he to give what she did crave;
   But when her lips were ready for his pay,
   He winks, and turns his lips another way.   90

16

Never did passenger in summer's heat
More thirst for drink than she for this good turn.
Her help she sees, but help she cannot get;
She bathes in water, yet her fire must burn:
   'Oh pity,' gan she cry, 'flint-hearted boy,
   'Tis but a kiss I beg, why art thou coy?

17

'I have been woo'd, as I entreat thee now,
Even by the stern and direful god of war,
Whose sinewy neck in battle ne'er did bow,
Who conquers where he comes in every jar;　　　100
    Yet hath he been my captive and my slave,
    And begg'd for that which thou unask'd shalt have.

18

'Over my altars hath he hung his lance,
His batter'd shield, his uncontrolled crest,
And for my sake hath learn'd to sport and dance,
To toy, to wanton, dally, smile and jest,
    Scorning his churlish drum and ensign red,
    Making my arms his field, his tent my bed.

19

'Thus he that over-rul'd I over-sway'd,
Leading him prisoner in a red-rose chain;　　　110
Strong-temper'd steel his stronger strength obey'd.
Yet was he servile to my coy disdain.
    Oh, be not proud, nor brag not of thy might,
    For mast'ring her that foil'd the god of fight!

20

'Touch but my lips with those fair lips of thine—
Though mine be not so fair, yet are they red—
The kiss shall be thine own as well as mine.
What see'st thou in the ground? hold up thy head,
    Look in mine eyeballs, there thy beauty lies;
    Then why not lips on lips, since eyes in eyes?　　　120

21

'Art thou asham'd to kiss? then wink again,
And I will wink; so shall the day seem night.

Love keeps his revels where there are but twain:
Be bold to play, our sport is not in sight.
    These blue-vein'd violets whereon we lean
    Never can blab, nor know not what we mean.

22

'The tender spring upon thy tempting lip
Shews thee unripe; yet mayst thou well be tasted;
Make use of time, let not advantage slip;
Beauty within itself should not be wasted;   130
    Fair flowers that are not gather'd in their prime
    Rot and consume themselves in little time.

carpe diem

23

'Were I hard-favour'd, foul, or wrinkled-old,
Ill-nurtur'd, crooked, churlish, harsh in voice,
O'erworn, despised, rheumatic and cold,
Thick-sighted, barren, lean, and lacking juice,
    Then mightst thou pause, for then I were not for thee;
    But having no defects, why dost abhor me?

24

'Thou canst not see one wrinkle in my brow;
Mine eyes are grey, and bright, and quick in turning: 140
My beauty as the spring doth yearly grow,
My flesh is soft and plump, my marrow burning,
    My smooth moist hand, were it with thy hand felt,
    Would in thy palm dissolve, or seem to melt.

25

'Bid me discourse, I will enchant thine ear,
Or like a fairy trip upon the green,
Or like a nymph, with long dishevell'd hair,
Dance on the sands, and yet no footing seen.

Love is a spirit all compact of fire,
Not gross to sink, but light, and will aspire.   150

26

'Witness this primrose bank whereon I lie;
These forceless flowers like sturdy trees support me:
Two strengthless doves will draw me through the sky,
From morn till night, even where I list to sport me.
　　Is love so light, sweet boy, and may it be
　　That thou should think it heavy unto thee?

27

'Is thine own heart to thine own face affected?
Can thy right hand seize love upon thy left?
Then woo thyself, be of thyself rejected:
Steal thine own freedom, and complain on theft.   160
　　Narcissus so himself himself forsook,
　　And died to kiss his shadow in the brook.

28

'Torches are made to light, jewels to wear,
Dainties to taste, fresh beauty for the use,
Herbs for their smell, and sappy plants to bear.
Things growing to themselves are growth's abuse,
　　Seeds spring from seeds, and beauty breedeth beauty;
　　Thou wast begot; to get it is thy duty.

29

'Upon the earth's increase why shouldst thou feed,
Unless the earth with thy increase be fed?   170
By law of Nature thou art bound to breed,
That thine may live when thou thyself art dead:
　　And so in spite of death thou dost survive,
　　In that thy likeness still is left alive.'

30

By this, the love-sick queen began to sweat,
For where they lay the shadow had forsook them,
And Titan, tired in the midday heat,
With burning eye did hotly over-look them,
　　Wishing Adonis had his team to guide,
　　So he were like him, and by Venus' side.　　　　180

31

And now Adonis, with a lazy sprite,
And with a heavy, dark disliking eye,
His louring brows o'erwhelming his fair sight,
Like misty vapours when they blot the sky,
　　Souring his cheeks, cries, 'Fie, no more of love!
　　The sun doth burn my face; I must remove.'

32

'Ay, me, (quoth Venus) young, and so unkind!
What bare excuses mak'st thou to be gone!
I'll sigh celestial breath, whose gentle wind
Shall cool the heat of this descending sun:　　　　190
　　I'll make a shadow for thee of my hairs;
　　If they burn too, I'll quench them with my tears.

33

'The sun that shines from heaven shines but warm,
And lo, I lie between that sun and thee:
The heat I have from thence doth little harm;
Thine eye darts forth the fire that burneth me,
　　And were I not immortal, life were done
　　Between this heavenly and earthly sun.

34

'Art thou obdurate, flinty, hard as steel?
Nay, more than flint, for stone at rain relenteth:　　200

Art thou a woman's son and canst not feel
What 'tis to love, how want of love tormenteth?
  O, had thy mother borne so hard a mind,
  She had not brought forth thee, but died unkind.

35

'What am I that thou shouldst contemn me this?
Or what great danger dwells upon my suit?
What were thy lips the worse for one poor kiss?
Speak, fair, but speak fair words, or else be mute:
  Give me one kiss, I'll give it thee again,
  And one for int'rest, if thou wilt have twain.   210

36

'Fie, lifeless picture, cold and senseless stone,
Well-painted idol, image dull and dead,
Statue contenting but the eye alone,
Thing like a man, but of no woman bred!
  Thou art no man, though of a man's complexion,
  For men will kiss even by their own direction.'

37

This said, impatience chokes her pleading tongue,
And swelling passion doth provoke a pause;
Red cheeks and fiery eyes blaze forth her wrong:
Being judge in love, she cannot right her cause.   220
  And now she weeps, and now she fain would speak,
  And now her sobs do her intendments break.

38

Sometimes she shakes her head, and then his hand,
Now gazeth she on him, now on the ground;
Sometime her arms enfold him like a band;
She would, he will not in her arms be bound:

And when from thence he struggles to be gone,
She locks her lily fingers one in one.

39

'Fondling,' she saith, 'since I have hemm'd thee here
Within the circuit of this ivory pale,   230
I'll be a park, and thou shalt be my deer:
Feed where thou wilt, on mountain or in dale;
   Graze on my lips, and if those hills be dry,
   Stray lower, where the pleasant fountains lie.

40

'Within this limit is relief enough,
Sweet bottom-grass, and high delightful plain,
Round rising hillocks, brakes obscure and rough,
To shelter thee from tempest and from rain:
   Then be my deer, since I am such a park;
   No dog shall rouse thee, though a thousand bark.' 240

41

At this Adonis smiles as in disdain,
That in each cheek appears a pretty dimple;
Love made those hollows, if himself were slain,
He might be buried in a tomb so simple;
   Foreknowing well, if there he came to lie,
   Why, there Love liv'd, and there he could not die.

42

These lovely caves, these round enchanting pits,
Open'd their mouths to swallow Venus' liking:
Being mad before, how doth she now for wits?
Struck dead at first, what needs a second striking?   250
   Poor Queen of Love, in thine own law forlorn,
   To love a cheek that smiles at thee in scorn!

I

43

Now which way shall she turn? what shall she say?
Her words are done, her woes the more increasing;
The time is spent, her object will away,
And from her twining arms doth urge releasing:
   'Pity,' she cries, 'some favour, some remorse!'
   Away he springs, and hasteth to his horse.

44

But lo, from forth a copse that neighbours by,
A breeding jennet, lusty, young and proud,   260
Adonis' trampling courser doth espy
And forth she rushes, snorts, and neighs aloud.
   The strong-neck'd steed, being tied unto a tree,
   Breaketh his rein and to her straight goes he.

45

Imperiously he leaps, he neighs, he bounds,
And now his woven girths he breaks asunder;
The bearing earth with his hard hoof he wounds,
Whose hollow womb resounds like heaven's thunder,
   The iron bit he crusheth 'tween his teeth,
   Controlling what he was controlled with.   270

46

His ears up-prick'd; his braided hanging mane
Upon his compass'd crest now stand on end;
His nostrils drink the air, and forth again,
As from a furnace, vapours doth he send:
   His eye, which scornfully glisters like fire,
   Shows his hot courage and his high desire.

47

Sometime he trots, as if he told the steps,
With gentle majesty and modest pride,

Anon he rears upright, curvets, and leaps,
As who should say, 'Lo, thus my strength is tried.   280
   And this I do to captivate the eye
   Of the fair breeder that is standing by.'

48

What recketh he his rider's angry stir,
His flattering 'holla', or his 'stand, I say'?
What cares he now for curb or pricking spur,
For rich caparisons or trappings gay?
   He sees his love, and nothing else he sees,
   For nothing else with his proud sight agrees.

49

Look when a painter would surpass the life.
In limning out a well-proportion'd steed,   290
His art with Nature's workmanship at strife,
As if the dead the living should exceed:
   So did this horse excel a common one
   In shape, in courage, colour, pace and bone.

50

Round-hoof'd, short-jointed, fetlocks shag and long,
Broad breast, full eye, small head, and nostril wide,
High crest, short ears, straight legs and passing strong,
Thin mane, thick tail, broad buttock, tender hide:
   Look what a horse should have he did not lack,
   Save a proud rider on so proud a back.   300

51

Sometimes he scuds far off, and there he stares;
Anon he starts at stirring of a feather:
To bid the wind a base he now prepares,
And whe'r he run, or fly, they know not whether:

For through his mane and tail the high wind sings,
Fanning the hairs, who wave like feather'd wings.

52

He looks upon his love, and neighs unto her;
She answers him as if she knew his mind;
Being proud, as females are, to see him woo her,
She puts on outward strangeness, seems unkind: 310
  Spurns at his love, and scorns the heat he feels,
  Beating his kind embracements with her heels.

53

Then like a melancholy malcontent,
He vails his tail, that like a falling plume
Cool shadow to his melting buttock lent;
He stamps, and bites the poor flies in his fume:
  His love, perceiving how he was enrag'd,
  Grew kinder, and his fury was assuag'd.

54

His testy master goeth about to take him,
When, lo, the unback'd breeder, full of fear,   320
Jealous of catching, swiftly doth forsake him,
With her the horse, and left Adonis there:
  As they were mad unto the wood they hie them,
  Outstripping crows that strive to overfly them.

55

All swoln with chafing, down Adonis sits,
Banning his boist'rous and unruly beast;
And now the happy season once more fits
That lovesick love by pleading may be blest:
  For lovers say the heart hath treble wrong
  When it is barr'd the aidance of the tongue.   330

56

An oven that is stopp'd, or river stay'd,
Burneth more hotly, swelleth with more rage:
So of concealed sorrow may be said,
Free vent of words love's fire doth assuage;
    But when the heart's attorney once is mute,
    The client breaks, as desperate in his suit.

57

He sees her coming, and begins to glow,
Even as a dying coal revives with wind,
And with his bonnet hides his angry brow,
Looks on the dull earth with disturbed mind: 340
    Taking no notice that she is so nigh,
    For all askance he holds her in his eye.

58

O, what a sight it was, wistly to view
How she came stealing to the wayward boy;
To note the fighting conflict of her hue,
How white and red each other did destroy:
    But now her cheek was pale, and by and by
    It flash'd forth fire, as lightning from the sky.

59

Now was she just before him as he sat,
And like a lowly lover down she kneels;   350
With one fair hand she heaveth up his hat,
Her other tender hand his fair cheek feels:
    His tenderer cheek receives her soft hand's print
    As apt as new-fall'n snow takes any dint.

60

O, what a war of looks was then between them,
Her eyes petitioners to his eyes suing!

His eyes saw her eyes as they had not seen them,
Her eyes woo'd still, his eyes disdain'd the wooing:
   And all this dumb play had his acts made plain
   With tears which Chorus-like her eyes did rain.   360

61

Full gently now she takes him by the hand,
A lily prison'd in a gaol of snow,
Or ivory in an alabaster band;
So white a friend engirts so white a foe:
   This beauteous combat, wilful and unwilling,
   Show'd like two silver doves that sit a-billing.

62

Once more the engine of her thoughts began:
'O fairest mover on this mortal round,
Would thou wert as I am, and I a man,
My heart all whole as thine, thy heart my wound;   370
   For one sweet look thy help I would assure thee,
   Though nothing but my body's bane would cure thee.'

63

'Give me my hand (saith he), why dost thou feel it?'
'Give me my heart (saith she), and thou shalt have it.
O, give it me lest thy hard heart do steel it,
And being steel'd, soft sighs can never grave it.
   Then love's deep groans I never shall regard,
   Because Adonis' heart hath made mine hard.'

64

'For shame,' he cries, 'let go, and let me go;
My day's delight is past, my horse is gone,   380
And 'tis your fault I am bereft him so.
I pray you hence, and leave me here alone,

For all my mind, my thought, my busy care,
Is how to get my palfrey from the mare.'

65

Thus she replies: 'Thy palfrey, as he should,
Welcomes the warm approach of sweet desire.
Affection is a coal that must be cool'd;
Else, suffer'd, it will set the heart on fire;
   The sea hath bounds, but deep desire hath none,
   Therefore no marvel though thy horse be gone.   390

66

'How like a jade he stood tied to the tree,
Servilely master'd with a leathern rein!
But when he saw his love, his youth's fair fee,
He held such petty bondage in disdain:
   Throwing the base thong from his bending crest,
   Enfranchising his mouth, his back, his breast.

67

'Who sees his true-love in her naked bed,
Teaching the sheets a whiter hue than white,
But when his glutton eye so full hath fed,
His other agents aim at like delight?   400
   Who is so faint that dares not be so bold
   To touch the fire, the weather being cold?

68

'Let me excuse thy courser, gentle boy,
And learn of him, I heartily beseech thee,
To take advantage on presented joy;
Though I were dumb, yet his proceedings teach thee:
   O, learn to love, the lesson is but plain,
   And once made perfect, never lost again.'

69

'I know not love (quoth he) nor will not know it,
Unless it be a boar, and then I chase it.   410
'Tis much to borrow, and I will not owe it;
My love to love is love but to disgrace it,
    For I have heard it is a life in death,
    That laughs and weeps, and all but with a breath.

70

'Who wears a garment shapeless and unfinish'd?
Who plucks the bud before one leaf put forth?
If springing things be any jot diminish'd,
They wither in their prime, prove nothing worth;
    The colt that's back'd and burden'd being young
    Loseth his pride, and never waxeth strong.   420

71

'You hurt my hand with wringing; let us part,
And leave this idle theme, this bootless chat;
Remove your siege from my unyielding heart;
To love's alarms it will not ope the gate,
    Dismiss your vows, your feigned tears, your flattery,
    For where a heart is hard they make no battery.'

72

'What, canst thou talk (quoth she), hast thou a tongue?
O, would thou hadst not, or I had no hearing!
Thy mermaid's voice hath done me double wrong;
I had my load before, now press'd with bearing;   430
    Melodious discord, heavenly tune harsh sounding,
    Ear's deep-sweet music, and heart's deep-sore wounding.

73

'Had I no eyes but ears, my ears would love
That inward beauty and invisible;

Or were I deaf, thy outward parts would move
Each part in me that were but sensible;
  Though neither eyes nor ears, to hear nor see,
  Yet should I be in love by touching thee.

74

'Say that the sense of feeling were bereft me,
And that I could not see, nor hear, nor touch,   440
And nothing but the very smell were left me,
Yet would my love to thee be still as much;
  For from the stillitory of thy face excelling
  Comes breath perfum'd, that breedeth love by smelling.

75

'But O, what banquet wert thou to the taste,
Being nurse and feeder of the other four!
Would they not wish the feast might ever last,
And bid suspicion double-lock the door;
  Lest jealousy, that sour unwelcome guest,
  Should by his stealing in disturb the feast?'   450

76

Once more the ruby-colour'd portal open'd,
Which to his speech did honey passage yield,
Like a red morn that ever yet betoken'd
Wrack to the seaman, tempest to the field,
  Sorrow to shepherds, woe unto the birds,
  Gusts and foul flaws to herdmen and to herds.

77

This ill presage advisedly she marketh.
Even as the wind is hush'd before it raineth,
Or as the wolf doth grin before he barketh,
Or as the berry breaks before it staineth,   460

Or like the deadly bullet of a gun,
His meaning struck her ere his words begun.

78

And at his look she flatly falleth down,
For looks kill love, and love by looks reviveth;
A smile recures the wounding of a frown,
But blessed bankrupt that by loss so thriveth!
   The silly boy, believing she is dead,
   Claps her pale cheek, till clapping makes it red.

79

And all amaz'd brake off his late intent,
For sharply he did think to reprehend her,   470
Which cunning love did wittily prevent;
Fair fall the wit that can so well defend her:
   For on the grass she lies as she were slain,
   Till his breath breatheth life in her again.

80

He wrings her nose, he strikes her on the cheeks,
He bends her fingers, holds her pulses hard,
He chafes her lips, a thousand ways he seeks
To mend the hurt that his unkindness marr'd;
   He kisses her, and she, by her good will,
   Will never rise, so he will kiss her still.   480

81

The night of sorrow now is turn'd to day.
Her two blue windows faintly she upheaveth,
Like the fair sun when in his fresh array
He cheers the morn, and all the earth relieveth:
   And as the bright sun glorifies the sky,
   So is her face illumin'd with her eye;

82

Whose beams upon his hairless face are fix'd,
As if from thence they borrow'd all their shine;
Were never four such lamps together mix'd,
Had not his clouded with his brow's repine.   490
    But hers, which through the crystal tears gave light,
    Shone like the moon in water seen by night.

83

'O, where am I (quoth she), in earth or heaven,
Or in the ocean drench'd, or in the fire?
What hour is this, or morn or weary even?
Do I delight to die or life desire?
    But now I liv'd, and life was death's annoy.
    But now I died, and death was lively joy.

84

'O, thou didst kill me; kill me once again.
Thy eyes' shrewd tutor, that hard heart of thine,   500
Hath taught them scornful tricks, and such disdain
That they have murd'red this poor heart of mine;
    And these mine eyes, true leaders to their queen,
    But for thy piteous lips no more had seen.

85

'Long may they kiss each other for this cure!
Oh, never let their crimson liveries wear,
And as they last, their verdure still endure.
To drive infection from the dangerous year!
    That the star-gazers, having writ on death,
    May say, the plague is banish'd by thy breath.   510

86

'Pure lips, sweet seals in my soft lips imprinted,
What bargains may I make still to be sealing?

To sell myself I can be well contented,
So thou wilt buy, and pay, and use good dealing;
    Which purchase if thou make, for fear of slips,
    Set thy seal manual on my wax-red lips.

87

'A thousand kisses buys my heart from me,
And pay them at thy leisure, one by one.
What is ten hundred touches unto thee?
Are they not quickly told, and quickly gone?   520
    Say for non-payment that the debt should double,
    Is twenty hundred kisses such a trouble?'

88

'Fair queen (quoth he), if any love you owe me,
Measure my strangeness with my unripe years;
Before I know myself, seek not to know me;
No fisher but the ungrown fry forbears;
    The mellow plum doth fall, the green sticks fast,
    Or being early pluck'd is sour to taste.

89

'Look, the world's comforter with weary gait
His day's hot task hath ended in the west;   530
The owl (night's herald) shrieks; 'tis very late,
The sheep are gone to fold, birds to their nest,
    And coal-black clouds, that shadow heaven's light,
    Do summon us to part, and bid good night.

90

'Now let me say good night, and so say you;
If you will say so, you shall have a kiss.'
'Good night' (quoth she), and ere he says adieu,
The honey fee of parting tender'd is;

Her arms do lend his neck a sweet embrace,
Incorporate then they seem, face grows to face.   540

91

Till breathless he disjoin'd, and backward drew
The heavenly moisture, that sweet coral mouth,
Whose precious taste her thirsty lips well knew,
Whereon they surfeit, yet complain on drouth.
  He with her plenty press'd, she faint with dearth,
  Their lips together glued, fall to the earth.

92

Now quick desire hath caught the yielding prey,
And glutton-like she feeds, yet never filleth;
Her lips are conquerors, his lips obey,
Paying what ransom the insulter willeth: 550
  Whose vulture thought doth pitch the price so high,
  That she will draw his lips' rich treasure dry.

93

And having felt the sweetness of the spoil,
With blindfold fury she begins to forage;
Her face doth reek and smoke, her blood doth boil,
And careless lust stirs up a desperate courage,
  Planting oblivion, beating reason back,
  Forgetting shame's pure blush and honour's wrack.

94

Hot, faint and weary with her hard embracing,
Like a wild bird being tam'd with too much handling,   560
Or as the fleet-foot roe that's tir'd with chasing,
Or like the froward infant still'd with dandling,
  He now obeys, and now no more resisteth,
  While she takes all she can, not all she listeth.

95

What wax so frozen but dissolves with temp'ring,
And yields at last to every light impression?
Things out of hope are compass'd oft with vent'ring,
Chiefly in love, whose leave exceeds commission:
  Affection faints not like a pale-fac'd coward,
  But then woos best when most his choice is froward. 570

96

When he did frown, oh, had she then gave over,
Such nectar from his lips she had not suck'd.
Foul words and frowns must not repel a lover;
What though the rose have prickles, yet 'tis pluck'd?
  Were beauty under twenty locks kept fast,
  Yet love breaks through, and picks them all at last.

97

For pity now she can no more detain him;
The poor fool prays her that he may depart.
She is resolv'd no longer to restrain him;
Bids him farewell, and look well to her heart,   580
  The which by Cupid's bow she doth protest
  He carries thence incaged in his breast.

98

'Sweet boy,' she says, 'this night I'll waste in sorrow,
For my sick heart commands mine eyes to watch.
Tell me, Love's master, shall we meet tomorrow?
Say, shall we? shall we? wilt thou make the match?'
  He tells her no; tomorrow he intends
  To hunt the boar with certain of his friends.

99

'The boar' (quoth she): whereat a sudden pale,
Like lawn being spread upon the blushing rose,   590

Usurps her cheek; she trembles at his tale,
And on his neck her yoking arms she throws.
  She sinketh down, still hanging by his neck,
  He on her belly falls, she on her back.

100

Now is she in the very lists of love,
Her champion mounted for the hot encounter,
All is imaginary she doth prove;
He will not manage her, although he mount her;
  That worse than Tantalus' is her annoy,
  To clip Elysium and to lack her joy.   600

101

Even as poor birds deceiv'd with painted grapes
Do surfeit by the eye, and pine the maw:
Even so she languisheth in her mishaps
As those poor birds that helpless berries saw;
  The warm effects which she in him finds missing
  She seeks to kindle with continual kissing.

102

But all in vain, good queen, it will not be,
She hath assay'd as much as may be prov'd;
Her pleading hath deserv'd a greater fee;
She's Love; she loves, and yet she is not lov'd: 610
  'Fie, fie,' he says, 'you crush me, let me go;
  You have no reason to withhold me so.'

103

'Thou hadst been gone (quoth she), sweet boy, ere this,
But that thou told'st me thou wouldst hunt the boar.
O, be advis'd, thou know'st not what it is
With javelin's point a churlish swine to gore,

Whose tushes never sheath'd he whetteth still,
Like to a mortal butcher bent to kill.

104

'On his bow-back he hath a battle set
Of bristly pikes that ever threat his foes;   620
His eyes like glow-worms shine when he doth fret;
His snout digs sepulchres where'er he goes;
    Being mov'd he strikes what'er is in his way,
    And whom he strikes his crooked tushes slay.

105

'His brawny sides, with hairy bristles arm'd,
Are better proof than thy spear's point can enter;
His short thick neck cannot be easily harm'd;
Being ireful, on the lion he will venter;
    The thorny brambles and embracing bushes,
    As fearful of him, part, through whom he rushes.   630

106

'Alas, he nought esteems that face of thine,
To which Love's eyes pays tributary gazes;
Nor thy soft hands, sweet lips and crystal eyne,
Whose full perfection all the world amazes;
    But having thee at vantage (wondrous dread!)
    Would root these beauties as he roots the mead.

107

'O, let him keep his loathsome cabin still;
Beauty hath nought to do with such foul fiends;
Come not within his danger by thy will;
They that thrive well take counsel of their friends: 640
    When thou didst name the boar, not to dissemble,
    I fear'd thy fortune, and my joints did tremble.

108

'Didst thou not mark my face, was it not white?
Saw'st thou not signs of fear lurk in mine eye?
Grew I not faint? and fell I not downright?
Within my bosom, whereon thou dost lie,
  My boding heart pants, beats and takes no rest,
  But like an earthquake shakes thee on my breast.

109

'For where Love reigns, disturbing Jealousy
Doth call himself Affection's sentinel;   650
Gives false alarms, suggesteth mutiny,
And in a peaceful hour doth cry, "Kill, kill!";
  Distemp'ring gentle Love in his desire,
  As air and water do abate the fire.

110

'This sour informer, this bate-breeding spy,
This canker that eats up Love's tender spring,
This carry-tale, dissentious Jealousy,
That sometime true news, sometime false doth bring,
  Knocks at my heart, and whispers in mine ear
  That if I love thee, I thy death should fear;   660

111

'And more than so, presenteth to mine eye
The picture of an angry chafing boar,
Under whose sharp fangs on his back doth lie
An image like thyself, all stain'd with gore;
  Whose blood upon the fresh flowers being shed
  Doth make them droop with grief and hang the head.

112

'What should I do, seeing thee so indeed,
That tremble at th' imagination?

The thought of it doth make my faint heart bleed,
And fear doth teach it divination; 670
  I prophesy thy death, my living sorrow,
  If thou encounter with the boar tomorrow.

113

'But if thou needs wilt hunt, be rul'd by me;
Uncouple at the timorous flying hare,
Or at the fox which lives by subtlety,
Or at the roe which no encounter dare:
  Pursue these fearful creatures o'er the downs,
  And on thy well-breath'd horse keep with thy hounds.

114

'And when thou hast on foot the purblind hare,
Mark the poor wretch, to overshoot his troubles, 680
How he outruns the wind, and with what care
He cranks and crosses with a thousand doubles;
  The many musits through the which he goes
  Are like a labyrinth to amaze his foes.

115

'Sometime he runs among a flock of sheep,
To make the cunning hounds mistake their smell,
And sometime where earth-delving conies keep,
To stop the loud pursuers in their yell:
  And sometime sorteth with a herd of deer;
  Danger deviseth shifts, wit waits on fear. 690

116

'For there his smell with others being mingl'd,
The hot scent-snuffing hounds are driven to doubt,
Ceasing their clamorous cry till they have singl'd
With much ado the cold fault cleanly out;

Then do they spend their mouths; Echo replies,
As if another chase were in the skies.

117

'By this poor Wat, far off upon a hill,
Stands on his hinder-legs with list'ning ear,
To hearken if his foes pursue him still;
Anon their loud alarums he doth hear, 700
    And now his grief may be compared well
    To one sore sick that hears the passing-bell.

118

'Then shalt thou see the dew-bedabbled wretch
Turn and return, indenting with the way;
Each envious brier his weary legs do scratch,
Each shadow makes him stop, each murmur stay;
    For misery is trodden on by many,
    And being low, never reliev'd by any.

119

'Lie quietly, and hear a little more;
Nay, do not struggle, for thou shalt not rise. 710
To make thee hate the hunting of the boar,
Unlike myself thou hear'st me moralize,
    Applying this to that, and so to so;
    For love can comment upon every woe.

120

'Where did I leave?' 'No matter where (quoth he);
Leave me, and then the story aptly ends,
The night is spent.' 'Why, what of that?' (quoth she).
'I am (quoth he) expected of my friends;
    And now 'tis dark, and going I shall fall.'
    'In night (quoth she) desire sees best of all. 720

121

'But if thou fall, O, then imagine this,
The earth, in love with thee, thy footing trips,
And all is but to rob thee of a kiss.
Rich preys make true men thieves: so do thy lips
    Make modest Dian cloudy and forlorn,
    Lest she should steal a kiss and die forsworn.

122

'Now of this dark night I perceive the reason;
Cynthia for shame obscures her silver shine,
Till forging Nature be condemn'd of treason
For stealing moulds from heaven that were divine;   730
    Wherein she fram'd thee, in high heaven's despite,
    To shame the sun by day, and her by night.

123

'And therefore hath she brib'd the Destinies
To cross the curious workmanship of Nature,
To mingle beauty with infirmities,
And pure perfection with impure defeature,
    Making it subject to the tyranny
    Of mad mischances and much misery;

124

'As burning fevers, agues pale and faint,
Life-poisoning pestilence and frenzies wood,   740
The marrow-eating sickness whose attaint
Disorder breeds by heating of the blood,
    Surfeits, imposthumes, grief and damn'd despair,
    Swear Nature's death for framing thee so fair.

125

'And not the least of all these maladies
But in one minute's fight brings beauty under;

Both favour, savour, hue and qualities,
Whereat th' impartial gazer late did wonder,
   Are on the sudden wasted, thaw'd and done,
   As mountain snows melts with the midday sun.   750

126

'Therefore, despite of fruitless chastity,
Love-lacking vestals and self-loving nuns
That on the earth would breed a scarcity,
And barren dearth of daughters and of sons,
   Be prodigal; the lamp that burns by night
   Dries up his oil, to lend the world his light.

127

'What is thy body but a swallowing grave,
Seeming to bury that posterity
Which by the rights of time thou needs must have,
If thou destroy them not in dark obscurity?   760
   If so, the world will hold thee in disdain,
   Sith in thy pride so fair a hope is slain.

128

'So in thyself, thyself art made away;
A mischief worse than civil home-bred strife,
Or theirs whose desperate hands themselves do slay,
Or butcher sire that reaves his son of life:
   Foul cank'ring rust the hidden treasure frets,
   But gold that's put to use more gold begets.'

129

'Nay then (quoth Adon) you will fall again
Into your idle over-handled theme;   770
The kiss I gave you is bestow'd in vain,
And all in vain you strive against the stream;

For by this black-fac'd night, desire's foul nurse,
Your treatise makes me like you worse and worse.

130

'If love have lent you twenty thousand tongues,
And every tongue more moving than your own,
Bewitching like the wanton mermaid's songs,
Yet from mine ear the tempting tune is blown;
   For know my heart stands armed in mine ear,
   And will not let a false sound enter there;   780

131

'Lest the deceiving harmony should run
Into the quiet closure of my breast;
And then my little heart were quite undone,
In his bedchamber to be barr'd of rest.
   No, lady, no, my heart longs not to groan,
   But soundly sleeps, while now it sleeps alone.

132

'What have you urg'd that I cannot reprove?
The path is smooth that leadeth on to danger;
I hate not love, but your device in love,
That lends embracements unto every stranger.   790
   You do it for increase! O, strange excuse
   When reason is the bawd to lust's abuse!

133

'Call it not love, for Love to heaven is fled
Since sweating Lust on earth usurp'd his name;
Under whose simple semblance he hath fed
Upon fresh Beauty, blotting it with blame;
   Which the hot tyrant stains and soon bereaves,
   As caterpillars do the tender leaves.

134

'Love comforteth like sunshine after rain,
But Lust's effect is tempest after sun;   800
Love's gentle spring doth always fresh remain,
Lust's winter comes ere summer half be done:
   Love surfeits not, Lust like a glutton dies:
   Love is all truth, Lust full of forged lies.

135

'More I could tell, but more I dare not say;
The text is old, the orator too green.
Therefore in sadness now I will away;
My face is full of shame, my heart of teen;
   Mine ears that to your wanton talk attended
   Do burn themselves for having so offended.'   810

136

With this he breaketh from the sweet embrace
Of those fair arms which bound him to her breast,
And homeward through the dark lawnd runs apace;
Leaves Love upon her back, deeply distress'd.
   Look how a bright star shooteth from the sky,
   So glides he in the night from Venus' eye;

137

Which after him she darts, as one on shore
Gazing upon a late-embarked friend,
Till the wild waves will have seen him no more,
Whose ridges with the meeting clouds contend: 820
   So did the merciless and pitchy night
   Fold in the object that did feed her sight.

138

Whereat amaz'd as one that unaware
Hath dropp'd a precious jewel in the flood,

Or 'stonish'd, as night-wand'rers often are,
Their light blown out in some mistrustful wood;
 Even so confounded in the dark she lay,
 Having lost the fair discovery of her way.

139

And now she beats her heart, whereat it groans,
That all the neighbour caves, as seeming troubled,   830
Make verbal repetition of her moans;
Passion on passion deeply is redoubled;
 'Ay me,' she cries, and twenty times, 'woe, woe!'
 And twenty echoes twenty times cry so.

140

She, marking them, begins a wailing note,
And sings extemporally a woeful ditty:
How love makes young men thrall, and old men dote,
How love is wise in folly, foolish witty;
 Her heavy anthem still concludes in woe,
 And still the choir of echoes answer so.   840

141

Her song was tedious and outwore the night,
For lover's hours are long, though seeming short;
If pleas'd themselves, others, they think, delight
In such-like circumstances, with such-like sport:
 Their copious stories, oftentimes begun,
 End without audience and are never done.

142

For who hath she to spend the night withal,
But idle sounds resembling parasites;
Like shrill-tongued tapsters answering every call,
Soothing the humour of fantastic wits?   850

She says ' 'Tis so'; they answer all ' 'Tis so';
And would say after her, if she said 'no'.

143

Lo, here the gentle lark, weary of rest,
From his moist cabinet mounts up on high
And wakes the morning, from whose silver breast
The sun ariseth in his majesty,
   Who doth the world so gloriously behold
   That cedar-tops and hills seem burnish'd gold.

144

Venus salutes him with this fair good-morrow:
'O, thou clear god, and patron of all light,   860
From whom each lamp and shining star doth borrow
The beauteous influence that makes him bright,
   There lives a son that suck'd an earthly mother
   May lend thee light, as thou dost lend to other.'

145

This said, she hasteth to a myrtle grove,
Musing the morning is so much o'erworn,
And yet she hears no tidings of her love;
She hearkens for his hounds and for his horn.
   Anon she hears them chant it lustily,
   And all in haste she coasteth to the cry.   870

146

And as she runs, the bushes in the way
Some catch her by the neck, some kiss her face,
Some twin'd about her thigh to make her stay;
She wildly breaketh from their strict embrace,
   Like a milch doe, whose swelling dugs do ache,
   Hasting to feed her fawn hid in some brake.

147

By this she hears the hounds are at a bay;
Whereat she starts, like one that spies an adder
Wreath'd up in fatal folds just in his way,
The fear whereof doth make him shake and shudder;   880
    Even so the timorous yelping of the hounds
    Appals her senses and her spirit confounds.

148

For now she khows it is no gentle chase,
But the blunt boar, rough bear, or lion proud,
Because the cry remaineth in one place,
Where fearfully the dogs exclaim aloud;
    Finding their enemy to be so curst,
    They all strain court'sy who shall cope him first.

149

This dismal cry rings sadly in her ear,
Through which it enters to surprise her heart;   890
Who, overcome by doubt and bloodless fear,
With cold-pale weakness numbs each feeling part;
    Like soldiers when their captain once doth yield,
    They basely fly and dare not stay the field.

150

Thus stands she in a trembling ecstasy;
Till, cheering up her senses all dismay'd,
She tells them 'tis a causeless fantasy,
And childish error, that they are afraid;
    Bids them leave quaking, bids them fear no more.
    And with that word she spied the hunted boar,   900

151

Whose frothy mouth, bepainted all with red,
Like milk and blood being mingled both together,

A second fear through all her sinews spread,
Which madly hurries her, she knows not whither;
  This way she runs, and now she will no further,
  But back retires, to rate the boar for murder.

152

A thousand spleens bear her a thousand ways;
She treads the path that she untreads again;
Her more than haste is mated with delays,
Like the proceedings of a drunken brain,   910
  Full of respects, yet not at all respecting,
  In hand with all things, nought at all effecting.

153

Here kennell'd in a brake she finds a hound,
And asks the weary caitiff for his master;
And there another licking of his wound,
'Gainst venom'd sores the only sovereign plaster;
  And here she meets another, sadly scowling,
  To whom she speaks, and he replies with howling.

154

When he hath ceas'd his ill-resounding noise,
Another flap-mouth'd mourner, black and grim,   920
Against the welkin volleys out his voice;
Another, and another, answer him,
  Clapping their proud tails to the ground below,
  Shaking their scratch'd ears, bleeding as they go.

155

Look how the world's poor people are amaz'd
At apparitions, signs and prodigies,
Whereon with fearful eyes they long have gaz'd,
Infusing them with dreadful prophecies;

So she at these sad signs draws up her breath,
And sighing it again, exclaims on Death.   930

156

'Hard-favoured tyrant, ugly, meagre, lean,
 Hateful divorce of love, (thus chides she Death)
 Grim-grinning ghost, earth's worm, what dost thou mean
 To stifle beauty, and to steal his breath
     Who when he liv'd, his breath and beauty set
     Gloss on the rose, smell to the violet?

157

'If he be dead—O no, it cannot be,
 Seeing his beauty, thou shouldst strike at it—
 O yes, it may; thou hast no eyes to see,
 But hatefully at random dost thou hit;   940
     Thy mark is feeble age, but thy false dart
     Mistakes that aim, and cleaves an infant's heart.

158

'Hadst thou but bid beware, then he had spoke,
 And hearing him, thy power had lost his power.
 The Destinies will curse thee for this stroke;
 They bid thee crop a weed, thou pluck'st a flower;
     Love's golden arrow at him should have fled,
     And not Death's ebon dart, to strike him dead.

159

'Dost thou drink tears, that thou provok'st such weeping;
 What may a heavy groan advantage thee?   950
 Why hast thou cast into eternal sleeping
 Those eyes that taught all other eyes to see?
     Now Nature cares not for thy mortal vigour,
     Since her best work is ruin'd with thy rigour.'

160

Here overcome as one full of despair,
She vail'd her eye-lids, who like sluices stopp'd
The crystal tide that from her two cheeks fair
In the sweet channel of her bosom dropp'd:
 But through the flood-gates breaks the silver rain,
 And with his strong course opens them again. 960

161

O, how her eyes and tears did lend and borrow!
Her eye seen in the tears, tears in her eye;
Both crystals, where they view'd each other's sorrow,
Sorrow that friendly sighs sought still to dry;
 But like a stormy day, now wind, now rain,
 Sighs dry her cheeks, tears make them wet again.

162

Variable passions throng her constant woe,
As striving who should best become her grief;
All entertain'd, each passion labours so
That every present sorrow seemeth chief, 970
 But none is best, Then join they all together,
 Like many clouds consulting for foul weather.

163

By this, far off she hears some huntsman holla;
A nurse's song ne'er pleased her babe so well.
The dire imagination she did follow
This sound of hope doth labour to expel;
 For now reviving joy bids her rejoice,
 And flatters her, it is Adonis' voice.

164

Whereat her tears began to turn their tide,
Being prison'd in her eye like pearls in glass. 980

Yet sometimes falls an orient drop beside,
Which her cheek melts, as scorning it should pass
  To wash the foul face of the sluttish ground,
  Who is but drunken when she seemeth drown'd.

165

O, hard-believing love, how strange it seems
Not to believe, and yet too credulous!
Thy weal and woe are both of them extremes;
Despair and hope makes thee ridiculous:
  The one doth flatter thee in thoughts unlikely,
  In likely thoughts the other kills thee quickly.   990

166

Now she unweaves the web that she hath wrought;
Adonis lives, and Death is not to blame:
It was not she that call'd him all to nought;
Now she adds honours to his hateful name.
  She clepes him king of graves, and grave for kings,
  Imperious supreme of all mortal things.

167

'No, no,' quoth she, 'sweet Death, I did but jest;
Yet pardon me, I felt a kind of fear
Whenas I met the boar, that bloody beast
Which knows no pity but is still severe.   1000
  Then, gentle shadow, (truth I must confess)
  I rail'd on thee, fearing my love's decease.

168

' 'Tis not my fault; the boar provok'd my tongue;
Be wreak'd on him (invisible commander);
'Tis he, foul creature, that hath done thee wrong;
I did but act, he's author of thy slander.

Grief hath two tongues, and never woman yet
Could rule them both without ten women's wit.'

169

Thus, hoping that Adonis is alive,
Her rash suspect she doth extenuate;   1010
And that his beauty may the better thrive,
With Death she humbly doth insinuate;
   Tells him of trophies, statues, tombs, and stories
   His victories, his triumphs and his glories.

170

'O Jove,' quoth she, 'how much a fool was I
To be of such a weak and silly mind
To wail his death who lives, and must not die
Till mutual overthrow of mortal kind!
   For he being dead, with him is Beauty slain,
   And Beauty dead, black Chaos comes again!   1020

171

'Fie, fie, fond Love, thou art as full of fear
As one with treasure laden, hemm'd with thieves;
Trifles unwitnessed with eye or ear
Thy coward heart with false bethinking grieves.'
   Even at this word she hears a merry horn,
   Whereat she leaps that was but late forlorn.

172

As falcons to the lure, away she flies;
The grass stoops not, she treads on it so light;
And in her haste unfortunately spies
The foul boar's conquest on her fair delight;   1030
   Which seen, her eyes as murd'red with the view,
   Like stars asham'd of day, themselves withdrew;

173

Or as the snail, whose tender horns being hit,
Shrinks backward in his shelly cave with pain,
And, there all smother'd up, in shade doth sit,
Long after fearing to creep forth again:
  So at his bloody view her eyes are fled
  Into the deep-dark cabins of her head;

174

Where they resign their office and their light
To the disposing of her troubled brain,   1040
Who bids them still consort with ugly night,
And never wound the heart with looks again;
  Who, like a king perplexed in his throne,
  By their suggestion gives a deadly groan,

175

Whereat each tributary subject quakes;
As when the wind, imprison'd in the ground,
Struggling for passage, earth's foundation shakes,
Which with cold terror doth men's minds confound.
  This mutiny each part doth so surprise,
  That from their dark beds once more leap her eyes; 1050

176

And being open'd, threw unwilling light
Upon the wide wound that the boar had trench'd
In his soft flank, whose wonted lily white
With purple tears that his wound wept was drench'd.
  No flower was nigh, no grass, herb, leaf or weed,
  But stole his blood and seem'd with him to bleed.

177

This solemn sympathy poor Venus noteth;
Over one shoulder doth she hang her head,

Dumbly she passions, franticly she doteth;
She thinks he could not die, he is not dead.   1060
   Her voice is stopp'd, her joints forget to bow;
   Her eyes are mad that they have wept till now.

178

Upon his hurt she looks so steadfastly
That her sight dazzling makes the wound seem three,
And then she reprehends her mangling eye
That makes more gashes where no breach should be:
   His face seems twain, each several limb is doubled;
   For oft the eye mistakes, the brain being troubled.

179

'My tongue cannot express my grief for one,
And yet (quoth she) behold two Adons dead!   1070
My sighs are blown away, my salt tears gone,
Mine eyes are turn'd to fire, my heart to lead;
   Heavy heart's lead, melt at mine eyes' red fire!
   So shall I die by drops of hot desire.

180

'Alas, poor world, what treasure hast thou lost!
What face remains alive that's worth the viewing?
Whose tongue is music now? what canst thou boast
Of things long since, or anything ensuing?
   The flowers are sweet, their colours fresh, and trim;
   But true sweet Beauty liv'd and died with him.   1080

181

'Bonnet nor veil henceforth no creature wear,
Nor sun nor wind will ever strive to kiss you;
Having no fair to lose, you need not fear
The sun doth scorn you, and the wind doth hiss you.

L

But when Adonis liv'd, sun and sharp air
Lurk'd like two thieves to rob him of his fair.

182

'And therefore would he put his bonnet on,
 Under whose brim the gaudy sun would peep;
The wind would blow it off, and being gone,
Play with his locks. Then would Adonis weep;   1090
  And straight, in pity of his tender years,
  They both would strive who first should dry his tears.

183

'To see his face the lion walk'd along
Behind some hedge, because he would not fear him:
To recreate himself when he hath song,
The tiger would be tame and gently hear him,
  If he had spoke, the wolf would leave his prey,
  And never fright the silly lamb that day.

184

'When he beheld his shadow in the brook,
The fishes spread on it their golden gills;   1100
When he was by, the birds such pleasure took
That some would sing, some others in their bills
  Would bring him mulberries and ripe-red cherries;
  He fed them with his sight, they him with berries.

185

'But this foul, grim and urchin-snouted boar,
Whose downward eye still looketh for a grave,
Ne'er saw the beauteous livery that he wore;
Witness the entertainment that he gave.
  If he did see his face, why then I know
  He thought to kiss him, and hath kill'd him so.   1110

186

' 'Tis true, 'tis true, thus was Adonis slain;
He ran upon the boar with his sharp spear,
Who did not whet his teeth at him again,
But by a kiss thought to persuade him there;
   And nuzzling in his flank, the loving swine
   Sheath'd unaware the tusk in his soft groin.

187

'Had I been tooth'd like him, I must confess
With kissing him I should have kill'd him first;
But he is dead, and never did he bless
My youth with his; the more am I accurst.'   1120
   With this she falleth in the place she stood,
   And stains her face with his congealed blood.

188

She looks upon his lips, and they are pale;
She takes him by the hand, and that is cold,
She whispers in his ears a heavy tale,
As if they heard the woeful words she told;
   She lifts the coffer-lids that close his eyes,
   Where, lo, two lamps, burnt out, in darkness lies;

189

Two glasses where herself herself beheld
A thousand times, and now no more reflect;   1130
Their virtue lost wherein they late excell'd,
And every beauty robb'd of his effect.
   'Wonder of time, (quoth she), this is my spite,
   That, thou being dead, the day should yet be light.

190

'Since thou art dead, lo, here I prophesy
Sorrow on love hereafter shall attend:

It shall be waited on with jealousy,
Find sweet beginning but unsavoury end;
  Ne'er settled equally, but high or low,
    That all love's pleasure shall not match his woe.   1140

191

'It shall be fickle, false and full of fraud;
Bud, and be blasted, in a breathing while;
The bottom poison, and the top o'erstraw'd
With sweets that shall the truest sight beguile;
  The strongest body shall it make most weak,
  Strike the wise dumb, and teach the fool to speak.

192

'It shall be sparing, and too full of riot,
Teaching decrepit age to tread the measures;
The staring ruffian shall it keep in quiet,
Pluck down the rich, enrich the poor with treasures;   1150
  It shall be raging-mad, and silly-mild,
  Make the young old, the old become a child.

193

'It shall suspect where is no cause of fear;
It shall not fear where it should most mistrust;
It shall be merciful and too severe,
And most deceiving when it seems most just;
  Perverse it shall be where it shows most toward,
  Put fear to valour, courage to the coward.

194

'It shall be cause of war and dire events,
And set dissension 'twixt the son and sire;   1160
Subject and servile to all discontents,
As dry combustious matter is to fire,

Sith in his prime Death doth my love destroy,
They that love best their loves shall not enjoy.'

195

By this the boy that by her side lay kill'd
Was melted like a vapour from her sight,
And in his blood that on the ground lay spill'd
A purple flower sprung up, chequer'd with white,
  Resembling well his pale cheeks, and the blood
  Which in round drops upon their whiteness stood. 1170

196

She bows her head the new-sprung flower to smell,
Comparing it to her Adonis' breath,
And says within her bosom it shall dwell,
Since he himself is reft from her by death;
  She crops the stalk, and in the breach appears
  Green-dropping sap, which she compares to tears.

197

'Poor flower (quoth she), this was thy father's guise—
Sweet issue of a more sweet-smelling sire—
For every little grief to wet his eyes.
To grow unto himself was his desire;   1180
  And so 'tis thine; but know, it is as good
  To wither in my breast as in his blood.

198

'Here was thy father's bed, here in my breast;
Thou art the next of blood, and 'tis thy right.
Lo, in this hollow cradle take thy rest;
My throbbing heart shall rock thee day and night;
  There shall not be one minute in an hour
  Wherein I will not kiss my sweet love's flower.'

199

Thus weary of the world, away she hies,
And yokes her silver doves, by whose swift aid   1190
Their mistress, mounted, through the empty skies
In her light chariot quickly is convey'd,
    Holding their course to Paphos, where their queen
    Means to immure herself and not be seen.

MICHAEL DRAYTON

Endymion and Phoebe:
Idea's Latmus

(1595)

In Ionia whence sprang old poets' fame,
From whom that sea did first derive her name,
The blessed bed whereon the Muses lay,
Beauty of Greece, the pride of Asia,
Whence Archelaus, whom times historify,
First unto Athens brought philosophy:
In this fair region on a goodly plain,
Stretching her bounds unto the bord'ring main,
The mountain Latmus overlooks the sea,
Smiling to see the ocean billows play: 10
Latmus, where young Endymion us'd to keep
His fairest flock of silver-fleeced sheep,
To whom Silvanus often would resort,
At barley-break to see the Satyrs sport;
And when rude Pan his tabret list to sound,
To see the fair nymphs foot it in a round,
Under the trees which on this mountain grew,
As yet the like Arabia never knew:
For all the pleasures Nature could devise
Within this plot she did imparadise;   20
And great Diana, of her special grace,
With vestal rites had hallow'd all the place:
Upon this mount there stood a stately grove,
Whose reaching arms to clip the welkin strove,
Of tufted cedars and the branching pine,
Whose busy tops themselves do so entwine
As seem'd, when Nature first this work begun,

She then conspir'd against the piercing sun;
Under whose covert (thus divinely made)
Phoebus' green laurel flourish'd in the shade: 30
Fair Venus' myrtle, Mars his warlike fir,
Minerva's olive, and the weeping myrrh,
The patient palm, which thrives in spite of hate,
The poplar, to Alcides consecrate;
Which Nature in such order had dispos'd,
And therewithal these goodly walks enclos'd,
As serv'd for hangings and rich tapestry
To beautify this stately gallery.
Embroid'ring these in curious trails along,
The cluster'd grapes, the golden citrons hung,
More glorious than the precious fruit were these,
Kept by the dragon in Hesperides;
Or gorgeous arras in rich colours wrought,
With silk from Afric or from Indy brought.
Out of this soil sweet bubbling fountains crept,
As though for joy the senseless stones had wept,
With straying channels dancing sundry ways,
With often turns, like to a curious maze:
Which, breaking forth, the tender grass bedew'd,
Whose silver sand with orient pearl was strew'd,   50
Shadow'd with roses and sweet eglantine,
Dipping their sprays into this crystalline:
From which the birds the purple berries prun'd,
And to their loves their small recorders tun'd:
The nightingale, woods' herald of the spring,
The whistling woosel, mavis carolling,
Tuning their trebles to the waters' fall,
Which made the music more angelical:
Whilst gentle Zephyr, murmuring among,
Kept time, and bare the burthen to the song: 60
About whose brims, refresh'd with dainty showers,
Grew amaranthus, and sweet gillyflowers,
The marigold, Phoebus' beloved friend,
The moly, which from scorcery doth defend,

Violet, carnation, balm and cassia,
Idea's primrose, coronet of may.
Above this grove a gentle fair ascent,
Which by degrees of milk-white marble went:
Upon the top, a paradise was found,
With which Nature this miracle had crown'd;   70
Impal'd with rocks of rarest precious stone,
Which like the flames of Etna brightly shone,
And serv'd as lanthorns furnished with light,
To guide the wand'ring passengers by night:
For which fair Phoebe, sliding from her sphere,
Us'd oft-times to come and sport her there,
And from the azure, starry-painted sky
Embalm'd the banks with precious lunary:
That now her Maenalus she quite forsook,
And unto Latmus wholly her betook,   80
And in this place her pleasure us'd to take,
And all was for her sweet Endymion's sake:
Endymion, the lovely shepherd boy,
Endymion, great Phoebe's only joy,
Endymion, in whose pure-shining eyes
The naked fairies danc'd the hay-de-guys.
The shag-hair'd Satyrs, mountain-climbing race,
Have been made tame by gazing in his face.
For this boy's love, the water-nymphs have wept,
Stealing oft-times to kiss him whilst he slept,   90
And tasting once the nectar of his breath,
Surfeit with sweet, and languish unto death;
And Jove oft-times bent to lascivious sport,
And coming where Endymion did resort,
Hath courted him, inflamed with desire,
Thinking some nymph was cloth'd in boy's attire,
And often-times the simple rural swains,
Beholding him in crossing o'er the plains,
Imagin'd Apollo from above
Put on this shape, to win some maiden's love.   100
This shepherd, Phoebe ever did behold,

Whose love already had her thoughts controll'd;
From Latmus' top (her stately throne) she rose,
And to Endymion down beneath she goes.
Her brother's beams now had she laid aside,
Her horned crescent, and her full-fac'd pride:
For had she come adorned with her light,
No mortal eye could have endur'd the sight;
But like a nymph, crown'd with a flow'ry twine,
And not like Phoebe, as herself divine.   110
An azur'd mantle purfled with a veil,
Which in the air puff'd like a swelling sail,
Embosted rainbows did appear in silk,
With wavy streams as white as morning's milk:
Which ever as the gentle air did blow,
Still with the motion seem'd to ebb and flow;
About her neck a chain twice-twenty fold,
Of rubies, set in lozenges of gold;
Truss'd up in trammels, and in curious pleats,
With sphery circles falling on her teats;   120
A dainty smock of cypress, fine and thin,
O'ercast with curls, next to her lily skin:
Through which the pureness of the same did show
Like damask roses strew'd with flakes of snow,
Discovering all her stomach to the waist,
With branches of sweet-circling vines enchas'd.
A coronet she ware of myrtle boughs,
Which gave a shadow to her ivory brows.
No smother-beauty mask did beauty smother;
Great lights dim less, yet burn not one another;   130
Nature abhors to borrow from the mart;
Simples fit beauty, fie on drugs and art!
    Thus came she where her love Endymion lay,
Who with sweet carols sang the night away;
And as it is the shepherd's usual trade,
Oft on his pipe a roundelay he play'd.
As meek he was as any lamb might be,
Nor never liv'd a fairer youth than he:

His dainty hand the snow itself did stain,
Or her to whom Jove show'r'd in golden rain: 140
From whose sweet palm the liquid pearl did swell,
Pure as the drops of Aganippe's well,
Clear as the liquor which fair Hebe spilt;
His sheep-hook silver, damask'd all with gilt;
The staff itself, of snowy ivory,
Studied with coral, tipp'd with ebony;
His tresses, of the raven's shining black,
Straggling in curls along his manly back;
The balls which Nature in his eyes had set,
Like diamonds enclosing globes of jet;   150
Which sparkl'd from their milky lids out-right,
Like fair Orion's heaven-adorning light;
The stars on which her heavenly eyes were bent,
And fixed still with lovely blandishment;
For whom so oft disguised she was seen,
As she celestial Phoebe had not been:
Her dainty buskins lac'd unto the knee,
Her pleated frock, tuck'd up accordingly:
A nymph-like huntress, arm'd with bow and dart
About the woods she scours the long-liv'd hart.   160
She climbs the mountains with the light-foot Fauns
And with the Satyrs scuds it o'er the lawns.
In music's sweet delight she knows her skill,
Quavering the cithron nimbly with her quill.
Upon each tree she carves Endymion's name
In Gordian knots, with Phoebe to the same:
To kill him ven'son now she pitch'd her toils,
And to this lovely ranger brings the spoils;
And thus whilst she by chaste desire is led
Unto the downs where he his fair flocks fed,   170
Near to a grove she had Endymion spied,
Where he was fishing by a river side
Under a poplar, shadow'd from the sun;
Where merrily to court him she begun:
'Sweet boy,' quoth she, 'Take what thy heart can wish;

When thou dost angle would I were a fish;
When thou art sporting by the silver brooks,
Put in thy hand, thou need'st no other hooks;
Hard-hearted boy, Endymion, look on me!
Nothing on earth I hold too dear for thee: 180
I am a nymph and not of human blood,
Begot by Pan on Isis' sacred flood:
When I was born, upon that very day
Phoebus was seen the reveller to play:
In Jove's high house the gods assembl'd all,
And Juno held her sumptuous festival,
Oceanus that hour was dancing spied,
And Tithon seen to frolic with his bride;
The halcyons that season sweetly sang,
And all the shores with shouting sea-nymphs rang;   190
And on that day, my birth to memorize,
The shepherds hold a solemn sacrifice:
The chaste Diana nurs'd me in her lap,
And I suck'd nectar from her down-soft pap.
The well wherein this body bathed first,
Who drinks thereof shall never after thirst;
The water hath the lunacy appeas'd,
And by the virtue, cureth all diseas'd;
The place wherein my bare feet touch the mould,
Made up in balls, for pomander is sold.   200
See, see, these hands have robb'd the snow of white,
These dainty fingers, organs of delight:
Behold these lips, the lodestones of desire,
Whose words enchant like Amphion's well-tun'd lyre;
This foot art's just proportion doth reveal,
Signing the earth with heaven's own manual seal.
Go, play the wanton, I will tend thy flock,
And wait the hours as duly as a clock;
I'll deck thy ram with bells, and wreaths of bay,
And gild his horns upon the shearing day;   210
And with a garland crown thee shepherds' king,
And thou shalt lead the gay girls in a ring;

Birds with their wings shall fan thee in the sun,
And all the fountains with pure wine shall run;
I have a choir of dainty turtle-doves,
And they shall sit and sweetly sing our loves:
I'll lay thee on the swan's soft downy plume,
And all the wind shall gently breathe perfume,
I'll plait thy locks with many a curious pleat,
And chafe thy temples with a sacred heat;   220
The Muses still shall keep thee company,
And lull thee with enchanting harmony.
If not all these, yet let my virtues move thee;
A chaster nymph, Endymion, cannot love thee.'
    But he imagin'd she some nymph had been,
Because she was apparelled in green;
Or happily, some of fair Flora's train,
Which oft did use to sport upon the plain.
He tells her, he was Phoebe's servant sworn,
And oft in hunting had her quiver borne,   230
And that to her virginity he vow'd,
Which in no hand by Venus was allow'd;
Then unto her a catalogue recites
Of Phoebe's statutes, and her hallow'd rites,
And of the grievous penalty inflicted
On such as her chaste laws had interdicted:
Now, he requests that she would stand aside,
Because the fish her shadow had espied;
Then he entreats her that she would be gone,
And at this time to let him be alone;   240
Then turns him from her in an angry sort,
And frowns and chafes that she had spoil'd his sport.
And then he threatens her, if she did stay,
And told her great Diana came this way.
But for all this, this nymph would not forbear,
But now she smoothes his crispy-curled hair,
And when he (rudely) will'd her to refrain,
Yet scarcely ended, she begins again:
'Thy ewes,' quoth she, 'with milk shall daily spring,

And to thy profit yearly twins shall bring;   250
And thy fair flock, (a wonder to behold)
Shall have their fleeces turn'd to burnish'd gold;
Thy batful pasture, to thy wanton thews,
Shall be refresh'd with nectar-dropping dews,
The oak's smooth leaves, syrup'd with honey fall,
Trickle down drops to quench thy thirst withal:
The cruel tiger will I tame for thee,
And gently lay his head upon thy knee;
And by my spells, the wolves' jaws will I lock,
And (as good shepherds) make them guard thy flock;   260
I'll mount thee bravely on a lion's back,
To drive the foamy-tusked boar to wrack:
The brazen-hoofed yelling bulls I'll yoke,
And with my herbs the scaly dragon choke.
Thou in great Phoebe's ivory coach shalt ride,
Which drawn by eagles in the air shall glide:
I'll stay the time, it shall not steal away,
And twenty moons as seeming but one day.
Behold (fond boy), this rosin-weeping pine,
This mournful larix, dropping turpentine,   270
This mounting teda, thus with tempests torn,
With inky tears continually to mourn;
Look on this tree, which blubbereth amber gum,
Which seems to speak to thee, though it be dumb:
Which being senseless blocks, as thou dost see,
Weep at my woes, that thou might'st pity me:
O thou art young, and fit for love's profession,
Like wax which warmed quickly takes impression;
Sorrow, in time, with floods those eyes shall wear
Whence pity now cannot extort a tear.   280
Fond boy, with words thou might'st be overcome,
But love-surpris'd the heart, the tongue is dumb.
But as I can, I'll strive to conquer thee;
Yet tears and sighs my weapons needs must be.
My sighs move trees, rocks melting with my tears,
But thou art blind and, cruel, stopp'st thine ears.

Look in this well. If beauty men allow,
Though thou be fair, yet I as fair as thou;
I am a vestal, and a spotless maid,
Although by love to thee I am betray'd:　　290
But sith (unkind) thou dost my love disdain,
To rocks and hills myself I will complain.'
　　Thus with a sigh her speeches off she broke,
The while her eyes to him in silence spoke;
And from the place this wanton nymph arose,
And up to Latmus all in haste she goes;
Like to a nymph on shady Citheron,
The swift Ismaenus, or Therodon,
Gliding like Thetis, on the fleet waves borne;
O'er she which trips upon the ears of corn,　　300
Like swallows when in open air they strive,
Or like the fowl which tow'ring falcons drive.
But whilst the wanton thus pursu'd his sport,
Deceitful Love had undermin'd the fort,
And by a breach (in spite of all deniance),
Enter'd the fort which lately made defiance:
And with strong siege had now begirt about
The maiden sconce which held the soldier out.
Love wants his eyes, yet shoots he passing right,
His shafts our thoughts, his bow he makes our sight.　　310
His deadly piles are temper'd by such art
As still directs the arrow to the heart:
He cannot love, and yet forsooth he will;
He sees her not, and yet he sees her still;
He goes unto the place she stood upon,
And asks the poor soul whither she was gone;
Fain would he follow her, yet makes delay;
Fain would he go, and yet fain would he stay,
He kiss'd the flowers depressed with her feet,
And swears from her they borrow'd all their sweet.　　320
Fain would he cast aside this troublous thought,
But still, like poison, more and more it wrought;
And to himself thus often would he say,

Here my love sat, in this place did she play;
Here in the fountain hath my goddess been,
And with her presence hath she grac'd this green.
    Now black-brow'd Night, plac'd in her chair of jet,
Sat wrapp'd in clouds within her cabinet,
And with her dusky mantle overspread
The path the sunny palfreys us'd to tread;   330
And Cynthia, sitting in her crystal chair,
In all her pomp now rid along her sphere;
The honey'd dew descended in soft show'rs,
Drizzled in pearl upon the tender flow'rs;
And Zephyr hush'd, and with a whispering gale
Seemed to hearken to the nightingale,
Which in the thorny brakes with her sweet song,
Unto the silent night bewray'd her wrong.
    Now fast by Latmus near unto a grove,
Which by the mount was shadow'd from above,   340
Upon a bank Endymion sat by night,
To whom fair Phoebe lent her friendly light:
And sith his flocks were laid them down to rest,
Thus gives his sorrows passage from his breast:
'Sweet leaves,' quoth he, 'which by the air do tremble,
Oh, how your motions do my thoughts resemble;
With that mild breath, by which you only move,
Whisper my words in silence to my love:
Convey my sighs, sweet civet-breathing air,
In doleful accents to my heavenly fair;   350
You murmuring springs, like doleful instruments,
Upon your gravel sound my sad laments,
And in your silent bubbling as you go,
Consort yourselves like music to my woe.'
And lifting now his sad and heavy eyes
Up towards the beauty of the burnish'd skies,
'Bright lamps,' quoth he, 'the glorious welkin bears,
Which clip about the planets' wand'ring spheres,
And in your circled maze do ever roll,
Dancing about the never-moving pole: 360

Sweet nymph, which in fair Elice dost shine,
Whom thy surpassing beauty made divine,
Now in the Arctic constellation,
Smile, sweet Callisto, on Endymion:
And thou, brave Perseus, in the northern air,
Holding Medusa by the snaky hair,
Jove's show'r-begotten son, whose valour tried,
In seventeen glorious lights art stellified;
Which once thy love left as a monster's prey;
And thou, the lovely fair Andromeda,   370
Born of the famous Ethiopian line,
Darting these rays from thy transpiercing eyne,
To thee the bright Cassiope, with these
(Whose beauty strove with the Nereides),
With all the troupe of the celestial band
Which on Olympus in your glory stand;
And you, great wand'ring lights, if from your spheres
You have regard unto a shepherd's tears,
Or as men say, if over earthly things
You only rule as potentates and kings,   380
Unto my love's event, sweet stars, direct
Your kindest revolution and aspect,
And bend your clear eyes from your thrones above
Upon Endymion, pining thus in love.'
    Now, ere the purple dawning yet did spring,
The joyful lark began to stretch her wing,
And now the cock, the morning's trumpeter,
Play'd hunts-up for the day star to appear;
Down slideth Phoebe from her crystal chair,
'Sdaining to lend her light unto the air,   390
But unto Latmus all in haste is gone,
Longing to see her sweet Endymion;
At whose departure all the planets gaz'd,
As at some seld-seen accident amaz'd,
Till reasoning of the same, they fell at odds,
So that a question grew amongst the gods,
Whether without a general consent
    M

She might depart their sacred parliament.
But what they could do was but all in vain,
Of liberty they could her not restrain: 400
For of the seven since she the lowest was,
Unto the earth she might the easiest pass;
Since only by her moisty influence,
Of earthly things she hath pre-eminence,
And under her, man's mutable estate
As with her changes doth participate;
And from the working of her waning source,
Th' uncertain waters held a certain course.
Throughout her kingdom she might walk at large,
Whereof as empress she had care and charge,   410
And as the sun unto the day gives light,
She is the only mistress of the night;
Which whilst she in her oblique course doth guide,
The glittering stars appear in all their pride,
Which to her light their friendly lamps do lend,
And on her train as handmaids do attend;
And thirteen times she through her sphere doth run,
Ere Phoebus full his yearly course have done:
And unto her of women is assign'd,
Predominance of body and of mind,   420
That as of planets she most variable,
So of all creatures they most mutable.
But her sweet Latmus which she lov'd so much,
No sooner once her dainty foot doth touch,
But that the mountain with her brightness shone
And gave a light to all the horizon:
Even as the sun, which darkness long did shroud,
Breaks suddenly from underneath a cloud,
So that the nymphs which on her still attended,
Knew certainly great Phoebe was descended;   430
And all approached to this sacred hill,
There to await their sovereign goddess' will;
And now the little birds, whom Nature taught
To honour great Diana as they ought,

Because she is the goddess of the woods
And sole preserver of their hallow'd floods,
Set to their consort in their lower springs,
That with the music all the mountain rings;
So that it seem'd the birds of every grove
Which should excel and pass each other strove,   440
That in the higher woods and hollow grounds,
The murmuring echo everywhere resounds;
The trembling brooks their sliding courses stay'd,
The whilst the waves one with another play'd,
And all the flocks in this rejoicing mood,
As though enchanted, do forbear their food:
The herds of deer down from the mountains flew,
As loth to come within Diana's view,
Whom piercing arrows from her ivory bow
Had often taught her powerful hand to know.   450
And now from Latmus looking towards the plains,
Casting her eyes upon the shepherds' swains,
Perceiv'd her dear Endymion's flock were stray'd
And he himself upon the ground was laid;
Whom late recall'd from melancholy deep,
The chanting birds had lulled now asleep:
For why the music in this humble kind,
As it first found, so doth it leave the mind;
And melancholy, from the spleen begun,
By passion mov'd into the veins doth run;   460
Which when this humour as a swelling flood
By vigour is infused in the blood,
The vital spirits doth mightily appal,
And weakeneth so the parts organical;
And when the senses are disturb'd and tir'd,
With what the heart incessantly desir'd,
Like travellers with labour long oppress'd,
Find release, eftsoons they fall to rest.
    And coming now to her Endymion,
Whom heavy sleep had lately seiz'd upon,   470
Kneeling her down, him in her arms she clips,

And with sweet kisses sealeth up his lips,
Whilst from her eyes, tears streaming down in show'rs
Fell on his cheeks like dew upon the flow'rs,
In globy circles like pure drops of milk
Sprinkl'd on roses or fine crimson silk:
Touching his brow, 'This is the seat,' quoth she,
'Where Beauty sits in all her majesty.'
She calls his eyelids those pure crystal covers
Which do include the looking-glass of lovers;   480
She calls his lips the sweet delicious folds
Which rare perfume and precious incense holds;
She calls his soft smooth alabaster skin
The lawn which angels are attired in;
'Sweet face,' quoth she, 'but wanting words I spare thee,
Except to heaven alone I should compare thee:'
And whilst her words she wasteth thus in vain,
Sporting herself the time to entertain,
The frolic nymphs with music's sacred sound
Enter'd the meadows, dancing in a round: 490
And unto Phoebe straight their course direct,
Which now their joyful coming did expect;
Before whose feet their flow'ry spoils they lay,
And with sweet balm his body do embay:
And on the laurels growing there along
Their wreathed garlands all about they hung:
And all the ground within the compass load
With sweetest flowers, whereon they lightly troad.
With nectar then his temples they bedew,
And kneeling softly kiss him all arew;   500
Then in brave galliards they themselves advance,
And in the thyas, Bacchus' stately dance;
Then following on fair Flora's gilded train,
Into the groves they thus depart again.
And now to show her powerful deity,
Her sweet Endymion more to beautify,
Into his soul the goddess doth infuse
The fiery nature of a heavenly muse,

Which in the spirit labouring, by the mind
Partaketh of celestial things by kind: 510
For why the soul being divine alone,
Exempt from vile and gross corruption,
Of heavenly secrets comprehensible,
Of which the dull flesh is not sensible;
And by one only powerful faculty
Yet governeth a multiplicity,
Being essential, uniform in all;
Not to be sever'd nor dividual,
But in her function holdeth her estate,
By powers divine in her ingenerate, 520
And so by inspiration conceiveth
What heaven to her by divination breatheth.
But they no sooner to the shades were gone,
Leaving their goddess by Endymion,
But by the hand the lovely boy she takes,
And from his sweet sleep softly him awakes,
Who being struck into a sudden fear,
Beholding thus his glorious goddess there,
His heart transpierced with this sudden glance,
Became as one last cast into a trance: 530
Wiping his eyes not yet of perfect sight,
Scarcely awak'd, amazed at the light,
His cheeks now pale, then lovely blushing red,
Which oft increas'd, and quickly vanished;
And as on him her fixed eyes were bent,
So to and fro his colour came and went;
Like to a crystal near the fire set,
Against the brightness rightly opposet,
Now doth retain the colour of the flame,
And lightly mov'd again, reflects the same; 540
For our affection, quicken'd by her heat,
Allay'd and strengthen'd by a strong conceit,
The mind disturbed forthwith doth convart
To an internal passion of the heart,
By motion of that sudden joy or fear

Which we receive either by the eye or ear;
For by retraction of the spirit and blood,
From those exterior parts where first they stood,
Into the centre of the body sent,
Returns again more strong and vehement: 550
And in the like extremity made cold,
About the same, themselves do closely hold,
And though the cause be like, in this repect
Works by this means a contrary effect.

   Thus whilst this passion hotly held his course,
Ebbing and flowing from his springing source,
With the strong fit of this sweet fever mov'd,
At sight of her which he entirely lov'd,
Not knowing yet great Phoebe this should be,
His sovereign goddess, queen of chastity,   560
Now, like a man whom love had learned art,
Resolv'd at once his secrets to impart:
But first repeats the torments he had pass'd,
The woes endur'd since time he saw her last;
Now he reports he noted whilst she spake,
The bustling winds their murmur often break,
And being silent, seem'd to pause and stay,
To listen to her what she meant to say:
'Be kind,' quoth he, 'sweet nymph, unto thy lover,
My soul's sweet essence, and my senses' mover,   570
Life of my life, pure image of my heart,
Impressure of conceit, invention, art,
My vital spirit receives his spirit from thee;
Thou art that all which ruleth all in me,
Thou art the sap and life whereby I live,
Which pow'rful vigour dost receive and give;
Thou nourishest the flame wherein I burn,
The North whereto my heart's true touch doth turn.
Pity my poor flock, see their woeful plight,
Their master perish'd living from thy sight,   580
Their fleeces rent, my tresses all forlorn;
I pine, whilst they their pasture have forborne;

Behold (quoth he) this little flow'r below,
Which here within this fountain brim doth grow;'
With that, a solemn tale begins to tell
Of this fair flow'r, and of this holy well,
A goodly legend, many winters old,
Learn'd by the shepherds sitting by their fold,
How once this fountain was a youthful swain,
A frolic boy and kept upon the plain.   590
'Unfortunately it happ'd to him,' quoth he,
'To love a fair nymph as I now love thee;
To her his love and sorrow he imparts,
Which might dissolve a rock of flinty hearts;
To her he sues, to her he makes his moan,
But she more deaf and hard than steel or stone;
And thus one day, with grief of mind oppress'd,
As in this place he laid him down to rest,
The gods at length upon his sorrows look,
Transforming him into this purling brook,   600
Whose murmuring bubbles softly as they creep,
Falling in drops, the channel seems to weep.
But she thus careless of his misery,
Still spends her days in mirth and jollity;
And coming one day to the river side,
Laughing for joy when she the same espied,
This wanton nymph in that unhappy hour
Was here transform'd into this purple flow'r,
Which towards the water turns itself again,
To pity him by her unkindness slain.'   610
    She, as it seem'd, who all this time attended,
Longing to hear that once his tale were ended,
Now like a jealous woman she repeats
Men's subtleties and natural deceits;
And by example strives to verify
Their fickleness and vain inconstancy,
Their hard obdurate hearts and wilful blindness,
Telling a story wholly of unkindness;
But he, who well perceived her intent,

And to remove her from this argument,   620
Now by the sacred fount he vows and swears,
By lovers' sighs, and by her hallow'd tears,
By holy Latmus now he takes his oath,
That all he spake was in good faith and troth;
And for no frail uncertain doubt should move her,
Vows secrecy, the crown of a true lover.
  She, hearing this, thought time that she reveal'd
That kind affection which she long conceal'd,
Determineth to make her true love known,
Which she had borne unto Endymion;   630
'I am no huntress, nor no nymph,' quoth she,
'As thou perhaps imagin'st me to be,
I am great Phoebe, Latmus' sacred queen,
Who from the skies have hither pass'd unseen,
And by thy chaste love hither was I led,
Where full three years thy fair flock have I fed,
Upon these mountains and these fertile plains,
And crown'd thee king of all the shepherds' swains:
Nor wanton nor lascivious is my love,
Nor never lust my chaste thoughts once could move. 640
But since thou thus hast offer'd at my shrine,
And of the gods hast held me most divine,
Mine altars thou with sacrifice hast stor'd,
And in my temples hast my name ador'd,
And of all other, most hast honour'd me,
Great Phoebe's glory thou alone shalt see.'
  This spake, she putteth on her brave attire,
As being burnish'd in her brother's fire,
Purer than that celestial shining flame
Wherein great Jove unto his leman came,   650
Which quickly had his pale cheeks overspread,
And tinted with a lovely blushing red.
Which whilst her brother Titan for a space,
Withdrew himself, to give his sister place,
She now is darken'd to all creatures' eyes,
Whilst in the shadow of the earth she lies;

For that the earth, of nature cold and dry,
A very chaos of obscurity,
Whose globe exceeds her compass by degrees,
Fixed upon her superficies;   660
When in his shadow she doth hap to fall,
Doth cause her darkness to be general.
    Thus whilst he laid his head upon her lap,
She in a fiery mantle doth him wrap,
And carries him up from this lumpish mould
Into the skies, whereas he might behold
The earth in perfect roundness of a ball,
Exceeding globes most artificial:
Which in a fixed point Nature dispos'd,
And with the sundry elements enclos'd,   670
Which as the centre permanent doth stay,
When as the skies in their diurnal sway
Strongly maintain the ever-turning course,
Forc'd alone by their first mover source;
Where he beholds the aëry regions,
Whereas the clouds and strange impressions,
Maintain'd by coldness, often do appear,
And by the highest region of the air,
Unto the clearest element of fire,
Which to her silver footstool doth aspire.   680
Then doth she mount him up into her sphere,
Imparting heavenly secrets to him there;
Where lighten'd by her shining beams, he sees
The pow'rful planets, all in their degrees,
Their sundry revolutions in the skies,
And by their working how they sympathize;
All in their circles severally prefix'd,
And in due distance each with other mix'd:
The mansions which they hold in their estate,
Of which by nature they participate;   690
And how those signs their several places take,
Within the compass of the zodiac:
And in their several triplicities consent,

Unto the nature of an element;
To which the planets do themselves disperse,
Having the guidance of this universe,
And do from thence extend their several pow'rs
Unto this little fleshly world of ours:
Wherein her Maker's workmanship is found,
As in contriving of this mighty round,   700
In such strange manner and such fashion wrought
As doth exceed man's dull and feeble thought,
Guiding us still by their directions;
And that our fleshly frail complexions
Of elemental natures grounded be,
With which our dispositions most agree;
Some of the fire and air participate,
And some of wat'ry and of earthy state,
As hot and moist, with chilly cold and dry,
And unto these the other contrary;   710
And by their influence pow'rful on the earth,
Predominant in man's frail mortal birth;
And that our lives' effects and fortunes are,
As is that happy or unlucky star
Which, reigning in our frail nativity,
Seals up the secrets of our destiny,
With friendly planets in conjunction set,
Or else with other merely opposet.
And now to him her greatest pow'r she lent,
To lift him to the starry firmament,   720
Where he beheld that milky-stained place,
By which the Twins and heavenly Archers trace
The Dog which doth the furious Lion beat,
Whose flaming breath increaseth Titan's heat;
The tear-distilling mournful Pleiades,
Which on the earth the storms and tempests raise;
And all the course the constellations run,
When in conjunction with the moon or sun,
When towards the fixed Arctic they arise,
When towards the Antarctic, falling from our eyes;   730

And having imp'd the wings of his desire,
And kindl'd him with this celestial fire,
She sets him down, and vanishing his sight,
Leaves him enwrapp'd in this true delight.
Now wheresoever he his fair flock fed,
The Muses still Endymion followed;
His sheep as white as swans or driven snow,
Which beautified the soil with such a show,
As where he folded in the darkest night,
There never needed any other light;   740
If that he hunger'd and desired meat,
The bees would bring him honey for to eat,
Yet from his lips would not depart away,
Till they were loaden with ambrosia;
And if he thirsted, often there was seen
A bubbling fountain spring out of the green,
With crystal liquor fill'd unto the brim,
Which did present her liquid store to him.
If he would hunt, the fair nymphs at his will
With bows and quivers would attend him still: 750
And whatsoever he desir'd to have,
That he obtain'd, if he the same would crave.

And now at length the joyful time drew on,
She meant to honour her Endymion,
And glorify him on that stately mount
Whereof the goddess made so great account.
She sends Jove's winged herald to the woods,
The neighbour fountains and the bord'ring floods,
Charging the nymphs which did inhabit there
Upon a day appointed to appear,   760
And to attend her sacred majesty
In all their pomp and great solemnity.
Having obtain'd great Phoebus' free consent,
To further her divine and chaste intent,
Which thus imposed as a thing of weight,
In stately troupes appear before her straight
The Fauns and Satyrs from the tufted brakes,

Their bristly arms wreath'd all about with snakes,
Their sturdy loins with ropes of ivy bound,
Their horned heads with woodbine chaplets crown'd,   770
With cypress javelins, and about their thighs
The flaggy hair disorder'd loosely flies:
Th' Oreades, like to the Spartan maid,
In murrey sendal gorgeously array'd:
With gallant green scarves girded in the waist,
Their flaxen hair with silken fillets lac'd,
Woven with flow'rs in sweet lascivious wreaths,
Moving like feathers as the light air breathes,
With crowns of myrtle, glorious to behold,
Whose leaves are painted with pure drops of gold: 780
With trains of fine byss chequer'd all with frets
Of dainty pinks and precious violets,
In branched buskins of fine cordiwin,
With spangled garters down unto the shin,
Fring'd with fine silk, of many a sundry kind,
Which like to pennons waved with the wind.
The Hamadryads from their shady bow'rs,
Deck'd up in garlands of the rarest flow'rs,
Upon the backs of milk-white bulls were set,
With horn and hoof as black as any jet,   790
Whose collars were great massy golden rings,
Led by their swains in twisted silken strings.
Then did the lovely Dryades appear,
On dappl'd stags which bravely mounted were,
Whose velvet palms, with nosegays rarely dight,
To all the rest bred wonderful delight.
And in this sort, accompanied with these,
In triumph rode the wat'ry Naiades,
Upon seahorses, trapp'd with shining fins,
Armed with their mail, impenetrable skins;   800
Whose scaly crests, like rainbows bended high,
Seem to control proud Iris in the sky.
Upon a chariot was Endymion laid,
In snowy tissue gorgeously array'd,

Of precious ivory cover'd oe'r with lawn,
Which by four stately unicorns was drawn.
Of ropes of orient pearl their traces were,
Pure as the path which doth in heaven appear,
With rarest flow'rs enchas'd and overspread,
Which serv'd as curtains to this glorious bed,   810
Whose seat of crystal in the sunbeams shone,
Like thunder-breathing Jove's celestial throne;
Upon his head a coronet install'd
Of one entire and mighty emerald;
With richest bracelets on his lily wrists,
Of heliotropium, link'd with golden twists;
A bevy of fair swans, which flying over,
With their large wings him from the sun do cover,
And easily wafting as he went along,
Do lull him still with their enchanting song;   820
Whilst all the nymphs on solemn instruments,
Sound dainty music to their sweet laments.
   And now great Phoebe in her triumph came,
With all the titles of her glorious name,
Diana, Delia, Luna, Cynthia,
Virago, Hecate, and Elythia,
Prothyria, Dictynna, Proserpine,
Latona, and Lucina, most divine;
And in her pomp began now to approach,
Mounted aloft upon her crystal coach,   830
Drawn o'er the plains by four pure milk-white hinds,
Whose nimble feet seem'd winged with the winds;
Her rarest beauty being now begun,
But newly borrow'd from the golden sun,
Her lovely crescent, with a decent space,
By due proportion beautifi'd her face,
Till having fully fill'd her circled side,
Her glorious fullness now appear'd in pride;
Which long her changing brow could not retain,
But fully wax'd, began again to wane;   840
Upon her brow (like meteors in the air)

Twenty and eight great gorgeous lamps she bare;
Some, as the welkin, shining passing bright,
Some not so sumptuous, other lesser light;
Some burn, some other let their fair lights fall,
Compos'd in order geometrical;
And to adorn her with a greater grace,
And add more beauty to her lovely face,
Her richest globe she gloriously displays;
Now that the sun had hid his golden rays,   850
Lest that his radiance should her suppress,
And so might make her beauty seem the less;
Her stately train laid out in azur'd bars,
Powder'd all thick with troops of silver stars:
Her aëry vesture yet so rare and strange,
As every hour the colour seem'd to change,
Yet still the former beauty doth retain,
And ever came unto the same again.
Then fair Astraea, of the Titans' line,
Whom equity and justice made divine,   860
Was seated here upon the silver beam,
And with the reins guides on this goodly team;
To whom the Charites led on the way,
Aglaia, Thalia, and Euphrosyne;
With princely crowns they in the triumph came,
Embellished with Phoebe's glorious name:
These forth before the mighty goddess went,
As prince's heralds in a parliament,
And in their true consorted symphony
Record sweet songs of Phoebe's chastity;   870
Then follow'd on the Muses, sacred nine,
With the first number equally divine,
In virgin's white, whose lovely maiden brows,
Were crown'd with triumphant laurel boughs;
And on their garments, painted out in glory,
Their offices and functions in a story,
Emblazoning the fury and conceit
Which on their sacred company await.

For none but these were suffer'd to approach,
Or once come near to this celestial coach,   880
But these two of the numbers, nine and three,
Which being odd include an unity,
Into which number all things fitly fall,
And therefore named theological:
And first composing of this number nine,
Which of all numbers is the most divine,
From orders of the angels doth arise,
Which be contain'd in three hierarchies,
And each of these three hierarchies in three,
The perfect form of true triplicity;   890
And of the hierarchies I spake of erst,
The glorious Epiphania is the first,
In which the high celestial orders been,
Of Thrones, Cherub, and the Seraphin;
The second holds the mighty Principates,
The Dominations and the Potestates;
The Ephionia, the third hierarchy,
Which Virtues, Angels and Archangels be;
And thus by threes we aptly do define,
And do compose this sacred number nine.   900
Yet each of these nine orders grounded be
Upon some one particularity;
Then as a poet I might so infer
Another order when I spake of her.
From these the Muses only are deriv'd,
Which of the angels were in nine contriv'd;
These heaven-inspired babes of memory,
Which by a like-attracting sympathy
Apollo's prophets in their furies wrought,
And in their spirit enchanting numbers taught,   910
To teach such as at poesy repine
That it is only heavenly and divine,
And manifest her intellectual parts,
Sucking the purest of the purest arts;
And unto these as by a sweet consent,

The sphery circles-are equivalent,
From the first mover, and the starry heaven,
To glorious Phoebe, lowest of the seven,
Which Jove in tuneful diapasons fram'd
Of heavenly music of the Muses nam'd;   920
To which the soul in her divinity,
By her Creator made of harmony,
Whilst she in frail and mortal flesh doth live,
To her, nine sundry offices do give;
Which offices united are in three,
Which like the orders of the angels be,
Prefiguring thus by the number nine,
The soul, like to the angels, is divine:
And from these nines those conquerors renown'd,
Which with the wreaths of triumph oft were crown'd. 930
Which by their virtues gain'd the Worthies' name
First had this number added to their fame;
Not that the worthiest men were only nine,
But that the number of itself divine,
And as a perfect pattern of the rest,
Which by this holy number are express'd;
Nor chivalry this title only gain'd,
But might as well by wisdom be obtain'd;
Nor in this number men alone included,
But unto women well might be alluded,   940
Could wit, could worlds, could times, could ages find,
This number of Eliza's heavenly kind;
And those rare men which learning highly priz'd,
By whom the constellations were devis'd,
And by their favours learning highly grac'd,
For Orpheus' harp nine stars in heaven plac'd:
This sacred number to declare thereby
Her sweet consent and solid harmony;
And man's heroic voice, which doth impart
The thought conceived in the inward heart,   950
Her sweetness on nine instruments doth ground,
Else doth she fail in true and perfect sound.

Now of this three in order to dispose,
Whose trinary doth justly nine compose:
First in the form of this triplicity
Is shadowed that mighty Trinity,
Which still in steadfast unity remain,
And yet of three one Godhead do contain;
From this eternal living deity,
As by a heaven-inspired prophecy,   960
Divinest poets first derived these,
The fairest Graces, Jove-born Charites;
And in this number music first began,
The Lydian, Dorian, and the Phrygian,
Which ravishing in their soul-pleasing vein,
They made up seven in a higher strain;
And all those signs which Phoebus doth ascend,
Before he bring his yearly course to end,
Their several natures mutually agree,
And do concur in this triplicity;   970
And those interior senses with the rest,
Which properly pertain to man and beast,
Nature herself in working so devis'd,
That in this number they should be compris'd.
   But to my tale I must return again.
Phoebe to Latmus thus convey'd her swain,
Under a bushy laurel's pleasing shade,
Amongst whose boughs the birds sweet music made,
Whose fragrant branch-embosted canopy
Was never pierc'd with Phoebus' burning eye;   980
Yet never could this paradise want light,
Illumin'd still with Phoebe's glorious sight:
She laid Endymion on a grassy bed,
With summer's arras richly overspread,
Where from her sacred mansion next above
She might descend and sport her with her love;
Which thirty years the shepherd safely kept,
Who in her bosom soft and soundly slept;
Yet as a dream he thought the time not long,

Remaining ever beautiful and young,   990
And what in vision there to him befell,
My weary muse some other time shall tell.

Dear Colin, let my muse excused be
Which rudely thus presumes to sing by thee,
Although her strains be harsh, untun'd and ill,
Nor can attain to thy divinest skill.
     And thou the sweet Musaeus of these times,
Pardon my rugged and unfil'd rhymes,
Whose scarce invention is too mean and base,
When Delia's glorious muse doth come in place.   1000
     And thou my Goldey, which in summer days
Hast feasted us with merry roundelays,
And when my muse scarce able was to fly,
Didst imp her wings with thy sweet poesy.
     And you, the heirs of ever-living fame,
The worthy titles of a poet's name,
Whose skill and rarest excellence is such
As spiteful envy never yet durst touch,
To your protection I this poem send,
Which from proud Momus may my lines defend.   1010
     And if, sweet maid, thou deign'st to read this story,
Wherein thine eyes may view thy virtues' glory,
Thou purest spark of Vesta's kindled fire,
Sweet nymph of Anker, crown of my desire;
The plot which for their pleasure heaven devis'd,
Where all the Muses be imparadis'd,
Where thou dost live, there let all graces be,
Which want their grace if only wanting thee;
Let stormy winter never touch the clime,
But let it flourish as in April's prime;   1020
Let sullen night that soil ne'er overcloud,
But in thy presence let the earth be proud.
If ever Nature of her work might boast,
Of thy perfection she may glory most,
To whom fair Phoebe hath her bow resign'd,

Whose excellence doth live in thee refin'd;
And that thy praise time never should impair,
Hath made my heart thy never-moving sphere.
Then if my muse give life unto thy fame,
Thy virtues be the causers of the same;   1030
And from thy tomb some oracle shall rise,
To whom all pens shall yearly sacrifice.

JOHN MARSTON

The Metamorphosis of Pygmalion's Image

(1598)

Pygmalion, whose chaste mind all the beauties in Cyprus could
not ensnare, yet at the length having carved in ivory an excel-
lent proportion of a beauteous woman, was so deeply enamoured
on his own workmanship, that he would oftentimes lay the
image in bed with him, and fondly use such petitions and
dalliance, as if it had been a breathing creature. But in the end,
finding his fond dotage, and yet persevering in his ardent
affection, made his devout prayers to Venus, that she would
vouchsafe to inspire life into his love, and then join them both
together in marriage. Whereupon Venus graciously condescend-
ing to his earnest suit, the maid (by the power of her deity),
was metamorphosed into a living woman. And after, Pygmalion
(being in Cyprus) begat a son of her, which was called Paphus,
whereupon that island Cyprus, in honour of Venus, was after,
and is now, called by the inhabitants, Paphos.

I

Pygmalion, whose high love-hating mind
Disdain'd to yield servile affection
Or amorous suit to any womankind,
Knowing their wants, and men's perfection:
   Yet love at length forc'd him to know his fate,
   And love the shade whose substance he did hate.

2

For having wrought in purest ivory
So fair an image of a woman's feature,

That never yet proudest mortality
Could show so rare and beauteous a creature   10
  (Unless my mistress' all-excelling face,
  Which gives to beauty beauty's only grace),

3

He was amaz'd at the wondrous rareness
Of his own workmanship's perfection.
He thought that Nature ne'er produc'd such fairness
In which all beauties have their mansion;
  And thus admiring, was enamoured
  On that fair image himself portrayed.

4

And naked as it stood before his eyes,
Imperious Love declares his deity.   20
O, what alluring beauties he descries
In each part of his fair imagery!
  Her nakedness each beauteous shape contains,
  All beauty in her nakedness remains.

5

He thought he saw the blood run through the vein,
And leap and swell with all alluring means:
Then fears he is deceiv'd, and then again
He thinks he sees the brightness of the beams
  Which shoot from out the fairness of her eye:
  At which he stands as in an ecstasy.   30

6

Her amber-coloured, her shining hair,
Makes him protest, the sun hath spread her head
With golden beams, to make her far more fair.
But when her cheeks his amorous thoughts have fed,

Then he exclaims 'Such red and so pure white,
Did never bless the eye of mortal sight.'

7

Then views her lips—no lips did seem so fair
In his conceit—through which he thinks doth fly
So sweet a breath that doth perfume the air.
Then next her dimpl'd chin he doth descry,   40
    And views, and wonders, and yet views her still.
    Love's eyes in viewing never have their fill.

8

Her breasts like polish'd ivory appear,
Whose modest mount do bless admiring eye,
And makes him wish for such a pillowbeer.
Thus fond Pygmalion striveth to descry
    Each beauteous part, not letting overslip
    One parcel of his curious workmanship:

9

Until his eye descended so far down
That it descried love's pavilion: 50
Where Cupid doth enjoy his only crown,
And Venus hath her chiefest mansion:
    There would he wink, and winking look again;
    Both eyes and thoughts would gladly there remain.

10

Whoever saw the subtile City-dame
In sacred church, when her pure thoughts should pray,
Peer through her fingers, so to hide her shame,
When that her eye her mind would fain bewray:
    So would he view, and wink, and view again;
    A chaster thought could not his eyes retain.   60

11

He wonder'd that she blush'd not when his eye
Saluted those same parts of secrecy:
Conceiting not it was imagery
That kindly yielded that large liberty.
  (O that my mistress were an image too,
    That I might blameless her perfections view.)

12

But when the fair proportion of her thigh
Began appear: 'O, Ovid,' would he cry,
'Did e'er Corinna show such ivory
When she appear'd in Venus' livery?'   70
  And thus enamour'd, dotes on his own art,
    Which he did work to work his pleasing smart.

13

And fondly doting, oft he kiss'd her lip.
Oft would he dally with her ivory breasts.
No wanton love-trick would he overslip,
But still observ'd all amorous behests
  Whereby he thought he might procure the love
    Of his dull image, which no plaints could move.

14

Look how the peevish Papists crouch, and kneel
To some dumb idol with their offering,   80
As if a senseless carved stone could feel
The ardour of his bootless chattering,
  So fond he was, and earnest in his suit,
    To his remorseless image, dumb and mute.

15

He oft doth wish his soul might part in sunder,
So that one half in her had residence:

Oft he exclaims, 'O, beauty's only wonder,
Sweet model of delight, fair excellence,
   Be gracious unto him that formed thee,
   Compassionate his true love's ardency.'   90

16

She with her silence seems to grant his suit.
Then he all jocund, like a wanton lover,
With amorous embracements doth salute
Her slender waist, presuming to discover
   The vale of love, where Cupid doth delight
   To sport, and dally all the sable night.

17

His eyes, her eyes, kindly encounter'd,
His breast, her breast, oft joined close unto,
His arms' embracements oft she suffer'd,
Hands, arms, eyes, tongue, lips, and all parts did woo. 100
   His thigh with hers, his knee play'd with her knee,
   A happy consort when all parts agree.

18

But when he saw, poor soul, he was deceiv'd,
(Yet scarce he could believe his sense had fail'd)
Yet when he found all hope from him bereav'd,
And saw how fondly all his thoughts had err'd,
   Then did he like to poor Ixion seem,
   That clipp'd a cloud instead of heaven's queen.

19

I oft have smil'd to see the foolery
Of some sweet youths, who seriously protest   110
That love respects not actual luxury,
But only joys to dally, sport and jest:

Love is a child, contented with a toy;
A busk-point or some favour stills the boy.

20

Mark my Pygmalion, whose affection's ardour
May be a mirror to posterity.
Yet viewing, touching, kissing (common favour)
Could never satiate his love's ardency:
   And therefore, ladies, think that they ne'er love you
   Who do not unto more than kissing move you.   120

21

For my Pygmalion kiss'd, view'd and embrac'd,
And yet exclaims, 'Why were these women made,
O sacred gods, and with such beauties grac'd?
Have they not power as well to cool and shade
   As for to heat men's hearts? or is there none,
   Or are they all, like mine, relentless stone?'

22

With that he takes her in his loving arms,
And down within a down-bed softly laid her.
Then on his knees he all his senses charms,
To invocate sweet Venus for to raise her   130
   To wished life, and to infuse some breath
   To that which, dead, yet gave a life to death.

23

'Thou sacred queen of sportive dallying,'
(Thus he begins), 'Love's only emperess,
Whose kingdom rests in wanton revelling,
Let me beseech thee show thy powerfulness
   In changing stone to flesh! make her relent,
   And kindly yield to thy sweet blandishment!

24

'O, gracious gods, take compassion!
Instil into her some celestial fire,   140
That she may equalize affection,
And have a mutual love, and love's desire.
   Thou know'st the force of love! then pity me,
   Compassionate my true love's ardency.'

25

Thus having said, he riseth from the floor,
As if his soul divin'd him good fortune,
Hoping his prayers to pity mov'd some power,
For all his thoughts did all good luck importune.
   And therefore straight he strips him naked quite,
   That in the bed he might have more delight.   150

26

'Then thus, sweet sheets,' he says, 'which now do cover
The idol of my soul, the fairest one
That ever lov'd, or had an amorous lover,
Earth's only model of perfection:
   Sweet happy sheets, deign for to take me in,
   That I my hopes and longing thoughts may win.'

27

With that his nimble limbs do kiss the sheets,
And now he bows him for to lay him down,
And now each part with her fair parts do meet,
Now doth he hope for to enjoy love's crown: 160
   Now do they dally, kiss, embrace together,
   Like Leda's twins at sight of fairest weather.

28

Yet all's conceit, but shadow of that bliss
Which now my muse strives sweetly to display

In this my wondrous metamorphosis.
Deign to believe me, now I sadly say:
  The stony substance of his image feature
  Was straight transform'd into a living creature.

29

For when his hands her fair-form'd limbs had felt,
And that his arms her naked waist embrac'd,   170
Each part like wax before the sun did melt;
And now, oh now, he finds how 'he is grac'd
  By his own work. Tut, women will relent
  When as they find such moving blandishment.

30

Do but conceive a mother's passing gladness,
(After that death her only son hath seiz'd
And overwhelm'd her soul with endless sadness)
When that she sees him gin for to be rais'd
  From out his deadly swoon to life again:
  Such joy Pygmalion feels in every vein.   180

31

And yet he fears he doth but dreaming find
So rich content and such celestial bliss.
Yet when he proves and finds her wondrous kind,
Yielding soft touch for touch, sweet kiss for kiss,
  He's well assur'd no fair imagery
  Could yield such pleasing, love's felicity.

32

O, wonder not to hear me thus relate,
And say to flesh transformed was a stone.
Had I my love in such a wished state
As was afforded to Pygmalion,   190

Though flinty hard, of her you soon should see
As strange a transformation wrought by me.

33

And now methinks some wanton itching ear
With lustful thoughts and ill attention,
Lists to my muse, expecting for to hear
The amorous description of that action
    Which Venus seeks, and ever doth require,
    When fitness grants a place to please desire.

34

Let him conceit but what himself would do
When that he had obtained such a favour   200
Of her to whom his thoughts were bound unto,
If she, in recompense of his love's labour.
    Would deign to let one pair of sheets contain
    The willing bodies of those loving twain.

35

Could he, oh, could he, when that each to either
Did yield kind kissing, and more kind embracing,
Could he when that they felt, and clipp'd together,
And might enjoy the life of dallying,
    Could he abstain midst such a wanton sporting
    From doing that which is not fit reporting?   210

36

What would he do when that her softest skin
Saluted his with a delightful kiss?
When all things fit for love's sweet pleasuring
Invited him to reap a lover's bliss?
    What he would do, the self-same action
    Was not neglected by Pygmalion.

37

For when he found that life had took his seat
Within the breast of his kind beauteous love,
When that he found that warmth and wished heat
Which might a saint and coldest spirit move,   220
  Then arms, eyes, hands, tongue, lips and wanton thigh
  Were willing agents in love's luxury.

38

Who knows not what ensues? O, pardon me,
Ye gaping ears that swallow up my lines:
Expect no more. Peace, idle poesy,
Be not obscene, though wanton in thy rhymes;
  And chaster thoughts, pardon if I do trip,
  Or if some loose lines from my pen do slip.

39

Let this suffice, that that same happy night
So gracious were the gods of marriage,   230
Mid'st all their pleasing and long-wish'd delight
Paphus was got: of whom in after-age
  Cyprus was Paphos call'd, and evermore
  Those islanders do Venus' name adore.

NOTES TO THE POEMS

SAMUEL DANIEL (c. 1562-1619)

Daniel, the son of a music-master, was a Somerset man, born in a village near Taunton. In 1581 he entered Magdalen Hall, Oxford, and was tutored there by the Italian scholar John Florio, who had married his sister. He is said to have left without a degree, 'being more prone to easier and smoother studies than in pecking and hewing at logic'. In the following years he probably travelled in Europe, and he seems to have been a member of the English embassy to Paris in the critical year of 1586.

By about 1590 he was established in the Pembroke circle at Wilton, where the countess, Sir Philip Sidney's sister, was an inspiring patron of poets. Daniel was tutor to her son William Herbert, future Earl of Pembroke, to whom, and to his brother Philip, the Shakespeare First Folio was dedicated in 1623. A few years later he was at Skipton, in Yorkshire, now as tutor to the child Anne Clifford, heiress of the Earl of Cumberland, but he seems to have set his heart on a place at court, and in 1603 he greeted the new reign and the new king with a laudatory piece already prepared for the occasion.

These calculated approaches were successful, and although he was always 'at jealousies' with Ben Jonson, who superseded him as supervisor of court masques, Daniel remained at court for several years as a sort of unofficial laureate. For a time he had the duty of licensing the plays performed by the Children of the Queen's Revels, and he steadily received 'a fair salary' as a groom of the privy chamber. In fact he justly acknowledged that by good grace of James's queen, Anne of Denmark, he was able 'in quietness to eat the bread of rest'. According to Fuller's *Worthies*, he later 'turned husbandman, and rented a farm in Wiltshire, near to Devizes'. He also had a farm at Beckington in his native county, and it was there that he died and was buried in the parish church. Anne Clifford, his former pupil, erected a gracious memorial to his name.

Daniel thus had a more sheltered life than most of the Elizabethan poets. He seems never to have been in very good health, and probably he had neither the strength nor the inclination for their spendthrift Bohemianism.

For his early translations and sonnets he was hailed by Spenser as 'the new shepherd late upsprung', and in 1592 he acknowledged the compliment with his *Delia* sonnets, published together with *The Complaint of Rosamond*. *Cleopatra*, a Senecan tragedy, followed in 1594, and in the next year he published the first four books of his *Civil Wars*. At this point in his career Daniel had an indisputable influence on the artistic development of Shakespeare, who borrowed for his own sonnets the structure of three quatrains followed by a couplet which Daniel used in *Delia*, and reflected also upon the same theme of ill-rewarded love and of Beauty's helplessness before 'tyrant Time's desire'. In both form and subject *The Rape of Lucrece* owed something to Daniel's *Rosamond*, and the *Civil Wars* (of which four more books appeared before 1609, although the work was never completed) covered the same period of history, and drew the same lessons from the material, as Shakespeare's second tetralogy.

In 1599 Daniel published *Musophilus*, a philosophic poem in praise of learning and the literary life, and in *The Defence of Rhyme* (1601) he joined one of the great aesthetic controversies of the age, contending in defiance of Champion's *Art of Poesie* that English was a suitable language for rhyming verse. He held that poetry must always develop in the ways that were congenial and natural to it, and that Campion's insistence upon the imitation of classical metres would stifle its growth. Daniel demonstrated his point in the charming Horatian *Epistles* that came out in the following years.

His career was momentarily in danger when another Senecan drama, *Philotas* (1604), seemed to reflect dangerously upon Essex's recent rebellion, but he succeeded in persuading the authorities that this story about a Macedonian general who plotted against Alexander the Great was innocent of contemporary implications. Daniel produced a number of successful masques for performance at court, and he occupied his last years in a prose history of England.

In some ways Daniel was the most modern of the Elizabethans for we do not find in him the conceits, rhetorical extravagances, and artificial quaintness that tormented so much of the verse of his time. But although his fastidious mind rejected these amplifications and embellishments, he was technically master of many kinds of versification, and he wrote in a tone that was invariably sweet and stately. Critics say that he was deficient in passion and energy, but at his best he had the gift, rare in his own or any age, of writing melodiously of solemn and weighty matters. In his patriotism, his philosophic seriousness and moral elevation, he upheld the highest values of the Humanist tradition:

> unless above himself he can
> Erect himself, how poor a thing is man.

In *The Complaint of Rosamond* he bore out Spenser's prophecy that 'in tragic plaints and passionate mischance' his accent would particularly excel. The form was the complaint made familiar in *A Mirror for Magistrates*, and the story was one that had been told many times, most recently in William Warner's surprisingly popular *Albion's England* (1586–1606—some 10,000 lines of 'fourteeners').

This story, which was certainly founded on fact, was first related by Giraldus Cambrensis (*c.* 1146–1220), who was alive at the time. Rosamond was one of the six children of Walter de Clifford (*d.* 1190), she was undoubtedly Henry II's mistress, and she undoubtedly met an untimely death. Beyond that, it is impossible now to separate fact from the legendary accretions which gathered round her romantic story in its frequent retelling. Legend says that the king, jealous of his treasure, kept her in a house of 'Daedalian workmanship', hiding her in a labyrinth to which he gained access by a silken thread; and that Eleanor, his queen, presently found her way into the heart of the maze and there took her revenge. The earliest version of this part of the story says that she bled Rosamond to death in a hot bath; other lethal instruments later ascribed to her included a dagger and a bowl of poison. The chronicler Fabyan, writing early in the sixteenth century, says simply that Eleanor 'dealt with her in such manner that she lived not long after'. Daniel's version is that she made Rosamond take poison.

In his poem Rosamond returns to earth to lament that her soul cannot rest in peace until delivered from torment by the sighs of living lovers. Daniel writes in rhyme-royal, a seven-lined decasyllabic stanza rhyming *ababbcc*, which Shakespeare was shortly to use in *The Rape of Lucrece*.

The Complaint of Rosamond

l. 4 *spot:* blemish. *My kind:* the sort of person I was, my behaviour or course of action.

l. 7 *fame* is a word which Daniel uses loosely to mean good reputation, or bad reputation, infamy (as here), or report, rumour, gossip. The context always indicates which meaning is intended.

ll. 9–10 The *Elysian* fields were the resting-place after death of those who had lived virtuous lives or else were *repurified* by some form of atonement in the underworld.

l. 12 *Charon:* the boatman who ferried the souls of the dead across the Styx, the principal river of the underworld. (It is perhaps surprising to find Rosamond, an English maiden, adopting ancient Greek and Roman conceptions of the after-life.) *Waftage:* conveyance.

l. 16. *Procure this sacrifice:* persuade lovers to grieve for her, l.14.

l. 18 *life's unjust depriving:* my unjust end.

l. 19 She means here that no one any longer feels any pity or grief for her fate, although her own grief is always being reborn.

l. 22 None of the nine Muses (the goddesses of the arts) inspires poets to lament the wretchedness of her fate.

l. 23 *overpass:* ignore.

l. 25 *Shore's wife:* Jane Shore, wife of a London goldsmith, was the mistress of Edward IV. Richard III later charged her with sorcery and made her do penance. She died in great poverty some 40 years afterwards.

ll. 26–7 *The Legend of Shore's Wife*, by Thomas Churchyard, was one of the poems printed in the 1563 edition of *A Mirror for Magistrates*. Rosamond says that Jane Shore, who was just as bad a sinner as herself, found in Churchyard a poetic champion able to erase the stain of her offence (*attaint*). She hopes that Daniel will do the same for her.

l. 28 *pass'd:* to the Elysian fields.

l. 30 *Whilom:* in a former time. While she lived, her beauty was admired by all, and death causes her to bewail its loss.

l. 35 *register my wrong:* put on record the injury done to me. *Wrong* might also mean a sin committed, and this is implicit here.

l. 36 *just:* justly. Daniel is assuming the fashionable affectation of being stricken to the heart by the cruelty of woman.

l. 37 *Toil'd:* trapped, ensnared.

l. 52 Rosamond herself was beautiful when she died, and she hopes to be saved from her suffering *by the fairest* of living women, Delia.

l. 59 *deign'd to declare:* condescended to make known.

ll. 67–70 One of the recognized objects of the complaint was to act as a warning to others, particularly against the inscrutability of Fortune.

l. 79 *My birth had honour:* the Cliffords were an Anglo-Norman family who owned a castle on the Wye and estates in Herefordshire and Shropshire.

l. 84 Her fall was the more damnable because of her rich opportunities and expectations.

l. 97 *shelf:* a sandbank or a submerged ledge of rock.

ll. 99. Daniel subtly uses the form of the complaint to press the argument that Beauty is its own justification. Rosamond's beauty and tender heart were the cause of her fall, and although she occupies many stanzas in blaming herself for her natural surrender to sensuality, the poem almost asserts that her beauty, which even conquers kings, exempts her from moral censure. Stanza 15 asserts that it is not in the nature of lovely women to be unrelenting.

l. 106 *thither com'd:* there (to court) I went.

l. 108 *reviving:* awakening.

l. 110 *flower affections:* make passion grow.

ll. 113–14 The fancies of old men are chilled by the advancing years, so that they are no longer capable of the hot desires of youth.

l. 117 *I fram'd my look a liar:* I looked with an air of assumed innocence.

l. 120 *Look how:* just as.

l. 124 *rubies:* my ruby lips.

l. 127 *siren:* a nymph who lured men to destruction.

l. 131 *diapason:* concord.

l. 137 *bale:* torment. *lour:* frown.

l. 140 *admires:* beholds with wonder.

ll. 141–54 In most ages men have thus denounced artificial

aids to beauty. The Puritans in particular detested such extravagances of fashion, 'the fantastical folly of our nation'.

l. 144 *adulterate:* counterfeit, spurious.

l. 145 *Vild:* old form of vile. *eke:* also, moreover.

ll. 146–7 As Hamlet said when he picked up Yorick's skull: 'Now get you to my lady's chamber, and tell her, let her paint an inch thick, to this favour she must come' (V.i.211).

l. 175 *shame:* modesty, self-respect.

l. 176 *defends:* gives protection from.

l. 181 'Let no one think that other people are saints just because they appear so'.

l. 187 *hap:* chance, opportunity.

l. 192 *th' incompatible blood:* Henry II was born in 1133 and Rosamond's father was certainly married by 1138. So she may not have been more than a few years younger than her lover.

l. 199 *Sooth'd in their liking:* appeased in their desires.

l. 205 *Lethe:* a river in the underworld from which dead people drank and forgot their former lives.

l. 209 *serves and su'th:* submits himself and pleads.

l. 224 *conster:* understand.

l. 227 *authentic:* authoritative, entitled to respect.

l. 228 *subtilize:* argue subtly.

l. 235 *see thy hap:* perceive the opportunity that fate has given you.

l. 236 *fond respect:* foolish scruple; cf. l. 256, pedantic scruples.

l. 242 *shut thy lap:* we say that something bestowed without effort is 'laid in our lap'. Rosamond is accused of rejecting these easy gifts.

ll. 246–52 Here is the familiar argument of the sonneteers; cf. Daniel himself in one of the *Delia* poems: 'No April can revive thy withered flowers'. The old woman's speech is a typical *suasio* to unchastity, reason made 'the bawd to lust's abuse' (*Venus and Adonis*, l. 792).

l. 261 *beauty's:* three syllables.

ll. 262–3 The age-long apology for predatory man: 'It's the natural thing to do.'

l. 264 *weal:* material advantage.

l. 268 *lists:* limits, boundaries. They are *imaginary* because the temptress believes that one's honour and good name are no more than a puff of air; cf. *Hero and Leander*, I. 269–74.

l. 269 *cold severity:* bleak austerity.

l. 270 *Breath of the vulgar:* the opinion of low-bred people. (This is the old idea that respectability is only valued by the lower orders.)

l. 271 *Melancholy's opinion:* the views of dreary, puritanically minded people. *custom's relation:* conventional report.

l. 272 *To leave the sweet:* to deny oneself pleasure.

l. 274 *opinion but conceiv'd:* just an imaginary reputation.

l. 275 *without us:* external, conferred by other people.

l. 278 Many have acquired a good reputation without deserving it.

l. 281 *subtle:* cunning. These women of the town believe that the only sin is to be found out.

l. 288 *talent:* on this old woman's lips the scriptural overtone of the word is particularly obscene.

l. 291 *judge thy fact:* know the sort of person you really are.

l. 292 *closely:* secretly.

ll. 295, 297 People in high places can give pardon for sin. If the offender is eminent enough, the offence is excused.

l. 302 *stand:* base your refusal.

l. 304 'Your lack of pleasure will be compensated by the money you will receive'.

l. 308 *credit what it likes:* believe what it wants to believe.

l. 313 *make my party good:* uphold my case.

l. 318 *even in retiring:* made an orderly retreat.

l. 342 'The face in which Nature's providence has inscribed such rare excellences.'

l. 344 *constrain:* violate, force me to surrender. Whether she yields or not, the world will think she has, and will assume that the king has used his royal power to win her.

l. 350 If she refuses, the king will humiliate her, and people will still believe that she has yielded. The argument is specious and also ironic: the old woman has just urged her not to worry about her reputation, but here she does worry about it, and she still reaches the same conclusion that her temptress had intended her to reach.

l. 360 *partialize:* take sides. This completes the idea of scales being weighed in the balance: the thought of worldly advantage and pleasure brought her down on that side.

l. 363 *alleg'd:* pleaded in excuse.

l. 365 *the golden balls:* the weights in the scales.

l. 366 Until she made her decision, her course could have been easy or difficult.

l. 367 *wretchless:* reckless. *store me:* provide me with material benefits.

l. 370 *use the virtue:* exploit the inherent power.

l. 372 *train'd:* compelled to go.

ll. 379–413 Daniel is normally sparing of rhetorical embellishment, and this is one of the very few decorative passages in the poem.

l. 382 *curious:* exquisite.

l. 385 *Amymone:* one of the fifty daughters of Danaus, king of the Argives.

l. 388 *Lerna:* a marshy district in Argolis where, on another occasion, Hercules slew the Lernean Hydra.

l. 398 *careful:* sorely troubled.

l. 401 *Wrought hotter flames:* she turned from tears to passion.

l. 404 *affects to move:* to provoke desire.

ll. 405–6 This is a moral with which we have become very familiar, but it is a strange one to draw from the predicament of a girl who has been violated by a lascivious god.

ll. 409–13 *Io* was an Argive princess who was loved by Zeus. So that she might escape the jealousy of his wife Hera, Zeus changed her into a heifer. But Hera, on being informed of this metamorphosis, had her guarded by the hundred-eyed Argus, and later sent a gadfly which so tormented her that she fled in frenzy. During her wanderings she is said to have swum the Bosporus, which means ox-ford.

l. 414 In realistic terms these two stories are unlikely *precedents* for Henry to have set before his intended mistress on the eve of her *defeature*, since they describe enforced submission to rape, and not the sharing of a genuine passion. Rosamond now proceeds, most inconsistently, to draw a very different moral from the one just suggested to her by the experiences of Amymone.

ll. 419–20 So our fate may be in ourselves as well as in our stars. In the difficult matter of assessing human responsibility for predestined events, this may be as reasonable a

compromise as any. It reconciles the apparently conflict-
ing themes of the poem. See Introduction, pp. 16–17.

l. 421 *Witness the world:* let the world bear witness.

ll. 425–7 Even those who think they have been given glimpses
of the future have so often been proved false by the event
that they cannot doubt that heaven plays a decisive part
in human affairs.

ll. 431 *defend:* avert.

l. 444 'Compelled to experience the bitter-sweet pleasure that
I had never experienced before'.

l. 453 In the moment of ecstasy her senses had temporarily
deceived her. Shakespeare's 129th sonnet will explain how
she felt.

l. 461 Nature restrains our indulgence in an unfamiliar sin by
making us hate it.

l. 465 His age made him increasingly prone to jealousy.

l. 467 'Or else fearing that in time his stolen pleasures would
be made public'.

ll. 470–6 According to legend, Henry concealed Rosamond in a
house in the gardens at Woodstock and surrounded it with
a labyrinth, so that no one could reach her. The story was
related in the middle of the fourteenth century by Ralph
Higden, a Benedictine monk of Chester, who told how
Henry 'made her a house of wonderful working, so that no
man or woman might come to her'. It is also mentioned
by Scott in his novel *Woodstock*, and when Blenheim
Palace was built, there was still a subterranean maze
known as Rosamond's bower.

l. 484 *Minotaur:* a savage monster that inhabited a labyrinth
designed by Daedalus.

l. 500 *Argus:* the herdsman appointed by Hera to keep watch
on Io, see note on ll. 409–13. Hermes lulled him to sleep
with enchanting music and cut off his head, whereupon
Hera grafted his hundred eyes on to the tail of a pea-
cock.

l. 510 Her imprisonment, imposed on her by Henry's jealousy
and mistrust, was the price exacted for her unchastity.

l. 522 *to live most in sight:* to live where they can best be
seen.

l. 524 *dehort:* dissuade.

l. 530 *stay:* sustain.

l. 533 *the curious:* connoisseurs of beauty, the fastidious. The word seldom had a pejorative sense at this time.

l. 538 *discover:* reveal.

l. 542 *highly:* by someone in high estate.

l. 543 *brave:* vaunt myself.

ll. 566–7 It is an inescapable fact of court life that one can never do anything without being found out.

l. 576 *forfeit:* transgression.

l. 577 *the wronged queen:* Eleanor of Aquitaine (*c.* 1122–1204). She was formerly the wife of Louis VII of France, from whom she was divorced in 1152 on the ground of consanguinity. A few months later she married Henry, who was some ten years her junior. In 1173 he had her put under guard for conspiring with their sons to rebel against him, and after that he seems to have been at no pains to conceal his association with Rosamond. Giraldus Cambrensis says that they now lived together 'palam et impudenter' (openly and without shame). It is unlikely that Eleanor had any personal part in Rosamond's death.

l. 613 *steed:* stead, avail.

l. 615 *drench:* dose.

l. 619 *Rigour:* severity, harshness (of Eleanor).

l. 642 *Dictates:* indicates.

ll. 657–62 This is another significant reference to the due of Beauty. Its reward should not be to perish unseen and unknown; cf. stanza 74.

l. 665 *dead what thy death did:* in death she repented, but because she died alone, no one would ever know of this.

l. 680 *ingeniate:* plan, contrive.

l. 682 Were her beautiful eyes designed by Nature to be the malevolent stars that guided her evil destiny?

l. 683 *spoil:* despoil, ravage.

l. 687 At the beginning of this speech Rosamond was speaking to herself, but now she is addressing all those beautiful ladies of the court who might need to profit from her example.

l. 711 *honour:* persons of high rank, as *titles* in the next line.

ll. 713–14 Although they have husbands, they are really widows because they are deprived of real love; they are lacking (*wanting*) what formally they have, because mere shadows (wealth, rank, etc.) are not what they really desire.

l. 716 *plotting in the air:* having daydreams about the future.

l. 719 The inevitable and irreparable process of physical decay.

l. 729 *bed-brokers:* pimps, such as the old woman who gave her bad advice.

l. 740 'Who reveal the weakness of our defences'.

l. 746 *Factors:* agents.

ll. 750–1 Such women wear the false disguise of a grave demeanour and are trusted because of their venerable years.

l. 756 *revenue:* profit.

ll. 768–70 This warning against evil is her testament to women who might follow in her steps; but the degrading nature of this testament (*the example of my will*) makes her wish that she had had no such legacy to bequeath; she would rather have died intestate.

l. 774 Cf. *Romeo and Juliet*, V. iii. 94–6.

l. 775 *before his right:* death should have had no claim upon her yet, being so young.

l. 795 *affects:* emotions, feelings.

l. 808 *controll'd:* called to account.

l. 815 *to counterpoise annoy:* to compensate my hurt.

l. 816 *interdicted:* prohibited.

l. 819 The details do not matter here, but Henry II's reign was disturbed by his own reckless, intransigent spirit and by the sprawling unwieldiness of the territories he tried to control.

l. 821 *Dissension in my blood:* his sons were ambitious, quarrelsome, and disloyal. But the *jars* (disharmonies) in his bed were mostly of his own making.

l. 822 He was suspicious of the food set before him at table, fearing he would be poisoned.

ll. 825–6 Cf. *Henry V*, IV. i. 250–304.

l. 839 *Motives:* inspirations.

l. 841 This stanza may be compared with Romeo's lament for Juliet when he believes her to be dead. The poem was almost certainly earlier than the play: which shows how genius may improve upon competence.

l. 852 In fact, he lived until 1189. Nor is there any evidence that, apart from honouring her tomb, he fulfilled the

promises made in the following stanza. If he had, there
would have been no need for Rosamond to importune
Delia.

l. 859 It is said that her epitaph read thus:

Hic iacet in tumba Rosa mundi, non Rosa munda.

Non redolet, sed olet, quae redolere solet.

(Here in this grave lies a worldly Rose, not a modest
Rose. She is not fragrant but smells rank, who used to
smell so sweet.)

l. 871 She was buried by the altar at the nunnery church at
Godstow, on the Thames near Oxford. Then only a small
church, it was endowed by gifts from the king and also
from Rosamond's father, Walter de Clifford. It seems that
her mother was buried there too. In 1191 the church was
visited by St. Hugh of Avalon, the austere and saintly
Bishop of Lincoln, in whose diocese Oxford then lay.
He was scandalized to find her tomb honoured by silken
hangings, lamps, and waxen candles, and he ordered her
bones to be moved outside the church. They were later
re-buried in the chapter-house, but probably were dis-
turbed again at the Reformation.

l. 876–82 It is not Rosamond who is speaking here but the
characteristic voice of Tudor Protestantism.

l. 883–9 More pleasurably, these lines express the conviction of
all Elizabethan poets that their lines will long outlive the
grave. Rosamond hopes that they will prove to be the true
guarantee of her immortality.

ll. 890–6 The poem comes to a magnificent climax in the asser-
tion that Beauty, and the lovely memory of it, will prevail
over dumb mortality and oblivion. This is the conviction
which gives ultimate value to the poem and removes it
from the rather depressing category of the conventional
'complaint'. It is still valid even though, as here, human
frailty earns its inexorable punishment.

l. 892 In particular a reference to Spenser's *Prothalamion*, but
in general a tribute to the wonderful profusion of poets
writing in London in Daniel's time. In ll. 895–6 he regrets
that they did not receive the same patronage and encour-
agement as their Italian contemporaries, but as his own
career was to prove, this complaint was not altogether just.

l. 902 *those happy banks:* the Elysian fields.

THOMAS LODGE (*c.* 1558-1625)

Lodge was a Londoner, born at West Ham, and his father was Master of the Grocers' Company and Lord Mayor of London. He also seems to have been one of the earliest slave-traders, but his fortunes subsequently declined and he became a bankrupt.

The poet was educated at the Merchant Taylors' school in London and Trinity College, Oxford, and in 1578 he was admitted to Lincoln's Inn. But he soon abandoned law for literature and became one of the 'University Wits', a convenient label to indicate the fact that, like Lodge himself, Lyly, Nashe, Peele, Marlowe, and Greene were all university men. They were much too individualistic to form a coherent literary group, and they were not scholars in the strict sense of the term. But they were educated men all trying to make a living as professional writers, and their immense versatility, stimulated by economic pressures, made them the forcing-bed of Elizabethan literature. In the long run their greatest influence was in the theatre, because there had never previously been men of talent willing to write for the public stages, whose needs had hitherto been supplied by clowns, jugglers, and anyone capable of mouthing a few lines of ranting verse.

But this versatility also had its drawbacks. Poverty, not fame, was the spur, and it forced the University Wits, and others like them, to be too prolific for their own good. They ministered too often 'to penny-knaves' delight', and because they would put their hand to anything, they did few things supremely well.

Lodge's career illustrates this. His first published work was *Honest Excuses* (1580), a pamphlet defending poetry and drama against the psychopathic attack made by the Puritan Gosson in his *School of Abuse*. Various plays, pamphlets, and prose romances followed, but none of this can have been very profitable, for in 1588 Lodge went on a freebooting voyage to the Canaries and three years later he accompanied Cavendish on a similar expedition to Brazil. On the first of these voyages he beguiled the long days at sea by writing *Rosalynde, or Euphues' Golden Legacy*, a prose tale which is recognized as the best imitation of Lyly's intricate and highly artificial style, and also Shakespeare's only source for *As You Like It*.

It is characteristic of Lodge that he should be chiefly remembered for things that other men did better. This is true even of his poetry, for, although he wrote with great lyric charm, his *Phillis honoured with Pastoral Sonnets, Elegies and Amorous Delights* (1593) was a rather conventional contribution to a mode that had suddenly become popular, and the *Complaint for Elstred*, printed at the same time, again deferred to a prévalent, and much less rewarding, literary fashion. Most of his work for the theatre is probably lost, but *The Wounds of Civil War* and *A Looking-Glass for London and England*, this written in collaboration with Greene, do not suggest any particular talent for drama. Of his other prose romances only *A Margarite for America* shows his individual quality; and the Horatian satires in *A Fig for Momus* (1595) are neat and polished (for C. S. Lewis their style and versification were almost Augustan), but they have none of the bite and passion to be found in Joseph Hall and Marston.

Perhaps his most effective work was done in his pamphlets, because in these Lodge was most powerfully committed as a man. The early *Alarum against Usurers* (1584) shows a deep seriousness underlying the euphuistic affectations of the style. Lodge was at some time converted to Roman Catholicism, and his religious beliefs are reflected in two pamphlets published in 1596: *The Devil Conjured*, a plea for self-discipline and an attack on spurious astrology; and *Wit's Misery and World's Madness*, a sermon, presented through allegorical characters, on the seven deadly sins.

Like several other famous writers of this time, Lodge gradually turned from literature to more serious things. In about 1595 he went to Avignon to study medicine, and after returning to Oxford to take a medical degree, he practised as a doctor, mainly among his fellow-Catholics. He wrote *A Treatise of the Plague* in 1603, and the remainder of his literary output consisted of translations of the Jewish historian Josephus, the Roman philosopher Seneca, and, finally, du Bartas.

Lodge having been a writer who was content to follow literary fashions rather than initiate them, it is surprising to find that in *Scylla's Metamorphosis* he was something of a pioneer. The poem was printed in 1589 (and reissued, as *Glaucus and Scylla*, in 1610), but it was probably written some years earlier. Dedicated to 'the Gentlemen of the Inns of Court and Chancery', It started the vogue for Ovidian adaptations. Conceivably it was the first romantic treatment in verse of a classical subject, the first attempt to claim ancient mythology as a suitable topic for courtly poetry and the love complaint.

The story of Scylla existed in several forms, since mythology had a clear duty to explain the presence of dangerous rocks in the Straits of Messina, and Lodge gives an account that is loosely based on Books XIII and XIV of Ovid's *Metamorphoses*. Musing by the banks of the Thames on his own rejected love, the poet meets the sea god Glaucus, who is in a like predicament. Plaintively and lengthily Glaucus moans that the Nereid Scylla will have nothing to do with him. His grief so much distresses his mother Thetis that she invokes the help of Venus and Cupid. Cupid's darts simultaneously quench Glaucus's love and awake a belated passion in the nymph. Glaucus is now indifferent to her advances, and finally she is transformed into a submarine monster by Furies from the underworld.

The poem is in six-line stanzas, a quatrain followed by a couplet. In *Venus and Adonis* Shakespeare used the metre as well as the mode.

Scylla's Metamorphosis

l. 1 *all only:* entirely.

l. 2 *Isis' flood:* the Thames at Oxford. Following Lodge, several of the 'Ovidian' poets gave their legendary narratives an Elizabethan location. Lodge was an Oxford man and possibly wrote some of his poem there.

l. 3 'Bemoaning the things I lack, and complaining that this brings meagre comfort'. Such lamentation will continue: this is one of the most tearful poems ever written.

l. 4 *wood:* mad.

l. 5 *relenting at my moan:* softened by my grief.

l. 9 His *mother* (in this poem at any rate: there were other versions) was Thetis, a sea goddess, sister of the Nereids. She was *sad,* and so had stained or dyed the ocean with her tears, because the gods had made her marry Peleus against her will. Her son by him was Achilles.

l. 11 *frame:* make.

l. 12 *Scylla* was the nymph whom Glaucus loved—so far without response.

l. 14 Glaucus is here pictured as the shining adornment of his mother's home.

l. 20 *scope:* sphere. These two lines are an elaborate way of asking why he has allowed his peace of mind to desert him.

l. 21 *fond repent:* foolish grief.

l. 22 'And you can argue from experience of fluctuating fortune'. *Pelf:* strictly, fortune in the sense of wealth, which is often precarious.

l. 26 *straight:* immediately. The *sunny tract* is the course taken by the sun's chariot across the sky. The swift concealment of the morning sun by clouds is another example of fortune's changes.

l. 27 *pomp:* glory.

l. 29 *moist:* moisture. *take colour from his kind:* rob all things of their natural colour.

l. 30 This is the Elizabethan doctrine of Mutability, of a world endlessly ravaged by time and change. It received its finest statement from Spenser, who sought escape through the creation of a Platonic world of eternal beauty, but Lodge's remedy in this poem is that lovers should continue to exhibit constancy.

l. 31 *secret:* inward.

l. 33 To contemplate the fixed, unchanging universe (which is superior to human feeling) will soothe the agitated senses.

l. 34 *Respect:* examine.

ll. 35–6 He has grown from childhood to youth, but if youth is prematurely worn out (*forespent*), a miserable old age is the result.

l. 37 'In studying then the philsophers' learned observations'.

l. 38 *springing:* growing.

l. 39 *floats:* waves.

l. 40 *nurture:* discipline.

l. 43 *heavy:* careworn.

l. 45 *charm'd by dread:* subdued into silence by his fear.

l. 49 *channel's glide:* flowing stream.

l. 51 *dance a pleasant tide:* ripple softly.

l. 52 *weeds and sallows:* water-plants and willows.

l. 54 *fleeting ford:* swift-flowing current.

l. 56 *Themis,* like Clore and Chelis in st. 15, was a water-nymph, with perhaps the idea that she is a particularly appropriate resident of the Thames. For the various nymphs, see note on *Endymion and Phoebe,* l. 767.

l. 60 The ladies are standing waist-deep in the stream. *Tremble:* quiver.

l. 61 *featly:* neatly.

l. 62 *brightsome fairs:* shining beauties.

l. 64 When *Ariadne* married Dionysus (Bacchus), he gave her a *crown* which was later placed among the stars. *Repairs:* dwell around.

l. 67 *Nais:* in some stories the wife of Neptune. The Naiades, nymphs of lakes and rivers, were descended from her. *Bacchus' ivory touch:* Greek drama originated from the musical festivals of Dionysus, where the lutes were plucked with ivory.

l. 68 'Began to play a love-song with such sweet melodies'. In music a report was strictly a note answering or repeating another.

l. 70 *fed with such consorts:* accompanied by such harmonies.

l. 71 *the Delian harper:* Apollo, the god of music and song, born on the island of Delos.
bent: inclined, disposed.

l. 76 *prove:* put to the test.

l. 81 'When, before she could really know the bird was in the bush'.

l. 82 *woe the luck:* alas for her misfortune.

l. 83 *quick her:* hurry.

l. 85 *envious:* indignant.

l. 94 'In open agreement formulated this neat maxim'.

l. 100 *vail their crests:* lower their plumes.

l. 101 *sweet:* sweetest, i.e. they looked their loveliest.

l. 103 *passionate with painings:* moved with grief.

l. 104 *ruth:* lamentation.

l. 106 *nill:* will not. *Regard my truth:* take heed of my true love.

l. 107 *us two:* Glaucus and the poet.

l. 112 It is hard to know quite what the hills are expected to do here. Perhaps they sympathetically throw back (*store* = restore) the slender comfort available to the lovers.

l. 119 *surpris'd:* overtaken.

l. 121 *the sweet Arcadian boy:* Adonis.

l. 122 *forced:* violent.

l. 123 *pretty:* abundant. *annoy:* pain.

l. 126 *thrall:* distress.

l. 128 *her birds*: See *Venus and Adonis*, l. 1190.

l. 131 *wont:* are wont to.

l. 132 *wasteful:* destructive.

l. 133 *address'd:* Applying itself. *daw:* adaw, awake.

ll. 139–56 Lodge leaves classical mythology and finds instances in modern literature. Boiardo's *Orlando Innamorato* (1486), continued by Ariosto in *Orlando Furioso* (1552), told the story of Angelica, daughter of the King of Cathay. She was loved by Orlando (the Roland of the Charlemagne epics) but fell in love with a Moorish youth, Medoro, and married him. Sir John Harington's translation of Ariosto's poem appeared in 1591, and Robert Greene wrote a play with the same title, in which Orlando and Angelica were married.

l. 140 *Bestraught with fancy:* distraught with love.

l. 144 *rest:* interval of silence during a movement in music.

l. 150 *league:* bond.

l. 156 *amber-weeping:* amber is fossilized resin from trees.

l. 158 *Lucina:* goddess of light and of childbirth, sometimes identified with Juno and Diana.

l. 159 *her Latmian love:* Endymion, loved by Diana as the Moon. The text reads Latium, but Latmian must be intended.

l. 161 Aurora, goddess of the dawn, was in love with *Cephalus*, but he was already married and rejected her.

l. 163 *teen:* grief.

l. 165 *crosses:* afflictions.

l. 166 *fancy's power:* the bondage of love.

l. 170 *betime:* soon. *sable:* black.

l. 173 *whereas beforn:* where previously.

l. 175 *sound:* strait.

ll. 179–80 His divinity is of no avail because he is afflicted with everlasting grief.

l. 182 *coy in touching:* reluctant to touch.

l. 183 *Sibylla:* a wise woman who possessed certain prophetic books and was consulted in times of emergency when grave decisions were needed.

l. 184 *grutching:* grumbling.

l. 192 *advised:* intended. This long lament by Glaucus, which began at l. 105, is characteristic of the fashionable 'complaint' in expecting the streams, the fields and their shepherds, and all the nymphs and goddesses, to shed tears in sympathy with his grief. The pastoral convention, with its wealth of decoration and literary and mythological allusion, keeps genuine feeling at a distance.

l. 196 *Pallas' flower:* the olive was sacred to Pallas, but it is not a flower, nor particularly associated with pallor as grief.

l. 198 *languish:* grow faint, become dispirited.

l. 200 *moly:* a plant believed to have magic properties. Hermes gave it to Odysseus as a charm against the sorceries of Circe.

l. 203 *Amaranthus' flower:* the amaranth was believed to be unfading, and so to give immortality.

l. 204 *Ajax' blossom:* the hyacinth, which sprang from the blood of Ajax when he slew himself after an unsuccessful contest with Ulysses for the arms of Achilles. *stour:* time of stress.

l. 213 *vouching:* invoking.

l. 216 *doom upon:* give judgment on.

l. 219 *disdain'd:* coloured.

l. 225 *discover'd:* revealed.

l. 230 *sense:* instinct.

l. 232 *mine eyes' offence:* my tears.

l. 239 *Taurus:* mountains stretching from the Euphrates to the Aegean.

l. 240 They subdue their noisy cackle by the instinctive power (*secret art*) mentioned in l. 230.

l. 243 *prest:* eager.

l. 244 By dwelling so near to the sun they have a natural majesty.

l. 252 *wished waters of frequent:* the water where they want to settle.

l. 253 The *fond God* is Cupid, and Glaucus, himself a god, complains of the madness that love induces.

l. 255 *Whilom:* formerly.

l. 259 *Tritons:* sea monsters whose music stilled the restless waves.

l. 268 *fair:* beauty.

l. 272 *you floods can tell my chancing:* you waters can relate how it happened to me.

l. 275 *a beam of subtil firing:* a ray cunningly discharged (from her eye).

l. 284 *Hybla:* a town in Sicily famous for its honey.

l. 287 His eyes were then *judicial* because he had not previously lost his heart to anyone.

l. 295 *tenor:* quality, character. It will be observed that in these stanzas describing Scylla's beauty Lodge is neither elegant nor exact; the lines have little sensuous quality. But this may have been partly deliberate, to complement the extravagance of the preceding lamentation. The intention of the poem is largely satirical.

l. 308 *saples:* saplings.

l. 309 The *five lovely sprigs* are the fingers, each with nails like roses.

l. 313 *hide:* fail to mention.

l. 319 *Confounded with descriptions:* he is overwhelmed by the effort of listing these delights—or possibly the poet is admitting that the descriptions are themselves confused.

l. 322 *consort:* accompany.

l. 323 *these fairs attending:* her beauties.

l. 326 *Shrouded within:* concealed.

l. 328 *affect:* passion.

l. 329 *straight was flying:* was immediately elusive.

l. 341 *coying:* flirting.

l. 342 *toying:* dalliance.

ll. 349–54 The metre changes for this lament.

l. 358 *falsehood wrought my smart:* her treachery was the cause of my pain.

l. 365 *Eurotas:* the chief river of Laconia, where Sparta stood.

l. 367 'But a brief account is most appropriate for my lack of success': possibly another satirical touch, for he certainly has not been brief, and will not be.

l. 376 *fancy:* a loving disposition.

l. 388 *receipts:* shelters, retreats.

l. 394 *repair:* haunt, resting-place.

l. 398 *in view of:* within sight of.

l. 400 *to make me mickle sport:* to give me much entertainment.

l. 412 *dureless:* transitory.

l. 413 *Wanhope:* despair. He is saying that only despair gives him any comfort, and misfortune (*bad adventure*) is the only thing he can trust. His heart is entirely surrounded by grief.

l. 415 *Ate,* daughter of Eris (strife), was the deity who caused men to be infatuated and demented.

l. 422 *sequel:* narrative.

l. 423 This is a ponderous way of saying that they wept for pity.

l. 424 *his scant redress:* his slender relief (from his sufferings).

l. 427 After so long a time it is a shock to be reminded of the presence of the poet himself, whom we met at the beginning but may by now have forgotten. *bewept:* wept for.

l. 432 *fruitless fancy:* unrequited love.

ll. 433–4 The poet asks his muse to forbid him to be too discursive; because (l. 435) unnecessary pauses in a tragic narrative are a cause of pain.

l. 437 *working:* moving. *languish:* tenderness, compassion.

l. 439 *attainted:* affected.

l. 443 *Thetis:* see note to l. 9.

l. 450 *In states of worth:* in respect of your virtue and good qualities. *dote:* behave or talk in an infatuated way.

l. 451 *wend:* go.

l. 456 *by reason's level:* on a rational plane.

l. 460 *pretty:* ample.

l. 462 *amated:* dejected.

l. 466 *were not:* but for.

l. 467 *enjoy'd:* had the use of.

l. 471 'To admit that she was right and accept her advice'.

l. 477 *enur'd:* went to work.

l. 478 *vowed:* devoted.

l. 481 Venus, or Aphrodite, was believed to have been born from the sea at Paphos, a town in Cyprus.

l. 482 *conspiring:* perhaps best rendered by Shakespeare's nonce-word 'congreeing' (Henry V, I. ii. 182).

l. 483 *for whose sweet behove:* for whose tender sake.

l. 488 *Vulcan's rival:* Venus was married to Vulcan but cuckolded him with Mars; cf. l. 508.

l. 490 *twist:* garland.

l. 497 *So:* so long as.

l. 506 *Amyntas:* a shepherd-boy beloved of Venus.

l. 510 *carnation:* crimson (literally, flesh-coloured).

l. 513 *blaz'd:* emblazoned. *wrack:* ruin, overthrow.

l. 514 *Leda:* a queen of Sparta who was seduced by Zeus in the shape of a swan and bore (as eggs) Castor and Pollux.

l. 515 *her lovely son:* Cupid.

l. 522 *did shed:* was scattered.

l. 526 *that fancies bind:* this cannot be rendered literally, because a bow cannot tie loves. But the sense is plain enough: with his bow Cupid transfixes lovers and holds them fast.

l. 532 Venus had a temple at *Sestos,* see *Hero and Leander.*

l. 543 *taint:* balm, remedy. As well as being a great warrior, Achilles was taught the art of healing by the centaur Chiron.

l. 546 *cup:* used figuratively to mean lot, experience, portion; cf. 'the cup of their deservings' (*King Lear,* V. III. 304).

l. 550 *his bushy crest:* cf. l. 266, where he speaks in admiration of his 'bushy locks'. Proverbially Glaucus was bearded and shaggy.

l. 560 *kempt:* combed.

l. 561 *check'd him with his welladay:* taunted him for his lament.

l. 567 *coyly vaunts her crest:* proudly displays her colours. *Coyly* has an element of disdain; a *crest* was the figure or device worn by a knight on his helmet.

l. 569 *Palemon:* was made a sea-god by Neptune when his mother Ino jumped with him into the sea to save him from the demented wrath of his father, Athamas. He is mentioned in *The Faerie Queene* IV. xi, in the verse (13) in which Spenser also refers to Glaucus and his gift of prophecy.

l. 576 *the cause of Glaucus' blames:* the object of Glaucus's chidings.

l. 577 *the carriage of her eye:* her mien, deportment.

ll. 580–2 Clore condemns anyone who looks favourably upon a nymph who so despises avowals of love that nothing will move her disdainful heart. *lawless* means that she will not observe the rules or conventions that normally prevail in matters of love.

l. 583 *her:* the injury done to Thetis by Scylla's treatment of her son.

l. 588 *whom* refers to Scylla, the originator of her grief.

l. 595 *attainted:* affected.

l. 602 *affect:* passion. *recure:* remedy, assuagement.

l. 605 *weary with her harms:* sorely afflicted by the pangs of love.

l. 608 *stark:* unyielding. *list not prove her:* was unwilling to put her love to the test.

l. 618 *fatal haps:* dire misfortune.

l. 620 *looks for babies in his eyes:* among the poets of the time there are frequent references to the practice of lovers of looking closely into each other's eyes to see their own reflection there. This reflection was alluded to as a baby.

l. 621 *leeks:* likes.

l. 622 *envies:* hates, despises.

l. 623 *envious:* although they shared his hatred of Scylla, they could not help echoing her grief.

l. 625 *grace:* mercy.

ll. 629-30 Like the nymphs, the poet himself was affected by Scylla's suffering and almost wished to see her gain the object of her desire. The personification *Disdain* refers to her former attitude to Glaucus.

l. 633 *waits:* looks for.

l. 645 *sound:* swoon.

ll. 646-7 See note to l. 192. Poetic convention required all Nature to show sympathy in distresses of this kind.

ll. 649-50 Even Thetis is now stirred to pity.

l. 651 *lipping:* kissing.

l. 652 *nill list to moan her:* will give her no mercy.

ll. 653-4 'I who write have pity, because her distress deserves it. Hope must inevitably die when grief so intense can barely keep it alive'.

l. 656 *approved:* experienced.

l. 661 *Zephyrus:* the west wind.

l. 662 *In hapless tide:* at that unlucky time.

l. 670 *their vowed loves:* their pledges of mutual love.

l. 672 *Ca¨ster:* a river of Lydia and Ionia, famous for abundant water-fowl.

l. 681 *for want:* for his own suffering, in being neglected by his love; see l. 3. Glaucus says, by way of comfort, that time heals men's suffering, and a grief that is not admitted has little chance of earning sympathy.

l. 684 He blamed his wits because, although they had been advised of this remedy, they had failed to perceive it.

l. 685 *talk:* describe.

l. 686 *Discourse:* understanding.

l. 687 'Imagination was the ship that bore me and love was the harbour towards which I sailed'.

l. 689 *Hast:* which has.

l. 692 *The pomp of prime:* the glory of high summer.

l. 702 *the nymph:* Echo, who was personified as a nymph. When her love for Narcissus was not returned, she pined away until nothing remained but her voice.

l. 706 *sop:* bread.

l. 707 *admire:* wonder at.

l. 716 *Ditis' den:* the underworld, ruled by Dis.

l. 723 *repin'd:* muttered his displeasure.

l. 724 *Stygian:* infernal. Styx was a river of the underworld.

l. 725 *elf:* dwarf.

ll. 735–8 Her hair is turned into quicksands, her hands into rocks. There are several versions of Scylla's metamorphosis. In one she was beloved by Neptune, whose wife Amphritrite in revenge had her turned into a monster which devoured mariners. But in the *Odyssey* Homer says that Glaucus, when scorned by her, appealed to Circe to give her potions that would make her look more favourably upon him. But Circe herself fell in love with Glaucus and poisoned the fountain where Scylla went to bathe, changing her into a barking monster with twelve feet and six heads, each with three rows of teeth. On seeing her own horrifying reflection, Scylla threw herself into the sea and her teeth became rocks upon which many ships were wrecked. These rocks were on the Italian side of the Straits of Messina, opposite the whirlpool of Charybdis.

l. 741 *scout:* deride.

l. 746 *dispairing:* avoiding (the opposite of repair).

l. 747 *sirens:* monsters, part-bird and part-woman, whose singing lured sailors to destruction.

l. 753 *rest:* relief, content.

l. 755 *beck:* summons.

l. 758 *repast:* feed upon.

l. 761 *trick up:* dress. *woon:* would'n, wish.

l. 764 *bain:* vessel of water.

l. 773 *glide:* progress through the water.

ll. 777–80 These lines may be compared with Shakespeare's dedication accompanying *Venus and Adonis*, and the Latin couplet on the title-page. Lodge pledges himself to give up catchpenny writing which only brings discredit to its author, and devote himself to work which will bring him a better reputation.

l. 781 *I missay not:* I am telling you the truth. The envoy (postcript) indicates the purpose of the poem, which was to be a courtly persuasion against disdain. Coy ladies are warned that if they spurn their faithful lovers, they will share the fate of Scylla.

CHRISTOPHER MARLOWE (1564-93)

Marlowe was the son of a Canterbury shoemaker, and was educated there at the King's School and afterwards at Corpus Christi College, Cambridge. Little about his short life is definite, but at some time he joined the acting company whose nominal patron was the Earl of Nottingham (later Lord High Admiral—the company are best known as the Admiral's Men). Philip Henslowe was their business manger, and it was for their great tragedian Edward Alleyn that most of Marlowe's plays were written.

A fellow-playwright, Robert Greene, reproved Marlowe for his dangerous opinions and dissolute way of life, and in 1593 he was summoned before the Privy Council to answer charges of blasphemy brought against him by a common informer. He was accused of having said that 'Moses was but a juggler' whose tricks any competent conjuror could perform, and that the Jews acted rightly in crucifying Christ. His personal life was also criticized, and among other heterodoxies he was charged with holding that he had as much right as the Queen to mint coins, and that 'all they that love not tobacco were fools'.

But before Marlowe could answer the summons he was dead. To escape from the plague he had left London for Deptford, then a country village, and in May 1593 he was killed in a tavern brawl. Ostensibly the quarrel arose from a dispute about the bill, but Marlowe had been hired by the government as a spy, and it is possible that his death was engineered by the authorities because he had become in some way dangerous to them.

Marlowe was the first great English poet to write for the theatre. His most famous plays, *Tamburlaine, Dr. Faustus, Edward II*, and *The Jew of Malta*, all have as central characters men with high aspiring minds who sought power in one or other of its forms, conquest, knowledge, political dominion, or wealth. The plays are deficient in humour, construction, and even in humanity, and their gorgeous rhetoric is often uncontrolled. But this was a new voice in English poetry, and Marlowe's supreme achievement was to make blank verse (then a new form in England, and hitherto formal, stiff, and dull) an incomparable vehicle for dramatic speech. It could be lyrical or passionate, and with the suppleness and variety that Marlowe gave it, it could be colloquial too. With his greater technical discipline, Shakespeare later used it with a warmth and subtlety beyond Marlowe's powers; but Marlowe was the pioneer.

He acquainted himself with Ovid by translating the *Amores*, and *Hero and Leander* was essentially an Ovidian poem, even though his actual source was Musaeus, an Alexandrian poet of the sixth century. Hero was a priestess of Venus at Sestos, and Leander lived at Abydos on the opposite shore of the Hellespont. Leander used to swim the straits to visit her, Hero holding a torch to guide him. But one night he lost his way and was drowned, and Hero was so distressed that she threw herself into the sea. Ovid tells the story in *Heroides* xviii and xix.

It was a short and simple story, but Marlowe did not complete it. This may have been due to his early and unexpected death, and his *Desunt nonnulla* at the end of the second sestiad may have been a promise to continue. But there is nothing certain about that, and the artistic probabilities seem to point the other way. The poem is a pagan hymn to sensuous delight. When the lovers are united, Marlowe stops, and he might never have felt inclined to take them to the tragic conclusion that the traditional story demanded. He glories in the love that moves mountains—or in this case defies the perilous seas—and he may not have wanted to admit that it cannot ultimately defy the Fates as well.

So the poem was finished by someone else. *Hero and Leander* was registered for publication a few months after Marlowe's death, and there may have been one or two printings before the earliest surviving edition of 1598. At any rate, the poem was well known to contemporaries, and it was in 1598, the same year as the first books of his translation of Homer, that George Chapman completed it in a further 1558 lines.

Up to a point the continuation was a 'corrective' of the opening sestiads, just as *Endymion and Phoebe* may be thought to correct *Venus and Adonis*. More specifically, Chapman may have been anxious to rescue the Ovidian poem from the sort of treatment that Marston was just then giving it. Thus the story is a warning 'to shun love's stolen sports by that these lovers prove' (III. 16). 'Fear fills the chamber, darkness decks the bride' (III. 154) when lust is master, and he wants his readers to know that

> Joy graven in sense like snow in water wastes;
> Without preserve of virtue nothing lasts. (III. 35–6)

But Chapman's tone is not that of a narrow moralist. He had considerable skill in describing these 'stolen sports', and he acknowledged that beauty everywhere has this much grace, that 'It supples rigour and it lessens sin' (III. 396). It so much distressed him that youth and love and beauty would eventually have to be destroyed that on his own admission (V. 491–6) he introduced digressions to put off the hour when he must describe it.

But the 'nuptial honours' had been neglected and Chapman brings in Ceremony and Hymen to remind the lovers of their fault. In a fine appreciation of the poem (*English Literature in the Sixteenth Century*, pp. 513–16) C. S. Lewis calls Chapman's continuation 'essentially . . . a eulogy of marriage'. The lovers regard their mutual passion as sufficient justification in itself, but—and this had been the theme of Musaeus, ignored by Marlowe—'Love compels not Fate'. Ceremony addresses them in the sort of terms used by Friar Laurence when he reminded Romeo that 'violent delights have violent ends' (II. vi. 9 ff.). It is not a matter of morals only: they have neglected the ordinary civilized decencies of life by seizing so avidly on delights that merely assuage a passing hunger. In due season, and with due formality, they could have been enjoyed so much more richly.

Chapman is metaphysical, cryptic, and often clumsy, but his spirit is humane and generous. Lewis is surely right when he says that 'except for academic purposes the two parts, Marlowe's and Chapman's, should always be read together'.

Hero and Leander
First Sestiad

l. 1 *Hellespont*: the Dardanelles, the straits connecting the Sea of Marmora with the Aegean. The distance between the ancient cities of Sestos and Abydos was not much more than a mile, and it was here that Xerxes transported his army across a bridge of boats in 480 B.C. Alexander the Great also crossed at this point, and centuries later, in an attempt to relive the old legend, Byron swam it with a friend. *guilty of true love's blood:* because Hero and Leander were to die there.

l. 3 *disjoin'd:* separated.

l. 4 *hight:* named.

l. 10 *drawn:* adorned.

l. 13 *careless:* uncaring.

l. 15 *kirtle:* skirt.

l. 26 *lighten'd:* the whiteness of her neck made the stones shine all the brighter, so that they resembled diamonds.

l. 28 *to her mind:* at her wish or inclination.

l. 29 *Or . . . or:* either . . . or.

l. 31 *Buskins:* half-boots made of leather.

l. 32 *branch'd:* decorated with a figured pattern.

ll. 33–6 The idea here—as extravagant as the rest of the portrait of Hero—is that on the top of her boots she wore tiny gold and silver figures in the shape of birds; when filled with water, these would imitate birdsong as she moved.

l. 40 Cupid's mother was Venus. Hero was so beautiful that he could not distinguish her from the goddess herself.

l. 45 *Venus' nun:* Hero was a priestess in the temple of Venus at Sestos.

l. 46 *she:* Nature, who feared that Hero had robbed her of some of her own beauty.

ll. 49–50 It is because Nature was thus deprived of some of her radiance that half the world has been in darkness ever since; i.e. this was the origin of day and night.

l. 52 *Musaeus:* a Greek poet of about A.D. 500, author of a poem on Hero and Leander.

l. 54 *make greater moan:* lament more loudly.

ll. 56–8 It was to *Colchos,* or Colchis, that Jason and the Argonauts sailed to capture the golden fleece, which was guarded by a dragon. The suggestion is that Leander's hair would have been an even greater prize.

l. 59 *Cynthia:* the moon goddess.

l. 61 *Circe:* daughter of the sun, who lived on the island of Aeaea. She had magic powers which she exercised upon shipwrecked mariners.

l. 65 *Pelops*, son of Tantalus, was killed by his own father and his body was served to the gods. Only Demeter tasted the dish, and she ate his shoulder. When his body was put into a cauldron and restored to life, his shoulder was therefore missing, and Demeter replaced it with one made of ivory.

l. 70 *hardly*: with difficulty. *blazon*: literally, to explain in proper heraldic language; so to display in its proper colours.

l. 73 *orient*: resembling pearls, which came from the East.

ll. 73–6 Narcissus was so much in love with the reflection of his own beauty that he fell into the water and was drowned.

l. 77 *Hippolytus*, son of Theseus and Hippolyta, Queen of the Amazons, was renowned for his self-control.

l. 81 The soldiers of Thrace were notorious for their savagery and bloodthirsty habits. *moved with nought*: incapable of pity or any gentle emotion.

l. 85 *speaking*: eloquent, expressive.

l. 86 *brow*: often used for the features generally. *banquet*: feed on.

l. 90 *thrall*: slave; i.e. do not be so enslaved to your own beauty that no one else may share it.

l. 93 *Rose-cheek'd Adonis*: cf. *Venus and Adonis*, l. 3.

l. 98 *breathing stars*: living women who were as lovely as the stars and shone as brightly.

ll. 100–2 The sullen earth believed that the everlasting heavens were on fire, since it seemed that another Phaeton had charge of the sun-god's chariot. Phaeton persuaded his father, the sun, to allow him to drive his chariot across the sky just for one day; but he lost control of the horses, and the sun came so near to the earth as almost to set it on fire.

Marlowe says that the galaxy of beauty assembled at Sestos is so dazzling that there is almost a danger of a conflagration on earth. It is the sort of extravagant 'conceit' that he has been using about Hero and Leander. Yet such is his stylistic control that these excesses almost seem natural; there is no sense of strain, and it seems quite fitting that the world of nature should be prostrated by Hero's beauty.

l. 105 *inveigling*: enticing.

ll. 108–11 See the story of Endymion and Phoebe. *thirling:* literally, penetrating. The chariot is pictured as hurtling through the sky.

l. 111 The moon was believed to control the tides.

l. 114 After his union with a cloudy phantom which he believed to be Hera (see *Pygmalion's Image*, note to ll. 107–8), *Ixion* became the father of a Centaur, half-man, half-horse.

l. 127 *sharp satires:* here it probably just means rude lampoons, which Hero's disappointed admirers may have chalked on the walls.

l. 132 *thorough* was the original form of the adverb and preposition, still retained in the adjective.

l. 133 *As after chanc'd:* as later happened; or as was proved by the sequel. Marlowe does not name Leander here, but he does not need to: he has already established them as predestined lovers. Notice how he achieves dramatic suspense by immediately digressing into a description of the temple. He was much more skilful at this sort of description than at depicting human feelings; but we may also feel that the nature of the building is reflected in the characters' emotions.

l. 136 *discolour'd:* of different colours.

l. 137 *Proteus:* an old man who tended Neptune's flocks under the sea. He had the gift of prophecy and was able to turn himself into various shapes.

l. 146 *Danae:* the mother, by Zeus, of Perseus.

ll. 147–50 Zeus was married to his sister Hera, whose bed he left in order to seize *Ganymede*, a handsome Phrygian youth, from Mount Ida and carry him to Olympus to be cupbearer to the feasting gods. *Europa* was a Phoenician maiden whom he wooed disguised as a bull; and he also took liberties with Iris, goddess of the *rainbow*.

l. 151 *Blood-quaffing: Mars* was the god of war and therefore bloodthirsty. *Vulcan*, the god of fire, was lame because Zeus once hurled him from Olympus and he took a whole day to fall. He was the husband of Venus, who was unfaithful to him with the war-god. With the help of the *Cyclops*, one-eyed giants who helped him in his workshop in Sicily, he caught the guilty pair in an invisible net and exposed them to the ridicule of the gods.

l. 153 The destruction of Troy was due to Helen, who deserted her Greek husband Menelaus and went to Troy with her lover Paris.

ll. 154–6 *Silvanus:* a deity of the fields and forests. Cyparissus, a beautiful youth who was a favourite of Apollo, accidentally killed a sacred stag and at his own request was transformed into a *cypress*.

l. 157 *turtles:* turtle-doves, sacred to Venus.

l. 159 *Vail'd:* lowered herself.

l. 165 *relenting:* melting.

l. 166 *virtue:* strength.

ll. 167-8 In general the Elizabethans believed that human affairs were directed by destiny: Romeo and Juliet, for instance, were typical in attributing their misfortunes to the stars. But in his plays Marlowe was less orthodox. All his heroes aspire to be masters of their own fate.

l. 169 *course:* race.

l. 171 *especially:* more than the other. *affect:* favour.

l. 172 *like in each respect:* similar in all respects. Of two similar objects we prefer one to the other, and there is no accounting for such preferences.

l. 174 *censur'd:* judged, considered. Originally the word had no implication of disapproval.

l. 175 *deliberate:* take time to make up their minds.

l. 176 See *As you Like It*, III. v. 81–2.

l. 177 *but:* only.

l. 185 *parled:* spoke.

l. 186 *amazed:* in wonderment.

l. 189 *Acheron:* a river in the underworld.

l. 198 In Greece the Sophists were learned men or philosophers who gave instruction in return for payment, and their professional status was believed to influence their teachings. When Leander says that he is going to play the *sophister*, he means that he is going to furnish arguments in support of a certain course of action. In Rhetoric this was the *suasio*, or persuasion; and there is an implication that the reasoning will be specious.

l. 199 *accosted:* addressed, but with an additional sense of a physical approach, as in *coast*.

l. 199 *offence:* impropriety.

l. 200 *rude:* rough, ignorant. It was one of the devices of

Rhetoric to apologize for the supposed uncouthness of an argument that was highly subtle and sophisticated, cf. Antony in his address to the Roman mob.

l. 203 *misshapen stuff:* the meaning is not very clear, but this would seem to be a further apology for the ill-formed matter of his argument. Nor is it clear why in the next line the verb is in the plural.

l. 206 *force:* compel.

l. 210 *bending:* stooping. She is, or has been, kneeling at the altar.

l. 214 *flaring:* showy, gaudy.

l. 215 *worth:* quality, value. A diamond keeps its perfection even in a base setting.

l. 222 *Love's mother:* Venus was the mother of Cupid.

l. 230 Instruments will be tuneless (*harshly jar*) if they are neglected.

l. 233 *basest mould:* common earth.

l. 236 Money doubles itself if put out at interest.

l. 244 *drossy pelf:* worthless money.

l. 245 *earth:* here used for treasure.

l. 247 *sweet in the loss alone:* her virginity is enjoyed only if she loses it.

l. 248 *fleet:* pass away.

l. 251 *intestine broils:* civil war.

l. 258 'Although Hymen (the god of marriage) unites you in his indissoluble yoke'. *Never-singling:* never separating; i.e. joining eternally.

l. 265 We accept base metals as coinage if they bear an official stamp. Similarly we honour women if they bear the seal of marriage.

l. 270 *essence subject to the eye:* substance visible to the eye. For this argument, cf. *Complaint of Rosamond*, stanza 39.

l. 284 Men have *wrong'd Diana's name* by being impure, since she was the goddess of chastity.

l. 286 *So:* provided that. If a woman is beautiful, for that reason alone someone is sure to slander her.

l. 288 *debonair:* of gentle disposition.

l. 292 If she runs from him, her reputation will soon be blasted because (ll. 289–90) it will be assumed that she is someone else's kept woman. So she cannot win either way: sophistry designedly had this effect. Here again it is an argument that Rosamond uses to excuse her surrender, ll. 345–6.

l. 294 *heedless:* thoughtless, regardless of the consequences. So at last he is done, after nearly 100 lines, and in the latter part especially, his pleading has been sheer sophistry. For other examples, apart from those to be found elsewhere in this book, see Berowne in *Love's Labour's Lost*, IV. iii. 291 ff. and Milton's *Comus*, 706 ff.; or on a more scurrilous level *All's Well That Ends Well*, I. i. 122–64.

l. 296 In describing her eyes as *tralucent* (transparent) *cisterns* Marlowe is mocking the hyperbolic language of some of the writers of his day. This was the euphuistic style especially associated with John Lyly.

l. 300 *Love's beauteous empress:* Venus.

l. 301 *Doric music:* see note on *Endymion and Phoebe*, l. 964.

l. 302 *masques:* dramatic spectacles with music and dancing. *stern age:* the censoriousness of old age.

l. 308 *regular and formal:* observed as a matter of rule and convention.

l. 312 *put:* incited. *mo:* more.

l. 313 *reinforce:* give further support to.

l. 321 'Stony-hearted Pallas rejoices in living alone'. Pallas Athene, or Minerva, was the goddess of wisdom, usually represented as the goddess of virginity whose heart was inaccessible to love.

l. 325 Her *avarice* would be to hoard her beauty for her own delight alone, cf. *Venus and Adonis*, ll. 157–60.

l. 326 *nice:* coy.

l. 332 *jar:* be out of tune, and so quarrelsome.

l. 335 *evilly:* michievously.

l. 336 *would be:* wanted to be.

l. 346 *whist:* hushed.

l. 349 *Morpheus:* the god of dreams.

l. 353 *beldame:* old woman.

l. 356 *apish:* like a monkey, chattering, foolish.

l. 362 *assays:* attempts.

l. 371 *enrag'd:* maddened by passion.

l. 377 *Destinies:* the three goddesses who determined the fate of mankind.

l. 378 *languishment:* distress. Cupid grieves for the lovers because he knows that unless he can soften the hearts of the implacable Destinies, they are doomed to suffer.

ll. 385 ff. This digression into a mythical anecdote is very Ovidian. In explaining why the Fates are hostile to lovers, it hints at the unhappy sequel.

l. 387 *Argus*, who had a hundred eyes, was set to guard Io (beloved by Zeus and now turned into a heifer), but *Mercury* (Hermes) *enchanted* him with his lute and then cut off his head. It was one of the 'precedents' offered to Rosamond by her royal lover; see stanza 59.

l. 389 *careless*: disordered.

l. 392 *gloze*: talk speciously (like a sophister).

l. 396 *silver tincture*: lustrous complexion.

l. 398 *snaky rod*: the caduceus, Mercury's wand, with two serpents twined round it.

l. 402 *her fancy to assay*: to try to win her love.

l. 411 *Elysium*: the abode of the blessed after death, used figuratively for extreme happiness.

l. 412 *dower*: endowment.

l. 415 *fury*: passion.

l. 437 *he*: Jove. *inly*: in his heart.

l. 438 *Prometheus* stole fire from heaven and taught men other useful arts.

l. 439 *him . . . he*: Hermes.

l. 440 *cheer*: face, expression.

l. 444 *adamantine*: hard, pitiless, impervious to feeling.

l. 446 *deceitful*: crafty.

l. 447 *knife*: the Destinies had shears with which they snapped the thread of human life.

l. 449 *feather'd feet*: Mercury wore winged sandals which enabled him to travel with the speed of wind.

ll. 449–50 The Destinies were the daughters of Erebus (darkness) and Night, and Erebus was himself the son of *Chaos* (primeval space). To win Mercury's favour the three sisters laid at his feet death-dealing contrivances (*engines*) which had been brought up from Chaos.

l. 452 Jove dethroned Saturn, his own father.

l. 453 *presently*: immediately.

l. 455 *Ops*: wife of Saturn.

l. 458 *Stygian empery*: the underworld.

l. 460 *he*: Mercury.

l. 465 *but that:* were it not that. *Learning:* Mercury was, among other things, the author of many inventions, including music, astronomy, numbers, and the alphabet.

l. 471 A demonstration characteristic of myth. Because of this particular sin of Mercury, all his followers have to share his punishment.

l. 472 *boor:* countryman, peasant.

l. 475 *Midas' brood:* gold.

l. 477 *in aspiring:* ambitious.

l. 480 *surpris'd:* captivated.

l. 481 *lofty servile clown:* low-class peasant who gets above himself.

l. 482 *encroaching guile:* intrusive cunning.

l. 483 'Then do not wonder that Cupid's cause did not fare any better'.

Second Sestiad

l. 1 *sad:* grave.

l. 9 *parley:* conversation. *light:* loose.

l. 10 Her flight is *idle* (worthless, foolish) because she is always looking over her shoulder and does not really want to leave him.

l. 12 *train:* decoy.

l. 13 So he is a *novice* in practice (just as she is *with love unacquainted*), despite the accomplished skill of his earlier arguments. We do not have to look for consistency in myth, but in fact it would have been quite possible for an educated Elizabethan youth to have mastered these arguments as a rhetorical exercise without necessarily having any personal experience.

l. 26 *affied:* pledged.

l. 27 *look how:* just as.

l. 32 *peis'd:* weighed; where love is equally reciprocated.

l. 33 *rashness:* violent and powerful feeling; not necessarily with the modern sense of being ill-considered.

l. 40 *beguil'd:* cast a spell upon, with a slight implication of cheating or deceiving. Perhaps the best rendering here is 'teased'.

l. 43 *jealous:* anxious.

l. 46 *Salmacis:* a nymph who fell in love with a handsome boy called Hermaphroditus. The story, from *Metamorphoses*

Q

IV. 285–388, was retold in *Salmacis and Hermaphroditus* (1602), probably by Francis Beaumont; a poem in rhymed couplets which has very much the same attitude to the material as *Hero and Leander*.

l. 51 *Aesop's cock:* Aesop, a Greek who lived about 570 B.C., wrote some classic fables about animals, to which many spurious additions were made in later centuries. On finding a rare jewel, the cock observed that no doubt the owner would have been glad to recover it; but himself he would rather have a grain of corn than all the jewels in the world.

l. 56 *appetence:* desire.

l. 57 *wanting:* lacking. Animals act instinctively, not having the means to communicate with one another rationally.

l. 71 *cunningly:* eloquently.

l. 73 *a kind of granting:* apparent acquiescence. *put:* inflamed.

l. 75 *Tantalus:* see note on *Venus and Adonis*, l. 599.

l. 76 *seeming lavish:* although appearing to be generous.

l. 83 *though:* that.

l. 87 *Morn:* every morning Aurora, goddess of the dawn, drove up to Olympus to announce the ending of the night. Her *lover* was Tithonus.

l. 88 *weeds:* garments.

l. 92 *suddenly:* hastily.

l. 94 *use:* are accustomed.

l. 104 *habit:* dress.

l. 107 *largely:* widely.

l. 108 'Nor could the boy stop himself wearing'.

l. 113 *incorporeal Fame:* disembodied rumour.

ll. 115–16 The wind may be thought of as feathered because it is swift, but the idea here is that its progress is slowed by its contact with earth. *reeking:* giving off vapour (a verb used of Venus in moments of passion).

l. 117 Because his heart and mind were still with Hero and Sestos.

l. 120 *Alcides-like:* Alcides was a name for Hercules.

ll. 123–5 *diameter:* full extent, from one side to the other. When the full glare of the sun blazes on an object, it is set on fire; but from the side, i.e. when it is not directly overhead, the sun's heat is more temperate.

l. 133 *discovers:* reveals. If love is not thus evident, it means that the lovers are only half-hearted.

l. 135 *apparently:* clearly.

l. 141 See note on *Venus and Adonis,* l. 324.

l. 143 *ringled:* ringed.

l. 144 *Checks:* strikes. *submissive:* yielding.

l. 150 *toiling:* because it is rough, the water gives an appearance of exertion.

ll. 155–6 The *god* is Neptune, and *Triton,* his son, played on a trumpet made of shells to soothe the waves.

l. 157 *Ganymede:* a handsome mortal who was taken to Olympus to replace Hebe as the gods' cup-bearer.

ll. 159–64 The absence of feeling here has often been remarked upon. Leander must experience various emotions of shock and terror at being suddenly pulled below the surface, but they are not described. Instead there is just a picture of the sea-bed and its occupants, and they—significantly—are only interested in love. *careless sort:* uncaring way.

l. 172 *triple mace:* trident.

l. 172 *Which:* the waves.

l. 179 The Hellespont was named after *Helle,* who fell into the water there and was drowned. With her brother Phrixus she was riding through the air on a ram from which the golden fleece was later taken.

ll. 181 ff. The unsubtle advances of Neptune reinforce the erotic theme by showing that even the gods are subject to this powerful emotion; cf. l. 202.

l. 200 *satyrs, fauns:* see *Endymion and Phoebe,* l. 13 and l. 161. *up-staring:* wild-eyed.

l. 203 *Thetis:* a sea deity, mother of Achilles.

l. 212 *for darting it:* because he had used it as a dart.

ll. 215–18 This little piece of sententiousness burlesques the common trick of inserting a few lines of philosophical reflection in Ovidian narrative. It was Ovid's own habit of introducing such precepts that helped to recommend him to the serious-minded Golding (see pp. 3–4) But Marlowe overworks the joke when he plays it again three lines later, and again at ll. 225–6.

l. 223 'So in order to capture Leander's affection'.

l. 233 *timbrel:* an instrument resembling a tambourine.

l. 234 *crooked:* the dolphin, which was sacred to Neptune, had a curved back.

l. 242 *lawn:* the fine linen of her dress—no doubt diaphanous.

l. 250 *cheerly:* enthusiastically.

ll. 254 seq. There is deliberate irony here. Although Hero's bed is only *lukewarm*, presumably reflecting her undecided emotions, it is yet warm enough to excite the dispirited. *fet:* fetched. *base-declining souls:* sinking spirits. *dreary:* dire, cruel.

l. 260 *sallow:* pale.

l. 261 *Actaeon*, a famous huntsman, came upon *Diana*, the moon goddess, bathing with her nymphs. She changed him into a stag and he was devoured by his own hounds.

l. 266 *coverture:* coverlet, shelter.

l. 270 The three Harpies were fabulous monsters, with women's bodies but the wings and claws of birds, who carried off people and property. They thus became symbols of rapacity, and this is hardly an appropriate image here. Marlowe's intention would best be covered in some vernacular phrase suggesting that Hero began to act bitchily.

l. 274 *emphal'd:* surrounded.

l. 277 *Sisyphus toil'd in vain* because his punishment in the underworld was to push uphill a block of stone which always rolled down again.

l. 284 *alarm:* alarum, summons to battle.

l. 293 *Treason:* because she always intended to surrender to the enemy.

ll. 297–8 The eleventh labour of Hercules was to steal the golden apples from the garden of the *Hesperides*, see note to *Endymion and Phoebe*, l. 42.

ll. 301–2 Compare l. 1428 of Marlowe's play *Dr. Faustus*, where this erotic thought is used with striking effect in a very different context.

l. 305 *Erycina:* Venus. There was an ancient temple to Venus on Mt. Eryx in Sicily.

l. 309 *charily:* cautiously.

l. 320 *glims:* gleams.

l. 321 *this false morn:* the light from her countenance.

l. 325 *admiring:* wondering.

l. 326 *Dis*, or Pluto, the god of the underworld, was also the giver of wealth.

l. 329 *Hesperus:* usually the evening star but sometimes, as here, the morning star.

l. 331 *harbinger:* forerunner.
l. 334 *Dang:* drove violently.
    Desunt nonnulla: to be continued.

WILLIAM SHAKESPEARE (1564-1616)

In his own lifetime Shakespeare was at least as well known for his poems as for his plays. By 1617, a year after his death, there had been eleven registered editions of *Venus and Adonis* (there were five more by 1640), and six of *The Rape of Lucrece*.

Venus and Adonis first appeared in 1593, the printer being Richard Field, another Stratford man who came to London to earn his living. In a brief dedication to a fast-living young nobleman, the Earl of Southampton, Shakespeare describes the poem as 'the first heir of my invention', and promises to devote 'all idle hours' to the production of 'some graver labour'.

This graver labour was *The Rape of Lucrece*, dedicated to Southampton in the following year, and the idle hours were imposed on him by the forced suspension of his dramatic work: from August 1592 to April 1594 the London theatres were closed by a prolonged outbreak of plague. 'The first heir of my invention' has been more variously explained. The phrase was a discreet compliment to Southampton even if it was not strictly true. Some of Shakespeare's plays had already been acted and he was not, as older critics liked to suppose, here confessing that these plays were mere revisions of other people's work. None of them had yet been published, and in any case plays were the property of the companies who acted them, not of the men who wrote them.

He probably means, therefore, that while the poem was not the first work he had written, it was the first that he wished to be taken seriously. Mere playwriting was then an ill-regarded and ephemeral occupation. In turning to the popular fashion for narrative poetry he was perhaps aspiring to more substantial rewards and a higher kind of fame.

This is suggested by the couplet from Ovid's *Amores* that appeared on the title-page of the poem:

> *Vilia miretur vulgus; mihi flavus Apollo*
> *Pocula Castalia plena ministret aqua.*

Let vulgar people admire vulgar things. For me may golden-haired Apollo provide cups full of water from the Castalian spring (the fountain from which the Muses drank in search of inspiration).

Shakespeare seems to be apologizing for his past and pledging himself to more dignified undertakings than the hack-work of the professional stage.

None the less he returned to it as soon as the theatres opened again; and although the upstart actor-playwright from the midlands is here claiming attention for a self-consciously literary work in the current poetic mode, *Venus and Adonis* is unmistakably the production of a natural dramatist. The characters present themselves directly through speech (623 of the 1194 lines are dialogue); brief passages of description resemble the scene-setting devices of a theatre that functioned without artificial lighting or painted canvas; and in a mere six lines the opening stanza briefly disposes of the setting and establishes at least three major facts about the principal characters. In the same way Shakespeare the dramatist would get the action moving in a few sharp lines of dialogue.

The poem is written in six-line stanzas, a quatrain followed by a couplet. This was the metre used by Sidney in some of the verses in *Arcadia*, at times by Spenser, notably in *Astrophel*, his pastoral elegy on the death of Sidney, and by Lodge in *Scylla's Metamorphosis*.

Shakepeare's principal source was Book X of Ovid's *Metamorphoses*, lines 510-62 and 705-39, although he departs from Ovid in making Adonis refuse to be seduced. This reluctance may, however, be found in Ovid's story of Salmacis and Hermaphroditus (IV. 285–388). The episode of Narcissus and Echo (III. 341–510) was a further source. As well as reading Ovid in the original, Shakespeare was probably familiar with Golding's translation and with Spenser's treatment of the Adonis story in *The Faërie Queene*.

Venus, identified with the Greek Aphrodite and the Syrian Astarte, was the Roman goddess of love and beauty. She was given in marriage to Vulcan, but betrayed him for Mars and other gods. She also became enamoured of various mortals, including Adonis, and Anchises, the father of Aeneas.

Adonis, whose story was told by Theocritus, was identified

with the Assyrian Tammuz, the god who represented the decay and growth of natural life. For part of the year he descended into the nether world, but each year in the spring his bride Astarte brought him back to earth. In the Greek version of the story the grief of Aphrodite at his death was so great that the gods of the lower world allowed him to spend six months of every year with her on earth.

Shakespeare does not take the story as far as this. In his poem Venus falls passionately in love with the beauty of the young Adonis and detains him from the chase. But although she woos him ardently, he will not yield to her love, which he denounces as an unworthy passion. She then pleads with him to meet her on the following day, but he has promised to hunt the boar and will not be dissuaded. When the morning comes she hears his hounds at bay and tearfully goes to look for him. She finds that he has been killed by a boar, and the poem ends with his transformation into a flower.

Venus and Adonis

l. 3 *Rose-cheek'd Adonis:* Marlowe uses the same epithet in *Hero and Leander* (I. 93). The earliest extant edition of this was printed in 1598, but it was entered in the Stationers' Register in 1593, a few months after Marlowe's death, and there may have been earlier lost versions. So it is impossible to say which poem is the earlier. Probably they were written almost simultaneously, and as the two poets were acquainted through their work for the theatre (and see *As You Like It*, III. v. 81–2), they may have been familiar with each other's work in manuscript.

The colour of the face, and its rapid alternation of red and white under the stress of fear and excitement, occurs frequently in the poems in this book as a means of indicating emotion. It is especially common in *Venus and Adonis*. Even in the first stanza there are three references to the face.

l. 5 *amain:* in all haste.

l. 9 *Stain to:* one who so far eclipses others that he almost seems to put a blemish on them.

ll. 11–12 Nature, which struggled to surpass herself when she made Adonis, decrees that when he dies the world will come to an end.

l. 15 *meed:* reward.

l. 18 *set:* seated.

l. 19–21 Compare with *Antony and Cleopatra*, II. ii. 243–6, where the ideas of variety, appetite, and satiation all occur in the famous tribute of Enobarbus. In an article in *Shakespeare Survey 15* (1962) Adrien Bonjour suggestively indicates a number of resemblances between Venus and Cleopatra, e.g., the wind that fans the dying coal; Antony, the man of war, is ensnared by Cleopatra as Mars was ensnared by Venus; Venus and Cleopatra are both composed of the lighter elements of air and fire. Bonjour finds that Cleopatra is Venus transmuted, so that the vilest things become themselves in her, and even the priests bless her when she is riggish.

l. 20 In spite of the abundance of her kisses she will make him hungry for more.

l. 25 *sweating palm:* regarded as a sign of lust. Adonis is out hunting and naturally is hot with exercise, but Venus interprets this in accordance with her own lascivious desires.

l. 26 'The token of vigour and high spirits'.

l. 30 *Courageously:* lustfully.

l. 34 *unapt to toy:* disinclined to dally amorously.

l. 40 *prove:* put to the test.

l. 43 'No sooner was he down than she was at his side (*along*).'

l. 47 *with lustful language broken:* her words are interrupted by the 'lustful language' of kisses.

l. 53 *miss:* offending behaviour.

l. 55 *sharp by fast:* made eager by hunger.

l. 56 *Tires:* tears ravenously, feeds.

l. 61 *content:* acquiesce.

l. 64 *grace:* gift from the gods.

l. 66 *distilling:* falling in small drops.

l. 67 *Look how:* just as.

l. 69 His *resistance* is *aw'd* (overcome by his fear) because he he is mortal and she a goddess.

l. 71 *rank:* copious, full.

l. 82 *take truce with:* comes to terms with (contrasted with *contending*).

l. 86 *divedapper:* the dabchick or grebe, a timid water-bird. This is one of the many beautiful country images in the poem which have persuaded some critics that it was written at home in Warwickshire before Shakespeare came to London. This is unlikely. His boyhood memories of the midland countryside stayed with him all his life, and there are several passages which suggest his familiarity with town life and the literary world of London.

l. 90 *winks:* shuts his eyes, flinches.

l. 98 *god of war:* Mars, who had been one of her lovers.

l. 100 *jar:* broil.

l. 104 *uncontrolled crest:* unconquered helmet. Other meanings may suggest themselves.

l. 119 *there thy beauty lies:* because it is reflected in her eyes.

l. 124 *is not in sight:* cannot be overlooked by others.

l. 127 *tender spring:* downy hair.

l. 129 *advantage:* opportunity.

ll. 130–2 This is the familiar theme of 'Gather ye rosebuds while ye may'. Poets have always liked to compare the transience of human beauty with flowers that lose their bloom. See Introduction, pp. 11–14.

l. 135 *O'erworn:* worn out with age. *rheumatic:* the stress is on the first syllable.

l. 140 *grey* eyes were thought to be particularly attractive.

l. 142 *marrow:* strength, vitality.

l. 142 *moist hand:* cf. l. 25.

l. 148 *footing:* footprint. Being a goddess, she would leave no mark upon the sand; cf. l. 152, where the *forceless* (strengthless) primroses sustain her weight.

ll. 157–8 'Are you in love with your own beauty? Can your right hand find love by clasping your left?' These questions are inept, since it was unawareness, not self-love, that made Adonis unsatisfactory from the goddess's point of view.

ll. 161–2 *Narcissus* was a youth so beautiful that he fell in love with his own reflection in the water and was drowned when trying to embrace it.

l. 166 'Things which grow just for their own satisfaction frustrate the purpose of growth'.

l. 167–74 The belief that handsome men have a duty to breed children, and so preserve their beauty by reproducing it, was the theme of several of Shakespeare's sonnets, especially 1 to 17.

l. 177 *Titan:* the sun god, who drove a team of horses across the sky.

l. 181 *sprite:* spirit, mood.

l. 183 'His scowling expression darkening his handsome looks'.

l. 185 *Souring his cheeks:* giving him a sullen look.

l. 188 *bare:* threadbare, and so thin and insufficient.

l. 200 *relenteth:* is softened (by the constant dripping of water).

l. 202 *want of love:* love that is not reciprocated.

l. 204 *died unkind:* would have died without ever yielding to a lover. Adonis's parents were Cinyras, son of Apollo and king of Cyprus, and his daughter Myrrha. She was supposed to have been turned into a myrtle before his birth.

l. 205 *contemn me this:* contemptuously refuse me this favour.

l. 216 *even by their own direction:* on their own initiative, without being instructed.

l. 220 'Even though she is judge in love's disputes, she cannot plead her own cause successfully'.

l. 222 *her intendments break:* interrupt what she intended to say.

l. 229 *Fondling:* foolish one.

l. 230 In the clasp of her fair arms.

l. 235 *relief:* sustenance.

l. 236 *bottom-grass:* grass that grows in low valleys.

l. 240 *rouse:* stir an animal from its lair.

l. 243 *if himself:* so that if he himself.

l. 247 The *caves* and *pits* are Adonis's dimples.

l. 251 *in thine own law forlorn:* wretched in the kingdom where you should be sovereign.

l. 260 *breeding:* on heat. *jennet:* a small Spanish horse. *lusty:* vigorous. The digression on the jennet and the courser (a much larger horse) resembles the sub-plot which Shakespeare introduces into his plays to comment on the main action. Here the directness of the incident reflects ironically on Venus's long-winded and unsuccessful wooing.

l. 272 *compass'd:* arched. *crest:* neck. *stand:* plural because the mane consists of many hairs.

l. 276 *courage:* lust.

l. 277 *as if he told the steps:* with measured pace.

l. 279 *curvets:* prances on his hind legs.

l. 289 *Look when:* as when.

l. 295 *shag:* shaggy.

NOTES TO THE POEMS

l. 299 *Look what:* whatever.

l. 303 *To bid . . . a base:* to challenge. The reference is to the country game of prisoner's base.

l. 310 *strangeness:* estrangement, aloofness.

l. 314 *vails:* lowers.

l. 320 *unback'd;* not broken to a rider.

l. 321 *Jealous of catching:* afraid of being caught.

l. 324 Thus the human is echoed, with differences, in the animal kingdom. Like Marlowe in *Hero and Leander:* (II. 141–5), Shakespeare uses the horse as a symbol of the passion that can overcome reason. The ability to 'manage' a horse was equated with discipline and self-control, and Shakespeare was to make significant use of the idea to show how Prince Hal had conquered his youthful unruliness and was now master of his passions, *1 Henry IV.* IV. i. 104–10. But in the present context the purpose of the digression is perhaps to show how Adonis, having rejected Venus's arguments in favour of love, is offered an illustration by the natural uninhibited action of the horses. Even Spenser acknowledges that, under the influence of Venus, animals 'in generation seek to quench their inward fire' (*Faerie Queen* IV. x. 45–6).

l. 325 *swoln with chafing:* puffed with anger.

l. 326 *Banning:* cursing.

l. 331 *stopp'd:* filled with coal and closed. *stay'd:* blocked.

l. 336 *the heart's attorney:* the tongue, which presents the hearts's pleading.

l. 339 *angry:* flushed.

l. 342 *askance:* with a sidelong glance.

l. 343 *wistly:* attentively.

l. 347 *by and by:* the next moment.

l. 359 *his:* its. The reference is to the practice of the early theatres where the action was sometimes mimed before the scene began and the players' gestures were interupted by the Chorus, see *Hamlet,* III. iii.

ll. 361–6 In her discussion of the poem (*Shakespeare and Elizabethan Poetry*, 60–4) Miss M. C. Bradbrook remarks upon Shakespeare's boldness in using the cold whiteness of the lily, snow, ivory, and alabaster, all symbols of chastity, in a blatantly sensuous context.

l. 367 *the engine of her thoughts:* her tongue.

l. 368 *this mortal round:* the earth.

l. 370 *thy heart my wound:* your heart wounded as mine is.

l. 372 *bane:* destruction.

l. 376 *grave:* cut into.

l. 388 *suffer'd:* if allowed to get hot. See note on ll. 19–21.

l. 391 *jade:* a common nag.

l. 393 *his youth's fair fee:* the reward justly owed to his youth.

l. 396 *Enfranchising:* setting free.

l. 411 *'Tis much to borrow:* it is a serious matter to borrow love.
   owe: undertake the obligation.

l. 412 'My feeling towards love is only a desire to make it contemptible'.

l. 414 *all but with a breath:* all in the same moment.

l. 417 If blooms are picked or cut while they are still growing.

l. 419 *back'd and burden'd:* made to bear the weight of a rider.

l. 420 *pride:* mettle.

l. 424 *alarms:* attacks.

l. 426 *battery:* successful assault.

l. 430 *now press'd with bearing:* I am now overcome with the
   weight of it. Hearing him talk has made her suffering
   intolerable.

l. 443 *stillitory:* still.

l. 446 *the other four:* i.e. the senses.

l. 456 *flaws:* sudden gusts of wind.

l. 457 *ill presage:* bad omen. *advisedly:* carefully.

l. 471 *wittily:* ingeniously.

l. 472 *Fair fall:* good luck to.

l. 480 *so:* so long as.

l. 490 *his brow's repine:* the discontent he shows in his face.

l. 497 *death's annoy:* deathlike grief.

l. 500 *shrewd:* hard.

l. 506 She prays that the crimson livery or uniform of his lips
   shall never wear out.

l. 507 *verdure:* freshness.

l. 508 The poem was written during the *dangerous year* of
   1592–3, when there was a very serious outbreak of plague
   (*infection*) in London.

l. 509 *writ on death:* prophesied a fatal epidemic.

l. 514 *use good dealing:* trade honestly.

l. 515 *slips:* counterfeit money.

l. 516 *thy seal manual:* the impression of your seal.

l. 523 *owe:* bear.

l. 526 Every fisherman throws back the little fish.

l. 538 *The honey fee of parting:* the sweet reward that is due at parting.

l. 540 *Incorporate:* united in one body.

l. 550 *insulter:* one who exults in his triumph.

l. 551 Venus's *vulture thought* is one of several images that Shakespeare uses to represent her as a bird of prey, e.g. the eagle simile, ll. 55–60. It is the fate of Adonis the dedicated hunter to be himself hunted throughout the poem, first by Venus and then by the boar; and both are devourers. The story of Wat the hare (679 ff.) is a further comment on his situation.

l. 554 *fury:* passion. *forage:* eat ravenously.

l. 555 *reek* and *smoke* both have the meaning of 'give off moisture', i.e. sweat with desire. See note to l. 25.

l. 556 *careless:* reckless, unheeding.

l. 557 *Planting oblivion:* making her forget everything else.

l. 562 *froward:* spoiled, peevish. *still'd with dandling:* quietened by being picked up and cosseted.

l. 564 *listeth:* would like to have.

l. 568 *whose leave exceeds commission:* which takes more than has been laid down or prescribed.

l. 570 *when most his choice is forward:* when the object of his choice is being particularly perverse.

l. 583 *waste:* pass, spend.

l. 586 *match:* agreement.

ll. 589–96 It is ironical that it is through the sudden, uncontrolled gestures of fear that she comes as near to her desire as she will ever get.

l. 595 *lists:* the space enclosed for tilting on horseback. The idea of love as a tournament was a common one.

l. 597 'All that she experiences is only in her imagination'.

l. 599 *Tantalus* was punished in Hades by the torment of seeing fruit and water recede beyond his grasp just as he was about to eat and drink: hence 'tantalize'.

l. 600 *clip:* surround, embrace. *Elysium* was the abode of the blessed after death, often used figuratively for perfect happiness.

l. 602 They gorge their eyesight, but their bellies are starved.

l. 608 'She has attempted as much as may be experienced'.

l. 610 The line states one of the principal themes of the poem. But the detached irony of ll. 607–10, with the narrator standing at a distance from the action, will not allow her predicament to be tragic. A certain comic pathos is all that he grants her.

l. 612 *reason:* right. This couplet, with similar passages (e.g. ll. 523–8) has led some critics to observe that Adonis betrays himself as a country boy ill at ease in the presence of a fine lady. Hallet Smith (*Elizabethan Poetry*, p. 86) describes him as 'something of an adolescent lout' who does not know his way around; adding (p. 88) that this is a handicap he shares with his creator, whose 'rusticity shows through'.

l. 616 *churlish:* savage.

l. 617 *tushes:* tusks. The boar sharpens them although they have never been covered by a sheath, as swords were.

l. 619 *bow-back:* arched back. *battle:* figurative for the armament of bristling spikes mentioned in the next line. This stanza should be compared with Golding's translation of *Metamorphoses*, VIII. 375–9.

l. 622 *sepulchres:* holes in the ground—as tombs for his victims.

l. 626 *proof:* may be noun or adjective, suggesting impenetrability.

l. 628 *venter:* venture. Although the spelling was needed for the rhyme, this was the usual pronunciation of the word in Shakespeare's day.

l. 635 *at vantage:* in a favourable position to himself.

l. 636 *roots:* digs up with his snout.

l. 637 *cabin:* beast's lair, cave.

l. 639 *danger:* power to do harm.

l. 641 *not to dissemble:* to confess the truth.

l. 645 *downright:* could mean either 'on the spot' or 'immediately'.

l. 649 *jealousy:* mistrust, suspicion, apprehension of evil. It falsely pretends to be the protector of love or the loved one. Jealousy is similarly denounced by Daniel's Rosamond, ll. 491 ff.

l. 653 *distemp'ring:* disturbing.

l. 655 *bate-breeding:* causing dissension.

l. 656 The canker in the rose, destroyer of youth and beauty, was a frequent and deeply-felt image in Shakespeare's work.

l. 667 *indeed:* in reality, if you were really dead.

l. 668 *at th' imagination:* at the very idea of it.

l. 670 *divination:* the gift of prohecy.

l. 671 *my living sorrow:* a grief to me for the rest of my life.

l. 672 *encounter with:* meet as an adversary.

l. 674 *Uncouple:* release the hounds (which were leashed in pairs).

l. 678 *well-breath'd:* sound in wind.

ll. 679–708 These famous lines about Wat the hare are often cited to illustrate Shakespeare's familiarity with country pursuits and his ability to identify himself physically and emotionally with his creations. But the passage is not just one of the decorative digressions often found in Ovidian poetry. It is functional in reinforcing the theme of the hapless hunted creature, which Adonis has been and will be again; and it is further significant because it is Venus the huntress who speaks it.

l. 680 *overshoot:* run beyond.

l. 682 *cranks:* swerves.

l. 683 *musits:* gaps in the hedge.

l. 684 *amaze:* bewilder. There have been better puns.

l. 689 *sorteth:* keeps company with.

l. 690 *wit waits on fear:* fright stimulates one to make ingenious improvizations.

l. 694 *cold fault:* lost scent.

l. 695 *spend their mouths:* bark loudly.

l. 702 *passing-bell:* the church bell that was rung when a man was dying.

l. 704 *indenting with the way:* moving in zigzags along his path.

l. 705 *envious:* spiteful.

l. 712 *Unlike myself:* it is not characteristic of her to expound a situation in this way.

l. 715 *Where did I leave:* where did I break off my story?

ll. 725–6 Chaste Diana (the moon) hides behind the clouds, and so is melancholy, for fear that she should steal a kiss and so break her vow of chastity (*forsworn*).

l. 728 *Cynthia:* another name for the moon.

ll. 729–30 She is sulking because deceitful (*forging*) Nature has stolen from the gods the moulds or forms in which

Beauty was fashioned, and has used them to create Adonis.

l. 733 *the Destinies:* the three Fates, or Parcae, sister goddessess who determined the fate of men.

l. 734 *cross:* frustrate. *curious:* highly-wrought, elaborate.

l. 736 *defeature:* disfigurement.

l. 740 *wood:* (adj.) mad, raging.

l. 741 *marrow-eating:* bone-wasting. *attaint:* infection.

l. 743 *surfeits:* sickness caused by excess. *imposthumes:* abscesses.

l. 747 *favour, savour, hue:* good looks, fragrance, complexion.

l. 748 *late did wonder:* marvelled until now.

ll. 751 ff. Venus returns to the argument of ll. 163–74, that Beauty must renew itself by breeding. It was one of the age's commonest persuasions against chastity, but she is perhaps prompted to it here by her intense visualization of the boar as a mindless instrument of destruction. Like Time itself, the boar indiscriminately preys on Beauty, and she begs Adonis to submit himself to love before it is too late.

l. 752 *vestals:* the priestesses of Vesta, in Rome, who were vowed to chastity.

l. 755 *prodigal:* generous, fruitful. The *lamp*, or candle, consumes itself in order to give light to others.

ll. 757–60 Unless he submits to love, his body is nothing better than an avaricious (*swallowing*) grave in which he is burying the son he should have begotten.

l. 762 *Sith:* since.

l. 763 When he dies, his posterity (unborn) will die with him; and she goes on to say that this is worse than civil war, suicide, or actually killing his sons.

l. 766 *butcher sire:* murderous father. *reaves:* deprives.

l. 767 *frets:* eats away. Rust is as great a destroyer as canker in the flower, and here the two ideas are powerfully combined.

l. 768 *put to use:* invested, so as to gain interest.

ll. 769 ff. To Venus's classic argument on Beauty's obligation to multiply itself Adonis replies with the equally classic arguments in favour of chastity. He tells her that her passion is merely lust, which is a degradation of love. The force and eloquence of his words should not lead us to suppose that the coy adolescent has grown to sudden maturity. These ideas had long been familiar as a rhetorical exercise, and this book contains several examples of it. If it produces some apparently inconsistent characterization, it is timely to be reminded that the poem is only a myth.

l. 769 *will*: are determined to.

l. 770 *idle*: empty.

l. 774 *treatise*: recital.

l. 777 Mermaids were believed to sing seductive songs to lure mariners to destruction on the rocks, cf. l. 429.

l. 778 *blown*: blown away.

l. 782 *closure*: enclosure,

ll. 785–6 His heart sleeps soundly while it sleeps alone, and does not wish to complain about it.

l. 787 *reprove*: refute.

l. 789 *your device in love*: your manner of thinking or behaving about love.

l. 791 *increase*: propagation, breeding.

l. 792 'When rational argument is prostituted into becoming an advocate for lust'; cf. Rosamond's 'bed-broker'; ll. 218–308.

l. 795 *Under whose simple semblance*: in whose innocent guise.

l. 797 *Which*: refers to beauty, *the hot tyrant* to lust. *bereaves*: takes away.

l. 803 *surfeits*: gives way to excess.
The text is old: see note to ll. 769 ff.

l. 806 *green*: inexperienced.

l. 807 *in sadness*: in all seriousness.

l. 808 *teen*: grief.

l. 813 *lawnd*: glade.

l. 826 *mistrustful*: dangerous.

l. 828 *the fair discovery of her way*: him whose beauty illumined her path.

l. 836 *extemporally*: impromptu.

l. 837 *thrall*: enslaved.

l. 838 *foolish witty*: foolish when witty.

l. 841 *outwore*: outlasted.

l. 848 *resembling parasites*: because they were only echoes. There is more comic pathos when she finds only echo to answer her griefs. Having put on mortal flesh in order to woo Adonis, she is obliged to suffer in the ordinary human way.

ll. 849–50 *tapsters*, young serving-men at the inns, had to put with a good deal of ridicule from the conceited gallants (*fantastic wits*) who patronized them; see the rather cruel mockery in *1 Henry IV*, II. iv.

l. 854 *cabinet:* nest. *moist:* because the lark nests in the grass.

l. 863 *suck'd* was suckled by. She is speaking of Adonis, whose beauty may even lend glory to the sun.

l. 865 ff. It can often be observed that at divisions in the narrative, as here, the verse changes its mood and seems to renew its energy. We can sense the dramatist consciously recharging his powers as he begins a new scene, and it is this art learned in the theatre that is largely responsible for the speed and constant freshness of the poem.

l. 866 *so much o'erworn:* so far advanced.

l. 870 *coasteth:* approaches.

l. 871 ff. This stanza is another example of Shakespeare's use of the natural background to make the story dramatic. His personal identification with Venus has become rather closer since Adonis left her at nightfall.

l. 877 *at a bay:* when a hunted animal turns to face its pursuers.

l. 885 *cry:* barking of the hounds.

l. 888 *strain courtesy:* stand on ceremony, i.e. hold back to allow others to attack first. *cope:* encounter.

l. 895 *ecstasy:* fit of emotion.

l. 907 *spleens:* impulses.

l. 909 *mated:* checked.

ll. 911–12 'Full of ideas but not giving complete attention to any of them; trying to do everything but accomplishing nothing.'

l. 914 *caitiff:* wretch.

l. 916 *sovereign plaster:* effective cure.

l. 920 *flap-mouth'd:* having the long hanging jowl of a hound.

l. 921 *welkin:* sky.

l. 928 *Infusing them:* filling themselves (the people).

ll. 931–54 Venus entreats Death in extravagant conceits as she had earlier entreated Adonis.

l. 932 *divorce of love:* that which separates lovers.

l. 943 *bid beware:* warned him of your approach.

l. 944 *his:* its. Death would have been merciful if only he had heard the sweetness of Adonis's voice.

l. 950 'How can grievous distress profit you?'

l. 952 The sense here is that Adonis awakened in other men's eyes a new conception of beauty.

l. 953 *mortal vigour:* deadly strength.

l. 954 *rigour:* cruelty.

l. 956 *vail'd:* lowered.

ll. 961–6 The verbal conceits in this highly artificial stanza indicate the complementary action of her eyes and her tears in expressing her grief; and when she turned from weeping to sighing, her tears soon broke out again.

l. 972 *consulting for:* taking counsel together in order to bring about. All her various and turbulent emotions only result in tears.

ll. 975–6 The huntsman's cry tries to drive away the foreboding fancies which have overwhelmed her.

l. 978 *flatters:* deceives her into thinking.

l. 981 *orient:* because pearls came from the East. But pearls were lustrous and brilliant, and so it here means 'glistening'.

l. 983 *sluttish:* squalid, dirty. Made newly brave by hope, she accuses the earth, which she has drenched with her tears, of being sodden with drink.

ll. 985–7 In the extremes of feeling which love produces, it is at one moment reluctant to believe (*hard-believing*), then it makes disbelief seem unreasonable, and finally it becomes over-credulous. *weal and woe:* prosperity and disaster; or perhaps comfort and grief.

ll. 989–90 'Hope deceives you with improbable fancies, despair swiftly destroys you with plausible forebodings'.

ll. 991–2 She unwinds the fabric of self-deception in which she accused Death of having seized Adonis.

l. 993 *call'd him all to nought:* reviled him.

l. 995 *clepes:* names.

l. 1004 *wreak'd:* avenged.

l. 1006 *author of thy slander:* responsible for your being falsely accused.

l. 1007 Grief's *two tongues* are sorrowing at the event and cursing the person responsible for it.

l. 1010 'She makes light of her over-hasty suspicions'.

l. 1011 *his:* Adonis's.

l. 1012 *insinuate:* ingratiate herself.

l. 1013 *stories:* recounts.

l. 1018 *mutual;* common—until all mankind are dead.

ll. 1019–20 Her wild and fanciful talks suddenly soars to a couplet that epitomises the whole myth. Adonis is the embodiment of Beauty, and if he were dead, the whole created world would lose its meaning. *Chaos*, a very powerful image, was the infinite, unpeopled space which existed before the creation of the world, a primeval darkness in which there was no life; cf. *Othello*, III. iii. 90–2.

l. 1024 *with false bethinking:* with baseless supposition.

l. 1027 *lure:* a dummy resembling a bird which falconers used to recall their hawks.

l. 1028 Contrast this with ll. 871–4, where brambles delayed her progress.

l. 1030 *her fair delight:* the beautiful boy who had so delighted her.

l. 1032 *asham'd of:* put to confusion by.

ll. 1033–4 Cf. *Love's Labour's Lost*, IV. iii. 337–8.

l. 1040 *disposing:* ordering.

l. 1041 *consort with:* keep company with.

l. 1042 'Never again to hurt her by resuming the office of sight'

l. 1043 *who:* the heart. *perplexed:* sorely troubled.

l. 1044 *their:* the eyes'. *suggestion:* prompting.

l. 1045 *each tributary subject:* the other parts of the body.

ll. 1046–7 It was traditionally believed that earthquakes were caused by winds that were imprisoned in underground caves and struggled to escape; cf. *1 Henry IV*, III. i. 25 ff.

l. 1049 *mutiny:* strife.

l. 1051 *threw unwilling light:* looked with reluctance.

l. 1052 *trench'd:* dug like a trench (with its tusks).

ll. 1053–4 Compare the contrast here of white flesh and crimson blood with earlier descriptions of pale cheeks suffused by amorous blushes, e.g. ll. 343–8.

l. 1057 *sympathy:* likeness in suffering.

l. 1059 *passions:* grieves. *doteth:* acts wildly.

l. 1062 *that they have wept till now:* that previously they have wept for so much less cause than this.

l. 1064 *dazzling:* dazing, becoming blurred.

ll. 1075 ff. The tone changes. She cannot abandon conceits entirely, but the direct and mostly unaffected pathos of her elegy was at the least a model for *Lycidas*.

l. 1083 *fair:* beauty. It was the mark of true beauty to have a complexion untanned by wind or sun. But with Adonis dead, men and women need no longer go to the trouble of protecting themselves with veils and bonnets.

l. 1094 *fear:* frighten.

l. 1099 *shadow:* reflected image.

l. 1105 *urchin-snouted:* having a snout like an urchin, or hedgehog.

l. 1106 *downward:* looking at the ground. She supposes that if the boar had looked up to see Adonis, it would not have killed him. This was the blind destructiveness, synonymous with Evil itself, that brought Beauty to the grave.

l. 1107 *livery:* dress, but here used figuratively of his personal beauty.

l. 1108 *entertainment:* treatment.

l. 1118 We may well believe her. See ll. 553–8 and similar passages describing the violence of her passion: she is herself as acquisitive as the boar.

l. 1128 *coffer-lids:* lids to the treasure-chest of his eyes.

l. 1133 *spite:* vexation.

ll. 1135–64 True to the function of myth, Venus here explains why, with Adonis slain, mortal love will be for ever flawed.

ll. 1139–40 Love will never run smoothly; there will always be extremes of ecstasy and suffering.

l. 1142 'Flower and wither in a moment's breath'.

l. 1143 *o'erstraw'd:* strewn over.

l. 1144 *the truest sight beguile:* deceive the clearest perception.

l. 1147 *sparing:* thrifty. *riot:* luxury.

l. 1148 *measures:* dances.

l. 1149 *staring:* bold-eyed.

l. 1151 *silly-mild:* simple and meek.

l. 1157 *toward:* docile.

l. 1168 *a purple flower:* according to legend the anemone sprang from his blood—a final blending of the red and the white of his cheeks.

l. 1175 *crops:* plucks.

l. 1177 *guise:* custom.

l. 1180 *To grow unto himself:* to live for his own sake; cf. l. 166.

l. 1193 *Paphos:* in Cyprus, the centre of the worship of Venus-Aphrodite. She was thought to have walked ashore there after her birth among the waves.

MICHAEL DRAYTON (1563–1631)

Drayton, like Shakespeare, was a Warwickshire man of yeoman stock. In boyhood he was page to Sir Henry Goodere of Polesworth, whose daughter Anne, later Lady Rainsford, is thought to have been the inspiration of his sonnet sequence *Idea's Mirror* and other works, including the present poem.

Little is known of Drayton's personal life, but he was one of the most prolific writers of a prolific age. He produced a vast quantity of historical, religious, and topographical verse, as well as sonnets, occasional odes, and satires; and he was even for a time a hack writer for the theatre, being part-author of a play which sought to vindicate Sir John Oldcastle from the slur of supposedly having been the original of Falstaff.

Drayton's verse, disciplined by careful craftmanship, is always mellow, sweet, and wholesome. His affections, like Shakespeare's, never strayed far from his midland home, and his unwillingness to attach himself to poetic coteries in London may be the reason why—less fortunate than Daniel—he failed to win the patronage of James's court. His patriotism, and his steady faith in the traditional virtues of poetry and of life, put him increasingly out of sympathy with the 'melancholy' discontents affected by the intellectuals of his day.

His most characteristic work is *Poly-Olbion*, a heroic panorama in which he praises the pastoral beauties of his country, its native customs, and its famous men. English history is also presented in the *Heroical Epistles*, *The Barons' Wars*, and *The Ballad of Agincourt*, and the sonnets will always be memorable for the magnificent 'Since there's no help, come let us kiss and part'. His last work, *The Muses' Elysium* (1630), is a triumph of both technique and character. The veteran poet felicitously combines the serenity of age with a young man's freshness in celebrating a golden world of youth and song.

Drayton died next year in relative poverty, and although financially, and even in the way of fame, his life was always something of a struggle, he was the admired friend of many famous men, commended for his 'virtuous disposition, honest conversation and well-governed carriage'. Typical, perhaps, was the famous anecdote of the 'merry meeting' at Shakespeare's home at Stratford, when the wine passed round the table while Drayton, Jonson, and their host relived old days through an enchanted veil. Drayton was buried in Westminster Abbey: a circumstance which was to draw an ignorant jibe from Goldsmith, but was not altogether unfitting.

Endymion and Phoebe was published in 1595 with a dedicatory sonnet to the Countess of Bedford, patron of numerous Elizabethan poets. The story come from Ovid's *Heroides* (XVIII. 59–74), but Drayton does not pursue it to the usual Ovidian conclusion. Although Phoebe makes a frankly sensual approach to the beautiful shepherd, she is really offering him the chaste love which transcends the body and reaches to higher things, to knowledge of the divine soul that is 'exempt from vile and gross corruption'. The poem is a Neo-Platonic allegory of the soul's awakening through love to a heavenly purity and wisdom; see Introduction, pp. 10–11.

But Drayton's intention was to please as well as to instruct, and however exalted his ultimate purpose, he used all his poetic artifice in a studied assault upon the senses: partly through Phoebe's catalogue of love's delights and partly through the continuous deployment of the rich treasures of pastoral and mythological decoration. In some degree Marlowe and Shakespeare must have served as models for the poem, although at the end Drayton delivers the tacit rebuke of leaving them out when he names the three poets who have been fruitful to his art (ll. 993–1004).

The poem's secondary title is *Idea's Latmus*. 'Idea' was Drayton's term for his idealization of Anne Goodere, the 'sweet nymph of Anker', and she stands here as a symbol of beauty and of his confidence in the immortality of his work.

> Peace, ho! the moon sleeps with Endymion,
> And would not be awak'd.
> *Merchant of Venice*, V. i. 109.

In the traditional story Endymion had the gift of perpetual sleep. His beauty warmed the cold heart of the moon goddess and she came down to Mount Latmus to embrace him and lie there by his side. In an expansion of the myth he was said to have acquired a knowledge of astronomy and discovered the course of the moon. In about 1585 Lyly wrote a comedy, *Endymion*, or *The Man in the Moon*, in which Cynthia's love for a mortal is allegorically equated with Elizabeth's love for Leicester, and an opportunity found for complimenting the

queen upon her chastity. More than 200 years later Keats
embellished and retold the story in one of the most richly
inventive of his poems.

In Drayton's version Endymion is a shepherd who has
dedicated himself to serve the moon as a symbol of chastity.
Adonis-like, he rebukes her passion when the goddess, en-
chanted by his beauty, comes down to earth to woo him.
Presently, however, he finds that Love has 'undermin'd the
fort', and after revealing her identity, Phoebe promises him
heavenly understanding (although this was not what he asked
for), and carries him off to the skies. There the action ends.
Subsequent passages about the planets, the angelic hierarchies,
and the mystic import of the numbers 3 and 9 are introduced
to demonstrate the interdependence of poetry, astronomy, and
the divine being. An account of the nature of Endymion's
celestial vision is dismissed by the poet's 'weary muse' to an
unspecified future. It was not made any clearer when the poem
was reworked and expanded in 1606 as *The Man in the Moon*.

Endymion and Phoebe

l. 1 *Ionia:* a district on the west coast of Asia Minor which was
    colonized by the Greeks in the eleventh century B.C. Its
    twelve cities reached a level of prosperity, culture, and
    learning second only to that of Athens.
l. 3 This is to be taken figuratively. The actual seats of the Muses
    were on Helicon and Parnassus.
ll. 5–6 *Archelaus* of Miletus (*c*. 450 B.C.) was reputed to have
    taught Socrates, but he was not the first man to bring
    philosophy to Athens. His master Anaxagoras, also an
    Ionian, preceded him. *historify:* record historically.
l. 9 Mt. *Latmus*, in the province of Caria, has a height of 4,500
    feet.
l. 12 *Silvanus:* a Roman god of fields and forests.
l. 13 *barley-break:* an old country game. *Satyrs:* woodland
    demons, partly human in appearance but with pointed
    ears, horns and a goat's tail. They were companions of
    Bacchus.
    Pan: the goat-footed god of flocks and shepherds.
l. 15 *tabret:* a small drum. *list:* was pleased.
l. 16 *round:* dance.
l. 20 *imparadise:* place as in Paradise.

l. 21 *Diana:* the moon goddess.

l. 22 *vestal:* chaste.

l. 24 *clip the welkin:* embrace the sky.

l. 28 Nature conspired against the sun by making a leafy shade which it could not penetrate.

ll. 30–2 Certain plants and trees particularly associated with various gods and goddesses. *warlike fir:* transferred epithet; it is Mars who is warlike. *myrrh:* a tree or shrub that is *weeping* because it exudes resin.

l. 34 *Alcides:* a name for Hercules, who was the grandson of Alcaeus.

ll. 37–8 Bordering the glade which they enclosed, the trees resembled the hangings and tapestry which adorn a gallery.

l. 42 *Hesperides:* the garden where nymphs, also called Hesperides, guarded the golden apples which Earth gave to Zeus on his marriage to Hera. A dragon aided them in their watch.

l. 50 *orient:* from the East.

l. 52 *crystalline:* an adjective referring to the crystal clearness of the water.

l. 54 *their small recorders:* their musical voices.

l. 56 *woosel:* ousel, blackbird. *mavis:* song-thrush.

l. 59 *Zephyr:* the west wind.

l. 60 *bare the burthen:* bore the refrain.

l. 64 *moly:* a plant believed to have magic properties against enchantment.

l. 65 *balm:* general name for a number of fragrant garden herbs. *cassia:* a tree or shrub having medicinal powers.

l. 66 *Idea's:* Beauty's.

l. 71 *Impal'd:* shut in.

l. 72 *Etna:* a volcanic mountain in Sicily, now Monte Gibello.

l. 75 *her sphere:* the moon. Phoebe, identified with Diana or Artemis, was the goddess of the moon.

l. 78 *lunary:* moonlight.

l. 79 *Maenalus:* a mountain in Arcadia.

l. 86 *hay-de-guys:* country dances.

l. 105 *her brother:* Phoebus, the sun god.

l. 106 The crescent and the full face are aspects of the moon. She is laying these aside so as to disguise herself as a nymph and woo Endymion, and at last we are to have some action. But these elaborate set-pieces, rich in artifice, were characteristic of romantic allegorical poetry, and Drayton would have found several models in Spenser, e.g. the April eclogue in *The Shepherd's Calendar*, or in *The Faerie Queene* the garden of Adonis (III. vi), the castle of the enchantress Busirane (III. xi), or the bower of bliss (II. xii), where Sir Guyon overcame Acrasia, the embodiment of unchaste love.

l. 109 *twine:* spray.

l. 111 *purfled:* bordered.

l. 113 *embosted:* embossed, i.e. rainbows embossed in silk.

l. 119 *Truss'd up in trammels:* fastened in pleats. *curious:* intricate.

l. 120 *sphery:* rounded.

l. 121 *cypress:* a light fabric that originated in Cyprus.

l. 125 *Discovering:* revealing.

l. 126 *vines:* the text reads *veynes;* perhaps a *vines-veins* pun is intended. *enchas'd:* embossed.

ll. 129–30 She did not conceal her beauty by wearing a polished mask; bright lights outshine lesser ones but do not extinguish one another.

ll. 131–2 Nature scorns to hire beauty-aids from the shops. Nature's own products are the best adornment to beauty, fie on lotions and artificial aids. *Simples:* medicinal herbs.

l. 135 *trade:* custom.

l. 136 *roundelay:* a simple song with a refrain.

l. 139 *hand* is the object: so pure in its whiteness that even snow would soil it.

l. 140 See note to ll. 365–7.

l. 142 *liquid pearl:* glistening water.

l. 142 *Aganippe* was the nymph of a fountain at the foot of Mount Helicon. Like the Castalian spring at Parnassus, it was sacred to the Muses and was believed to inspire those who drank from it; cf. Shakespeare's introductory couplet to *Venus and Adonis*, p. 237.

l. 143 *Hebe:* the goddess of youth, waited on the gods and filled their cups with nectar. *spilt:* poured.

l. 144 *damask'd:* ornamented.

l. 152 *Orion* was a Greek hero who at his death was placed among the stars.

l. 156 *As she:* as though she. She is in a disguise which is now described.

l. 157 *buskins:* half-boots, commonly worn by actors on the stage.

l. 158 *accordingly:* becomingly.

l. 160 *scours:* runs in search of.

l. 161 *Fauns:* spirits of the countryside, similar to Satyrs, l. 13.

l. 162 *lawns:* glades.

l. 164 *cithron:* cithern, the Greek cithara, a stringed instrument played with a plectrum formed of the *quill* of a feather.

l. 166 A *Gordian* knot was proverbially one which could not be untied.

l. 167 *toils:* nets, snares.

l. 169 *chaste desire:* Drayton's ultimate intention is to declare that the love of these two is of a Platonic nature; but it does not appear so at the moment.

l. 182 *Isis:* the Thames. It is not clear what Pan was doing so far from his Arcadian home, but this is her story.

l. 187 *Oceanus:* god of the ocean.

l. 188 *Tithon* (us) was allowed by the gods to have immortality but not eternal youth, and so he remained for ever in decrepit old age. The birth of Phoebe momentarily restored him to frolicsome juvenility.

l. 189 *halcyons:* kingfishers.

l. 191 *memorize:* commemorate.

l. 199 *mould:* earth.

l. 200 *pomander:* a ball of perfume, supposed to ward off infection.

l. 201 Compare l. 139: a rather feeble repetition of a poetic idea, especially when applied to another character.

l. 203 *lodestones:* iron ore that attracts other pieces of iron.

l. 204 *Amphion* received a lyre from Hermes and played it with such skill that the stones of Thebes moved of their own accord and built themselves into a wall.

l. 206 *manual seal:* signature.

l. 207 *play the wanton:* usually has a sexual implication, but here she is only inviting him to leave his flocks and amuse himself.

l. 208 *wait:* watch. *duly:* dutifully.

l. 220 *chafe:* warm by stroking.

l. 227 *happily:* perhaps. *Flora:* goddess of flowers.

l. 230 *quiver:* a case for arrows. Diana was also goddess of the chase.

l. 231–2 Because of her pale silvery light the moon was the goddess of chastity, and in her name Endymion had sworn to be continent. This was contrary to the persuasions of Venus, and ironically he now spurns Phoebe by quoting her own precepts against her.

l. 252 *batful:* fertile. *thews:* theaves, ewes.

l. 255 *syrup'd with honey fall:* sweetened by the dropping honey.

l. 269 *fond:* foolish. *rosin:* oil from the resin of the pine.

l. 270 *larix:* the larch. *turpentine:* resin from coniferous trees.

l. 271 *teda:* tead, the torch pine.

l. 289 *vestal:* virgin.

l. 297 *Citheron:* Cithaeron, a mountain range on the border of Boeotia.

l. 298 *Ismaenus* and *Thermodon:* rivers in Boeotia.

l. 299 *Thetis:* a sea-goddess, mother of Achilles, see *Scylla's Metamorphosis.*

l. 308 *maiden sconce:* unbreached fortress.

l. 309 *wants:* lacks. Cupid was proverbially blind, which was held to account for the incompatibility of some of his victims. *passing right:* with surpassing accuracy.

l. 310 He is accurate because he aims with our secret desires.

l. 311 *piles:* darts. *temper'd:* hardened.

l. 313 *He:* previously Love, now Endymion.

ll. 326–7 This quiet description of the night, with its soft rhythm and lovely contrasts, prepares the reader for the emotional change in Endymion. At first he had rejected Phoebe, but now his senses are bemused by deceitful Love.

l. 328 *cabinet:* bower, private retreat.

l. 330 The path formerly taken by the horses which drew the sun's chariot across the sky.

l. 331 *Cynthia:* another name for the moon.

l. 332 *rid:* rode.

l. 338 *bewray'd her wrong:* revealed (in her song) the injury done to her. The gods changed Procne into a nightingale to save her from the vengeance of her husband Tereus. (In this story, parts of which were used by Shakespeare in *Titus Andronicus,* her sister Philomela was deprived of her tongue, and she herself killed her son Itys and served him in a dish at his father's table; see Ovid *Metamorphoses* VI.)

l. 339 *fast:* close.

l. 349 *civet:* a perfume taken from the civet, a small carnivorous animal.

l. 354 *Consort:* sing together.

l. 358 *clip about:* surround.

l. 359 *circled maze:* the orbits followed by the stars (the *bright lamps* of l. 357).

l. 361 He is addressing the nymph Callisto who lived in Helice and was changed by Hera into a bear. To save her life Zeus turned her into a constellation, the Great Bear.

l. 363 Drayton's own note to this line is, 'The constellations near the pole Artic' (Arctic).

ll. 365–7 *Perseus* was the Greek hero who slew *Medusa*, one of the three snake-haired Gorgons. In order to beget him Zeus turned himself into a shower of gold and so entered the prison where his mother Danae was kept.

l. 368 *art stellified:* have become a star.

ll. 369–70 *Andromeda*, daughter of the king of Ethiopia, was bound to a rock, but Perseus rescued her from a sea-monster.

ll. 373–4 *Cassiope*, the mother of Andromeda, boasted that she or her daughter was more beautiful than the Nereids, the daughters of the sea-god Nereus. She too became a star.

l. 380 *only:* alone.

l. 381 *event:* outcome.

l. 387 *hunts-up:* an early-morning song.

l. 390 *'Sdaining:* disdaining.

l. 394 *seld-seen accident:* event seldom seen.

l. 395 'Until in seeking for an explanation of this, they fell into dispute'.

l. 400 'They could not deprive her of her freedom of movement'.

l. 401 She was the lowest of the seven planets, and so nearest to the earth.

ll. 402–6 The moon's *moisty influence* was its supposed control over the tides, which thus gave it authority over mortal affairs. Mankind's *mutable estate*, its liability to flux and change, was therefore influenced by the moon's changes.

ll. 419–22 Being the most variable of the planets, the moon has been conceded particular authority over women, they being the least predictable of mortals.

l. 437 *consort:* birdsong. *springs:* copse of young trees.

l. 438 *That:* so that.

l. 448: *Diana's:* Phoebe's.

l. 457 *For why:* for the reason that.

l. 463 *Appal:* weaken. Drayton notes that this is 'the effect of melancholy'. Melancholy, literally 'black bile', was believed to originate in the spleen and infect the blood. With choler, blood, and phlegm, it was one of the four 'humours' whose relative proportions in the body were held to determine a person's temperament.

l. 464 *parts organical:* physical organs.

l. 468 *eftsoons: presently.*

l. 480 *include:* shut in.

l. 487 *wasteth:* spends.

l. 489 *frolic:* playful.

l. 490 *round:* circular dance.

l. 494 *embay:* bathe.

l. 497 *compass:* area.

l. 500 *arew:* a row, in a line, one after the other.

l. 501 *galliards:* lively dances in fast time.

l. 502 *thyas:* dance associated with the followers of Bacchus.

l. 505 *deity:* godlike power. Phoebe is about to impart divine inspiration to the mortal whom she loves. This is the Platonic idea that love of physical beauty, so long as one is not enslaved to it, may lead to knowledge of things divine; see introduction, pp. 10–11.

l. 506 *beautify:* much stronger than merely to adorn to make pretty. It rather has the sense of 'beatitude', a state of blessedness.

l. 508 Of the four elements, fire and air were the two which had the properties of lightness and inspiration. *fiery* here does not have the modern meaning of hot-tempered, etc.

ll. 509–10 The effect of this inspiration is to enable the mind to acquire heavenly knowledge.

l. 511 The poet adds a footnote that it is 'the excellency of the soul', its unique quality, that it alone is divine.

l. 513 *comprehensible:* able to understand.

l. 516 *multiplicity:* manifold variety. Its single unique quality enables it to be master of an infinite number.

l. 517 'Being of the essence of all things and unvarying in all conditions'.

l. 518 *dividual:* divisible.

l. 519 'But in its operation preserves its special condition'.

l. 520 *ingenerate:* inborn.

ll. 521–2 By means of inspiration the soul is able to communicate its divine knowledge.

l. 523 *they:* the nymphs.

l. 531 *not yet of perfect sight:* bemused by sleep, his eyes cannot yet see things plainly.

l. 533–6 As in *Venus and Adonis*, a sign of emotion.

l. 537 *rightly:* directly.

l. 541 Drayton's note is: 'The causes of the external signs of passion'.

l. 542 *conceit:* idea, conception.

l. 546 *retraction:* withdrawal. *Spirit* (monosyllable, cf. l. 573): vital energy. According to the suppositions of medieval physiology, this was what happened at moments of extreme emotion.

ll. 555–6 *his:* its.

l. 561 *learned:* taught.

l. 572 *impressure:* impression. *conceit:* wit, fancy. *invention:* creative power.

l. 578 She is the pole to which his natural love is magnetized.

ll. 580–2 He is *perish'd*, though still *living*, in that he no longer has time or inclination to care for them. Their dishevelled fleeces resemble his own love-distracted hair, and both have, for different reasons, given up eating. *from thy sight:* in consequence of your beauty.

l. 590 *kept:* dwelt.

l. 600 *purling:* murmuring.

l. 620 To make her change the subject.

l. 625 *for:* in order that.

l. 650 *leman:* paramour; in this case Aegina, mother of Aeacus, whom Zeus visited as fire.

ll. 654–62 The moon's light is reflected from the sun, so that when Phoebus, her brother Titan, withdraws in deference to her, the whole world is dark.

ll. 659–60 The earth is too large to be wholly penetrated by the light of the moon, which is merely fixed on its surface (*superficies*, five syllables).

l. 665 *lumpish mould:* gross earth.

l. 668 Earth is seen from here to be a perfect round, unlike man-made representations.

264 NOTES TO THE POEMS

l. 669 *Fixed point:* the earth's axis.

l. 672 *diurnal:* daily.

l. 674 The *first mover* was God, who set the universe in motion and ordered it to obey certain fixed laws. The next forty lines describe the Elizabethan cosmology and the reputed influence of the stars on man's individual fortune. There are several modern accounts of this planetary system, which was emotionally very important to the contemporary mind. The most convenient summary is in E. M. W. Tillyard, *The Elizabethan World Picture.*

l. 676 *Whereas:* wherein.

ll. 678–9 See note to l. 508. Clear air and bright fire are the only elements which can aim at reaching (*aspire*) to the moon's exalted height.

l. 681 *mount:* carry.

l. 686 *sympathize:* move in harmony. This harmony of the planets was a necessary condition of corresponding harmony in the world below.

l. 687 *severally prefix'd:* prescribed for each.

l. 689 Their *mansions* were the fixed points which they successively occupied on their course.

ll. 691–2 The *zodiac* is the belt within which the apparent motions of the planets take place. Its *signs* are the twelve equal divisions through one of which the sun passes each month; they are named after the twelve constellations.

ll. 693–4 *triplicities:* threefold character; in astromony, the trigon, the junction of three signs of the zodiac. The zodiac is divided into four trigons, watery, earthy, airy, and fiery. Thus, as stated in Drayton's own explanatory note, 'The signs in their triplicities participate with the elements.'

l. 703 *their:* the planets'.

ll. 722–4 *Twins, Archers, Dog, Lion, Titan:* respectively Gemini, Sagittarius, Canis, Leo, the sun. The 'dog days' proverbially generated exceptional heat.

l. 731 *imp'd:* in falconry, feathers were grafted on to a damaged wing to restore a bird's power of flight.

l. 765 Her instructions were charged with importance and had to be obeyed.

ll. 767–98 Nymphs, who were female divinities of a lower rank, were classified by the different parts of Nature which they represented: the *Oreades* inhabited the mountains and grottoes; the *Hamadryads* and *Dryades* were tree nymphs who were believed to die with the trees which had been their abode; the *Naiades* were nymphs of fresh water, living in rivers, brooks, and springs.

l. 772 *flaggy:* drooping.

l. 774 *murrey:* purple (mulberry-coloured). *sendal:* a rich silken material.

l. 776 *fillets:* bands.

l. 781 *byss:* fine linen. *frets:* ornaments.

l. 783 *branched buskins:* boots adorned with a figured pattern. *cordiwin:* cordwain, leather of goatskin, originally from Cordova.

l. 784 *spangled:* decorated with small plates of shining metal.

l. 795 *palms:* the flattened parts of the antler. *dight:* adorned.

l. 797 *sort:* company.

l. 799 *trapp'd:* decked.

l. 802 *Iris:* the messenger of the gods. The rainbow was the path by which she travelled to and from the earth.

l. 804 *tissue:* rich cloth.

l. 814 *entire:* whole.

l. 816 *heliotropium:* the bloodstone.

ll. 835–8 Referring to the moon's gradual change from crescent to full. *due proportion:* proper form.

l. 855 *vesture:* dress.

l. 859 *Astraea*, who was descended from the Titans (the children of Heaven and Earth) was the goddess of justice in the golden age of man; but as the world's wickedness increased she returned to heaven and as Virgo took her place among the stars. (Her sister Chastity withdrew at the same time.)

ll. 863–4 The three *Charites*, or Graces, were the personification of grace and beauty. They were daughters of Zeus; see l. 962.

l. 872 *With the first number:* as those who had gone before.

l. 877 *fury and conceit:* inspired frenzy and imagination.

l. 878 *await:* attend.

ll. 879 ff. This should be the moment when Phoebe grants Endymion the divine vision which had been promised in ll. 505 ff. According to the myth he acquired power over Nature and a knowledge of astronomy. But for some reason Drayton did not take the story to this climax. Instead, following his earlier disquisition on the planets, he discusses the mystic significance of numbers.

l. 888 According to the system of Dionysius the Areopagite, evolved in the first century A.D., *hierarchies* were the three divisions of angels, each consisting of three orders. This was 'the perfect form of true triplicity'.

ll. 891–8 The three hierarchies of angels were: seraphim, cherubim, and thrones; dominions, virtues, and powers; principalities, archangels, and angels.

l. 902 *particularity:* special quality.

l. 903 *infer:* assume the existence of.

l. 904 Completely forgetting Endymion for the moment, Drayton proposes a tenth order of angels, to be occupied by Anne Goodere, to whom he addressed his *Idea* sonnets.

ll. 905 ff. Drayton supposes a natural connection between the angels and the Muses (of whom also there were nine). Their *like-attracting sympathy* was in particular the inspiration of poetry.

ll. 909 *Apollo's prophets* were the poets, who wrestled in creative frenzy.

l. 910 *numbers:* verse; but an allusion to the sacred numerical figures is probably implicit.

l. 911 *repine:* complain.

l. 913 *manifest:* exhibit. The *prophets* are the subject of the verb.

l. 914 *sucking:* suckling, giving life to.

l. 919 *Which:* the sphery circles. *diapasons:* harmonies. The planets were believed to make 'the celestial music of the spheres' as they moved on their courses.

l. 927 *Prefiguring:* representing beforehand.

l. 931 *Which:* those who. The nine *Worthies*, heroes of the ancient and the Christian worlds, were Hector, Alexander the Great, and Julius Caesar; Joshua, David, and Judas Maccabaeus; King Arthur, Charlemagne, and Godfrey of Bouillon. Being in three groups of three, they naturally fitted into the system that Drayton is describing. (Shakespeare's Worthies included Pompey and Hercules; see *Love's Labour's Lost*, V. ii).

l. 942 *Eliza's heavenly kind:* such complimentary references to the Queen were frequently made by her poets. She too would have been a Worthy had it been possible to find eight other women with comparable virtues.

l. 944 *devis'd:* conceived.

l. 946 When Orpheus died, his lyre was placed among the stars at the request of Apollo and the Muses.

l. 948 *consent:* musical accord, as in l. 915. *solid:* smooth.

l. 954 *trinary:* a set of three.

l. 964 The *Lydian* (minor scale, soft), *Dorian* (appropriate to solemn or warlike melodies), and *Phrygian* (passionate) were the three principal modes of Greek music.

l. 975 Yes.

l. 984 *arras:* tapestry.

ll. 987–90 Drayton combines two versions of the myth: that Phoebe consigned Endymion to perpetual sleep, so that she might come down and kiss him without his knowledge; and that Zeus granted hin the gift of sleep and eternal youth.

l. 993 *Colin:* Spenser, one of whose works was the pastoral *Colin Clout's Come Home Again.* He also used the name in *The Shepherd's Calendar.*

ll. 997–1000 Referring to Samuel Daniel, whose *Delia* sonnets were printed in 1592. *Musaeus:* the sixth-century Greek poet whose poem on Hero and Leander was used by Marlowe. *unfil'd:* unpolished.

l. 1001 *Goldey:* anagram and affectionate dimunitive for his friend Lodge.

l. 1006 *worthy titles:* poets deserve to be famous.

l. 1010 *Momus:* the licensed jester of the gods, until they expelled him for his constant mockery. Lodge used the title *A Fig for Momus* for his collection of verse satires (1595).

ll. 1011 ff. The poem ends with a salutation to the fair lady of his sonnets. The sub-title, *Idea's Latmus,* shows that it was designed as a tale to be dedicated to her beauty and perfection.

l. 1014 *Anker:* a river near Hartshill, where Drayton was born. Lower down the river is Polesworth, where Anne Godere spent her early years.

l. 1018 They have no grace if she is not of their company.

l. 1019 *clime:* region.

l. 1025 Phoebe's *bow* refers to her alternative role as goddess of the chase.

l. 1029 The constant hope of Elizabethan poets that their verse
  will give immortality to the fair.
ll. 1031-2 Her memory will be an inspiration to poets yet
  unborn.

JOHN MARSTON (c. 1575-1634)

Although he came of a family of Shropshire lawyers and had
an Italian mother, Marston was, at least by upbringing, another
Warwickshire man. He certainly went to school at Coventry
and may have been born there. After matriculating at Brasenose
College, Oxford, he entered the Middle Temple with the aim
of becoming a lawyer like his father.

But, like Lodge, he was presently drawn from the law to
literature and the theatre. *Pygmalion's Image*, printed with
various other satires, appeared in 1598, but was written some
years earlier than that; 1598 was also the date of *The Scourge
of Villainy*, a much riper (in the way that cheese ripens) display
of vituperation and maladjustment. These were the dark hours
of Elizabeth's long reign. There were many reasons for it,
political, religious, and economic, but the satirists of the
nineties—Donne, Joseph Hall, and Marston, with Lodge and
certain lesser figures—principally directed themselves against
the permissive society. They were very bitter about sexual
indulgence, and Marston, savage, incoherent, almost psychotic,
complained the loudest of them all. He seems to have found
some kind of personal release in it.

All these satires were laced with personal allusions, and
sooner or later the authorities had to bring them under control.
In June 1599 the Archbiship of Canterbury and the Bishop of
London prohibited the publication of certain books, and
Marston's two volumes were among those to be publicly burnt.

In the following years he was a fairly regular dramatist for
the boy companies, Hamlet's 'little eyases', who were flourish-
ing at the turn of the century. His surviving plays include the
tragedies *Antonio and Mellida* and *Antonio's Revenge*, and a
comedy, *The Malcontent*, in which he anatomised the fashion-
able affectation of melancholy. *Eastward Ho* (1605), in which he
collaborated with Chapman and his old enemy Jonson, gave
offence to James I, and all three had a term of imprisonment.

In the same year Marston married Mary Wilkes, daughter of one of the king's favourite chaplains, and after writing one or two more comedies he gave up his association with the theatre. Like Hall (who became a bishop) and Donne, he was ordained as an Anglican clergyman (1609), and from 1616 to 1631 he held the living of Christchurch, in Hampshire.

An unfriendly critic has called Marston 'a screech-owl among the singing birds'. His combativeness and relish for acrid personalities embroiled him first with his fellow-satirists and afterwards with Jonson, Dekker, and other playwrights in the *Poetomachia*, or war of the theatres. The perceptiveness and occasional felicities of his work were marred by the obscurity and harsh extravagance of his language. At least in his literary life, he was not a lover of his fellow-men.

Circulated first in manuscript, *The Metamorphosis of Pygmalion's Image* was apparently ill-received, since in the published version Marston printed a scornful repudiation of his original intention. Its 'Salaminian titillations' (Salamis was sacred to Venus) were only meant to be a joke, and he now describes his 'precedent poem' as a 'dissembling shift' designed to satirize the sexual licence which had come to pervade the Ovidian romance. Readers who had been taken in by it are now held up to ridicule.

His contemporaries do not appear to have been deceived by this clumsy attempt to salvage his reputation. In his two books of satires Marston adopted the pseudonym W. Kynsader, which is believed to refer to *kinsing*, an operation—possibly castration—for the cure of mad dogs. The impression he made on the literary world is indicated by the remark of a character in the anonymous *Return from Parnassus* (*c.* 1600): 'What, Monsieur Kynsader! lifting up your leg and pissing against the world!'

The story of Pygmalion is told by Ovid in *Metamorphoses* X. ix. Pygmalion was a king of Cyprus who was so disgusted by the debauchery of the island, and particularly of the town of Amathus, where prostitution virtually received a municipal subsidy, that he forswore women and devoted himself to art. He carved in ivory an image so beautiful that he begged Aphrodite to give it life; and when his prayer was granted, he married the maiden and became the father of Paphus.

The story was later used by William Morris in *The Earthly Paradise* (August), and, after his fashion, by Bernard Shaw.

The Metamorphosis of Pygmalion's Image

l. 3 *proportion:* shape.

l. 7 *finding his fond dotage:* realizing how foolish was his infatuation.

l. 11 *deity:* godlike power.

l. 8 *image:* statue.

l. 9 *mortality:* mankind.

ll. 11–12 The *mistress* has not been identified, but this is the personal reference that habitually appears in the Ovidian poetry of the time.

l. 13 *amaz'd:* struck with wonder.

ll. 17–18 *portrayed* has three syllables. Poets were often perfunctory about their rhymes, but seldom as casual as this. Compare ll. 26 and 28, 205 and 207, 206 and 208: if two words had common endings like -ed or -ing, that was good enough for Marston.

l. 20 'Masterful Love asserts his divine power'.

l. 22 *imagery:* the object which his imagination had created.

ll. 32 *spread:* strewn.

l. 38 *conceit:* fancy.

l. 44 *modest mount:* chaste swelling.

l. 45 *pillowbeer:* pillowcase.

l. 47 *overslip:* pass unnoticed.

l. 48 *curious:* skilfully wrought, delicate.

l. 51 *his only:* that is his alone.

l. 52 *mansion:* dwelling.

l. 53 *wink:* close the eyes, blink.

l. 55 *subtile City-dame:* refined lady of the City, i.e., the respectable wives of the gentry and leading tradesmen. These ladies gave themselves prim and proper airs that were frequently mocked by the dramatists and poets; cf. Hotspur's ridicule of the 'Sunday citizens' and their mealy-mouthed wives, *1 Henry IV*, III. i. 251–61.

l. 58 *bewray:* betray. Her eye wants to distract her mind from the pious thoughts that should be occupying it.

l. 63–4 Not reminding himself that it was just a piece of statuary that obligingly permitted this freedom.

l. 69 *Corinna* was Ovid's mistress.

l. 72 *to work his pleasing smart:* to contrive this delicious pain.

l. 79 *Look how:* just as. *peevish:* senseless.

l. 82 *bootless chattering:* futile incantation.

l. 84 *remorseless:* merciless.

l. 90 *Compassionate:* have pity on.

l. 93 *salute:* pay respect to.

l. 94 *presuming to:* believing that he will.

l. 102 *consort:* a musical harmony in which all the *parts* are blended.

ll. 107–8 *Ixion* was in love with Hera, wife of Zeus, but the angry husband created a phantom which Ixion mistakenly thought was his lover. *clipp'd:* embraced.

l. 111 *respects not:* has no regard for. *luxury:* lust.

l. 114 *busk-point:* the stiffening of a corset. *some favour:* a mark of favour such as a ribbon or a glove. *stills:* quietens, soothes.

l. 124 *shade:* shelter from heat.

l. 129 *charms:* puts a spell upon.

l. 130 *invocate:* invoke.

l. 132 *yet gave a life to death:* yet made death seem to be alive.

l. 135 *Whose kingdom rests in:* whose power is derived from.

l. 137 In l. 126 *stone* is used metaphorically, but here Marston seems to forget that he has several times said that the statue was carved in ivory.

l. 141 *equalize:* reciprocate.

l. 144 He had already used this phrase in l. 90.

l. 146 *divin'd:* prophesied.

l. 162 *Leda's twins:* Castor and Pollux, the Gemini, who were hatched from an egg after Zeus had made love to Leda disguised as a swan.

l. 167 *feature:* form, shape. Image would be sufficient by itself, and this is just added for the sake of the rhyme.

l. 172 *grac'd:* shown favour.

l. 175 *passing:* surpassing.

l. 178 *gin for:* begin.

l. 183 *proves:* puts her to the test.

l. 194 *ill attention:* evil expectation.

l. 198 *fitness:* favourable circumstances.

l. 233 *Paphos:* a town in Cyprus, was a seat of the worship of Aphrodite or Venus.

FURTHER READING

Texts

Except *The Complaint of Rosamond*, and *Venus and Adonis*, texts of all other poems in this book are printed in E. S. Donno, *Elizabethan Minor Epics*, (1963), Routledge & Kegan Paul. This selection also includes poems by Chapman, Heywood, Beaumont, and other contemporary writers, and may be consulted by students interested in reading other examples of popular Elizabethan romance.

SHAKESPEARE. Recent editions of *Venus and Adonis* are in Arden Shakespeare, *The Poems*, edited by F. T. Prince (1960), Methuen; and the New Cambridge Shakespeare, *The Poems*, edited by J. C. Maxwell (1966), Cambridge University Press.

DANIEL. The complete works of Daniel were edited by A. B. Grosart, 5 vols (1885–96), and the poems and *A Defence of Rhyme* by A. C. Sprague (1930), Harvard University Press.

DRAYTON. The standard edition of Drayton is that by J. W. Hebel, K. Tillotson, and B. H. Newdigate, 5 vols (1931–41), Blackwell. C. Brett's *Minor Poems* (1907) is also useful.

LODGE. Lodge's complete works were edited by E. W. Gosse, 4 vols (1883).

MARLOWE. There are several complete editions of Marlowe: e.g., by A. H. Bullen, 3 vols (1885); Havelock Ellis (1887); C. F. Tucker Brooke (1910); and R. H. Case, 6 vols (1930–3) Methuen.

MARSTON. Marston's satires were edited by G. B. Harrison (1925), the poems by A. B. Grosart (1879), and the complete works by A. H. Bullen, 3 vols (1887), Bodley Head.

Criticism

(*a*) General

Recent standard works are two volumes in the Oxford History of English Literature: C. S. Lewis, *English Literature in the Sixteenth Century* (1954), Oxford University Press; and Douglas Bush, *English Literature in the Earlier Seventeenth Century* (1945), Oxford University Press.

The poetry of the period is analysed and discussed in M. C. Bradbrook, *Shakespeare and Elizabethan Poetry* (1951),

Chatto and Windus; Douglas Bush, *Mythology and the Renaissance Literary Tradition* (1932), Minneapolis; and Hallet Smith, *Elizabethan Poetry* (1952), Harvard University Press.

The influence of Ovid is examined by F. S. Boas in an English Association pamphlet, 'Ovid and the Elizabethans' (n.d.). L. T. Golding, a descendant of the poet, discusses the work and importance of Golding in *An Elizabethan Puritan* (1937), New York: Richard R. Smith. The book contains the dedication and preface which Golding wrote for his translation of Ovid.

E. M. W. Tillyard, *The Elizabethan World Picture* (1943), Chatto and Windus, supplies a background to the thought of the period.

(b) More detailed biographical and critical studies

Daniel. There are introductory essays on Daniel by H. C. Beeching in a selection of the poems (1899), by A. H. Bullen in *Elizabethans* (1924), Chapman and Hall, and Sprague in the edition mentioned above.

Drayton. *See* Oliver Elton, *Michael Drayton* (1905), Constable; Brett's edition of his poems; Bullen, *Elizabethans*; and B. H. Newdigate, *Michael Drayton and his Circle* (1941). The fullest study is that of Joan Rees in *Samuel Daniel: A Critical and Biographical Study* (1964), Liverpool University Press.

Lodge. The standard biographical and critical studies of Lodge are those by N. B. Paradise (1931), Yale University Press; and E. A. Tenney (1935), Cornell University Press. See also C. J. Sisson *Thomas Lodge and Other Elizabethans* (1933), Harvard University Press.

Marlowe. The career and work of Marlowe have attracted many studies and many different approaches. The book most relevant here is F. P. Wilson, *Marlowe and the Early Shakespeare* (1953), Oxford University Press. Others include Una Ellis-Fermor, *Christopher Marlowe* (1927), Methuen; F. S. Boas, *Christopher Marlowe* (1940), Oxford University Press; J. Bakeless, *The Tragical History of Christopher Marlowe* (1938), Jonathan Cape; and C. Norman, *The Muses' Darling* (1948), Falcon Press. The intellectual world which Marlowe inhabited is described in M. C. Bradbrook, *The School of Night* (1936), Cambridge University Press.

Marston. There is a useful essay on Marston's satire in *Elizabethan Poetry*, edited by J. R. Brown and Bernard Harris (1960). Arnold. M. S. Allen, *The Satire of John Marston* (1920), Columbus, Ohio, is a more detailed study.

Shakespeare. Shakespeare's non-dramatic work is stimulatingly discussed in several article in *Shakespeare Survey XV* (1962), Cambridge University Press.